Financial Fair Hope

Decentralization and Democratization of the Distribution of Money

Marcus R Bowman

ISBN: 978-1981791163
ISBN-10: 1981791167

DEDICATION

To a better future. For all.

CONTENTS

THE GOOD AND THE BAD

CRONY CAPITALISM

BOLD STEPS

1

INTRODUCTION

ON THE ROAD TO
FINANCIAL FAIR HOPE

Charles Dickens included this famous line in his 1859 blockbuster novel, *A Tale of Two Cities.*

"It was the best of times. It was the worst of times."

As true today as it was when Charles Dickens wrote it.

That was the opening line of his book. And, the setting? The eve of the French Revolution.

The line also rings as true for the setting of his story: in the time of the French Revolution—the late 1700's.

We have, now, in the United States of America, the best economy in the history of the earth.

Our economy—our financial system—provides so much to so many. We have built, and are building, so many amazing things. The world over.

From impressive bridges and skyscrapers to amazing phones and awesome apps.

Still, our economy is broken.

Using an analogy: the car you see in the parking lot. It was made so impressively. It looks great; from your front-on vantage point. Nice… and shiny and clean. But the car—when it is running—putters with a little noise. And on the back-left side, and the rear, it is marred with scratches and visible dings. All of this you can't see from the front… while the car is turned off.

That is our economy today.

The point of this book is that it is time to 'do' the economy differently. It is time for a vastly improved financial system. The car was built nicely. It functioned awesome for a while. It looked great. And it still does. From the front. While it is off.

We could talk about fixing the car. And at a minimum, that is what we need. Fix the blight we occasionally see-- like helping those homeless people and fixing the abandoned house, empty low and the run-down warehouse near downtown.

All of that is great. Desperately necessary. It is a primary goal of this book. A lot of what is needed may only be common sense and small improvements. Taking good and great and making it perfect and awesome.

However, we also need to start thinking much bigger. We could talk about building a new, better car. That too is not big enough thinking.

The call in this book, is for a revolutionary improvement to how we do things. It is time.

Just like the bold ideas of today's prominent tech titans, we need that vision for our economy and financial system. Elon Musk talks about a futuristic hyperloop transport system speeding passengers from New York City to Washington, DC in a half hour. Jeff Bezos talks about drones delivering books and sending citizens into space.

Our economy can operate so much better.

We **_can_** have an economy that accomplishes so much more,
positively affecting a lot more people.
Our financial system can be vastly improved.

That is the point.

We need to start talking boldly. And then we need to embrace big— perhaps radical—new ideas and completely overhaul our financial system.

A big transformation is likely coming within the next ten years to how our financial system operates and how our economy is managed. Your contribution now and ahead of time is likely to shape the result. This book kind of outlines what is possible and preps you to be a part of making it turn out right. One thing you can guarantee is that the people in charge of our financial system today are thinking about how to stay in power tomorrow. Either by keeping the current system in place or by being the ones inventing the next mouse trap. Thus, it is imperative for an outside run—groups outside the current financial system working to promote an alternative.

Three principles are at the heart of this book.

And, one fundamental aspect lies behind the three principles.

The foundation for the future is that:

management of the economy—our financial system—

must involve more people.

First, decision making about the economy and management of our financial system is too centralized. We must decentralize financial decision-making.

Second, we have democracy as the guiding credo behind our representation in government—with voting for our representatives and voting on key decisions. We must have democracy in management of our economy and financial system.

Third, we spend too much time worrying about who has the money and who the 1% are and it misses a bigger issue. Who prints our money? Who gives it out? Where does it go? Who gets it? Who gets it… first? We need to fix how our money is distributed.

Decentralize finance.

Democratization of finance.

Distribution of money.

Distribution has a two-fold meaning of which we will cover.

First, you can think of distribution in the sense of a "distribution center" for moving and delivering goods. A mode of transportation capable of larger shipments (such as shipping containers and railcars) is used to bring a variety of different goods to a large warehouse. From that warehouse, the goods are then delivered by truck to where they need to go. Distribution centers are usually in a geographically central and convenient location. And this helps facilitate the efficient movement of goods and products through the economy.

The other meaning of distribution is like a Bell Curve. How is something distributed among the population? Did everyone get a box delivered from the distribution center? Was the box the same size? Or did different people get different amounts of boxes of varying sizes? In evaluating distribution of something among the population it does not need to be a physical object. It could be, for example, test scores of students in a class. What percentage of students received an 'A'? What percentage of students received a 'B' grade? Etc. Then you have a distribution you can measure whether it is balanced based on a number of variable factors and criteria. What might be a fair distribution for one scenario may not be how a distribution will look in another scenario. And putting together a graphical representation of the distribution can be used to start a discussion such as: How can this be better? And/or for comparison to other similar population samples. For example, are all the teachers in a school assigning grades in a similar manner? Are there—relatively speaking—about the same amount of 'A' and 'B' grades from every teacher? Or are there some outliers? And why? Or, what about, for example, test scores between two different schools in different locations of the country: Are the resulting scores distributed more-or-less the same? Are the students learning equivalently at each school? Or are there disparities that can be picked up from showing the distribution? And how can that be addressed?

For the financial system and economy, we are then looking at distribution first in the sense of who is physically distributing the money and how are they doing it. Where are the distribution centers? How is the money getting to the distribution centers? Who's in charge of the process? Who is getting the money?

And then second, once the money is out and about in the economy how is it ending up in its distribution among the population? What is the shape of the distribution of the money among the population? What is the distribution of accumulated savings and wealth? Are there reasons why the distribution is the way it is? Are there improvements and fixes that could be beneficial? Thus, we are looking at income inequality.

What is the ideology and solution of the future?

The future is not likely to be conservative. Or liberal. It probably won't be capitalist. It won't be socialist. In one or more ways it likely will be combinations of both. For example, both extremes could live side-by-side: one way or the other does not necessarily win out universally, but rather different countries/regions/localities do different things. Or, another way is that the future is a combination of the best of all the above. A bit conservative but also a bit liberal. A bit socialist but also a bit capitalist.

Or that is how it should be. That is what our goal here is to promote. The best future will be a combination of the best of everything. The best future will incorporate all perspectives and leave everyone feeling they have a part in it.

Beyond conservative or liberal, capitalist or socialist, the best economy and financial system of the future should likely have bits of a lot of ideas that we haven't even quite thought about yet.

People may like to brand a new idea as conservative or liberal, or socialist or capitalist. More important is for us to embrace the future for what it can be; without getting lost in labels and trying to define what we can establish.

Thus, the successful path forward should be introspection and frank conversation.

Can we listen to others? Can we appreciate their alternative perspectives and policies? Even if you do not yourself believe in or agree with them. Can we at least listen. The sooner we can act like adults together the better. Because beyond the important and tough step of listening to others, we need to then dialogue.

Can we dialogue and try to meet half way with an even better idea?

The point is not that you get to convince others of your own brilliance.

Again, your liberal brilliance isn't going to win over your "Neanderthal" conservative minds. And conservatives and capitalists are unlikely to convince liberals to have a totally free market.

If each of us can stand to listen to each other. Well, we can have a very bright future indeed.

The key driving focus needs to be that we can do better. We can do better. We must do better.

That is America. The American way. We continually look to improve. So why not radically transform—our financial system? And in so doing let's get an economy for the future that is astoundingly better—for a lot more people.

Ralph Waldo Emerson wrote "Always the seer is a sayer. Somehow his dream is told; somehow he publishes it with solemn joy."[1]

We deserve a better economy.

Or rather, we are capable of a much better economy.

What that exactly means… we will attempt to define here. We will lay out ideas we can work toward. If America is good at anything, it is continual improvement.

Time and time again throughout history Americans have invented, worked hard and innovated over and over. Now it is time to tackle our financial system. Build it stronger and better. Touching all lives. A democratic and decentralized economic system.

This is the path for which this country and our economy is inevitably heading. We must go in the direction toward the decentralization of financial decisions, including democracy in money.

The economy is not working for enough people.

It is not working for all people.

We are capable of better.

Our way of life and the successes we have witnessed in America and around the globe are proof that the work toward a new economy is about the future and not so much about upending a failed system. The point of this book—while uncovering massive collusion and corruption—is not to say everything is terrible, when we achieve so many great things. Technology, life expectancy and so many improvements to our standard of living.

The goal is to inspire us to much greater heights. We need to completely rethink and revamp our economy and how it works.

We need a lot more "hope" for a lot more people in our economy. And we need more people involved in financial decision making.

Life will go on without a small group of Goldman Sachs bankers running Wall Street and Washington, DC and really the world. Because the balance of power must change. We don't need to be afraid.

Just like our phones are much different than they were a decade ago. We still make calls with them while being able to do so much more. Such it will be with the financial system. It may not look much different but will behave and do so many more things. Time for a journey to Financial Fair Hope.

---

[1] *When Breathe Becomes Air*, Paul Kalanithi. Pp 217-218

2
INTRODUCTION

FAIR?

Fair? The goal for an economy of the future should not be "fair."

At least my goal is not to suggest the economy should be fair.

Closer to "fair." Closer to fair then we are today?

Life isn't fair. That is what I remember thinking while growing up. That was the conclusion I remember gathering from my parents, and especially my mom since she was the one around during the long days of playing with my sister and friends. My father worked hard for the family.

My younger sister (and only sister) would write about fairness in her secret diary: "It's not fair!" That is some of what she would write about when my mom would, say, send my sister to her room for an incident. My sister felt the event was my fault and, yet my mom sent *her* to her room. Maybe, something inside of me thought it really *was* my fault. How else did I end up concluding that life isn't fair?

The extension of this is that I came to also fundamentally believe that life really *should not* be fair.

Life does not have to be fair. This is not to say it is a guiding principle of my life. Simply, a little point relative to this conversation and of course important to define 'fair' with respect to the title of this book.

Fairness is about degrees. I like to view many of the problems or notions in the world along a spectrum.

So, for example: what degree of fairness should society have? Along a spectrum of say 0% to 100%. Since I don't really believe fair is an appropriate outcome, let's step back though. That does not mean I believe in 0% fairness. What I might believe right now is that the world is, say, 20% fair. And so

"Financial Fair Hope" might be a way to make the world thirty or forty percent fair. Fairer than it is today.

Making a society fair, or even "more fair" is a practical issue as well. Reality is simply that we all make different decisions.

And random things happen to us all.

Fair has kind of come to be known as "the outcome should be equal." Yet, there are definitions of "fair" that do not attribute to the idea of things being "equal."

For example, "My Fair Lady"? So "fair" can be "pleasing to the eye" such as "fair skin," i.e. "unblemished in appearance." Some might say, like Fairhope, Alabama.

Or what about related terms? Such as "fair-minded." "Reasonable and unbiased."

Can we have a "fair-minded economy," a "reasonable and unbiased economy," even an "unblemished" economy?

Or consider baseball. A "fair ball." When a batter hits the ball into fair territory it could still result in an out. The batter might get a hit; and even a home run. Hitting in fair territory just means you put the ball in play. The analogy with baseball could take us into all kinds of philosophy with respect to the organization of the financial system. Consider that hitting a ball that is not "fair" does not mean you are out. When the ball is hit into fair territory there are rules. The game is played according to those rules. And the outcome for each individual player and the team they play on can vary greatly. So, the economy of the future can permit the randomness and the win-or-loss realities of games such as baseball where you could hit a homer, or you could get an out. And if you get an out, you bat again and try again.

When we think of a fairer economy of the future we can look at the definition of "fair" that is "clear; discernible; gentle, civil; honest, open; legitimate, justifiable, or acceptable, as a course of action."

"Reasonable, or adequate, as quantity or amount." "Suitable." "Good, select, or promising, as a choice." These are all the quoted definitions from a 1975 copy of "The Living Webster Encyclopedic Dictionary of the English Language" that I have lying around.

That is the financial system that we need. Not the type of fair that divides everything up equally.

3
INTRODUCTION
FAIRHOPE, ALABAMA

In our current popular culture, I suppose the knee-jerk reaction of many is no way anything good for the future could possibly come out of Alabama.

The little town in lower Alabama that I happened to move to in late 2012 sits on the eastern shore of Mobile Bay. There is a waterfront park, a city pier extending into the bay, a jogging trail and walking path along the water. The small town of, say, 15,000 people is a quaint shopping and restaurant destination for tourists. The town is called Fairhope.

I liken much that occurs in the town of Fairhope, and its traditional ways, to Maybury—the fictional town from the 1950's TV show, Andy Griffith. And, the history of Fairhope is as magnificent as the huge live oak trees and the Spanish moss hanging from them.

Drawing attention to the name—Fairhope—for this book does not so much reflect this view of the past and tradition. Rather the name Fairhope seems to inspire a vision for the future. And that is precisely why the town got its name.

**The founders of Fairhope envisioned
an entirely different financial system
that would help more people.**

As this book will weave through the highest elements of world finance on a journey to an economy of the future, think back to your own childhood or favorite small town. The essence of any great solution will be in how well it connects us to the real world of life.

Fairhope, Alabama was founded in 1894. The original settlers followed Ernest Gaston from Iowa to the eastern shore of Mobile Bay. They organized the town to serve as a model community for America.

The concept behind Fairhope's founders was based on the economic model of Henry George, first published in his 1879 book, *Progress and Poverty*. The initial corporate constitution of Fairhope stated:

> "To establish and conduct a model community or colony, free from all forms of private monopoly, and to secure to its members therein equality of opportunity, the full reward of individual efforts, and the benefits of cooperation in matters of general concern."[2]

Fairhope happens to be among a small number of towns that was started as a "single tax" colony in 1887.[3] And Fairhope *still is* a single tax colony. A say-what? What is a single tax colony?

Henry George started a movement based on his "single-tax" economic ideas. The single tax was to be focused on land. Land was fundamentally the same to everyone. In other words, to George we are all born on to the same earth and thus each entitled to a share of land; or even more succinctly, that all land ultimately belongs to all the people. Economic principles associated with this are, first, that no one should be able to profit from land and, second, because land is finite (can't really create more of it) it could be utilized as an equalizer in the economy—that all people would be 'treated better' (so-to-speak) in the economy and that incomes for all people would rise instead of too much wealth concentration. These ideas published as they were in 1879 struck a chord with a public frustrated by the budding monopoly power of titans like John D. Rockefeller, whose Standard Oil corporation had steamrolled through the economy in the 1870's. Thus, a single-tax on land as an economic equalizer.

Thus, amid the monopoly power of the Gilded Age many Americans wanted a different direction. A few dared to try. Politically, there were also movements to win power in Washington, DC. In 1892 the Populist Party was a national uprising. However, the aspiring party failed in the 1892 election. The ballot box alone could not get it done. So, it was time for some to try to form "true cooperative individualism" another way.[4] So began a lot of small-scale experimentation. Among these 'start-ups', the creation of Fairhope,

---

[2] *Man and Mission: E.B. Gaston and the Origins of the Fairhope Single Tax Colony*, Paul Gaston. 1993. Pp 128 (from Appendix Two: Constitution of the Fairhope Industrial Association, Article II. Purpose)

[3] *Man and Mission*, Paul Gaston. 1993. Pp 66.

[4] *Man and Mission*, Paul Gaston. 1993. Pp 14-15.

Alabama. Lawrence Goodwyn said the founders of Fairhope were "ordinary Americans" that "gave themselves permission to think grandly about human possibility."[5]

Henry George "believed that land should be common property in a community" and that the level of poverty was "an evil that could be remedied by the abolition of private land ownership."[6]

"Land should be common property." – Henry George

Still, the philosophy of George was only a guiding principle—or inspiration—for Fairhope. A group of 28 people from Iowa—*unknown to George*—founded Fairhope to put his theory into practice. The community of Fairhope was formed to prove George's theory. Ernest B. Gaston (a newspaperman) was the "most impassioned member" of the group. Gaston "strongly felt" George's beliefs "deserved a demonstration" and hoped that Fairhope would become a "utopia."[7]

Today, Fairhope can seem frozen in time as goes family and conservative traditions. And at the same time a little 'weird' in the Austin, Texas sense with a heavy dose of art. Fairhope has every bit of the charm of the south. Quite a small town still.[8] In some senses, it is the quintessential southern town. And magazines like *Southern Living* occasionally call it as such.[9] It is an artsy kind of town. In fact, the biggest annual event is the Fairhope Arts & Craft Festival. Jimmy Buffett lived in Fairhope as did the author of *Forrest Gump*.

I ended up in Fairhope by chance. Living amid successful artists and authors re-ignited my creative side. Inspiration was fostered in Fairhope—the laid-back lifestyle, scenic waterfront park, jogging path and sunsets are utopian. Great energy for believing in a better future. The slower-pace of living in a small town also provided more time to write. So, did the economy here in Alabama—a state ranked 47th of 50 in income per capita in 2015.[10] Hard for me to find a well-paying job. My income crashed amid few opportunities. That and seeing many people around me working hard for meager money reignited a long inner desire of mine to make a difference. I lived 12 years in Washington, DC—an economically thriving metropolitan area with 7 of the 10 richest counties in the country located there. The

[5] *Man and Mission: E.B. Gaston and the Origins of the Fairhope Single Tax Colony*, Paul Gaston. 1993. Pp 150.
[6] *The Fair Hope of Heaven*. Mary Lois Timbes. Pp 2.
[7] *The Fair Hope of Heaven*. Mary Lois Timbes. Pp 2.
[8] Population of less than 20,000 people https://en.wikipedia.org/wiki/Fairhope,_Alabama
[9] See, for example: http://www.southernliving.com/travel/what-to-do-fairhope-alabama and http://www.southernliving.com/travel/2016-souths-best-small-towns.
[10] https://en.wikipedia.org/wiki/List_of_U.S._states_by_income

contrast of those in New York City and Washington, DC doing so well with what I was now experiencing was a wake-up call.

4
INTRODUCTION

WHO HAS THE MONEY?
WHO PRINTS THE MONEY? WHY?

Who has the money? They certainly have a lot more in and around Washington, DC then many other places around America.

Who *has* the money? Who has the money right now? That, really, is missing the point.

Yes, there are a lot of changes that can be made to address disparities in who has the money now. And, to address the question of why do they have so much? And we will get to that. However, for big change there are much bigger fish to fry.

Occupy Wall Street is a movement that misses this nuanced point.

It is hardly as much about who *has* the money but in *who prints the money* and what is the *process of distributing* money. In other words, it is not so much about existing income distribution as it is about the future of the distribution of money.

It is not so much about who *has* the money or how they got it. Because that is an evaluation of the past. It is: who creates the money in the first place? And how is *that* decided? How do we change that?

It is about getting to the root causes and ultimate sources of problems. We can do something about who has the money now. However, if we don't address how money is moving around the economy we will end up with the same problems. Slightly different people but the same system will yield the same results.

What needs to change is who oversees determining how much money is printed? And... who do they give it to?! And, why?

When we say 'printed' what we really are talking about now is money created out of thin air. We are not talking about dollar bills coming off the printing presses at the Treasury Department.

We are talking about money that is created out of thin air by the highest elements of power in our banks, our Federal Reserve and government. And these are simply numbers on a computer. Transferred and entered into an account via a computer. Frankly, we don't really know what happens right now, or how.

Changing who is in control of the money process starts with the biggest banks in the banking industry. The ones closest to Wall Street. And their relationships working in conjunction with their own revolving door of insiders working at the U.S. Treasury Department and the Federal Reserve.

This tight association is where money is largely created and controlled.

We will discuss these specifics in a chapter or two. Suffice it to say right now that money creation is tightly restricted to our central bank, the Federal Reserve, as well as the Treasury Department. Anyone else printing money it is called counterfeiting.

Is it reasonable to call the Federal Reserve legal counterfeiting? Congress authorized the Federal Reserve back in 1913. The money they print—out of thin air, literally just made up—is given directly to the world's biggest banks in New York City.

Yes, it is counterfeiting. The ability for a few to counterfeit money around a board room table needs to be taken away. Bold words? The truth. That is what they are doing. It is unjustified power. Never intended for America.

Counterfeiting is when it is unequal. Counterfeiters get the money first.

It took a law to set it up. A change in the law is all that is needed to take their power away. And, then a much better future for a lot more people.

Here are the questions we need to be asking as a society:

Who gives out the money? Why them?
Who gets it? Why and how?
In other words, what to do with the money that is printed?
Who 'prints' the money? Why them?
How? How does it get there? Where does it go?
How do they decide how much money to print?
Who decides how much money to 'print'?
Who gets the money? First.
Who is deciding who receives money first?
Who makes up the Federal Reserve?
Why?
Why is it this way?

"What is your why?" is so much the rage now in self-help books and motivational speeches. If you know *why* you are doing what you are doing it can overcome all how.

Well, then, *why* is money distributed the way it is now?

Why is money distributed the way it is now?

More importantly: can we do it a better way?

Yes, this is America. We innovate.
We can get this done a better way.

Why is one closed organization deciding how money is printed and distributed for society? This is indeed the crux of the entire issue. We need to have a completely different organization or method with a mission far outside the thoughts of money printing today. Why does the Federal Reserve print money for society? Why do they decide who gets the money?

Thus, it is hardly as much about who has the money but in who prints the money. In other words, it is not so much about income distribution as it is about the distribution of money.

Impacts of Who Gives the Money Away First

"Income distribution" versus the "Distribution of Money." One is the cause of inequity in the other. If one subset of bankers decides where the money goes, the money goes to their closest friends and allies.

Ron Paul said it best in 2007, "those that benefit the most are the ones that get to use the newly created credit first."[11] If you trust the management of the medium of exchange to bankers, it will be manipulated to the benefit of the bankers. Depending on who decides, and who they give the money to first, can have a huge impact on society.

It is two questions to answer and solve. Who decides where the money goes? Who do they give it to (who gets it first?)?

Proximity and access certainly serve the biggest banks on Wall Street, such as Goldman Sachs. The impacts run deeper.

Why is Facebook, *Facebook*? Why is Google, *Google*? They are run by liberals. Most of the big internet successes are run by liberals. Between the bankers, and our media, they were able to control who became the successful enterprises. The founders needed to have access to capital to take their good ideas up a notch. Look at the movie, *The Social Network*. Mark Zuckerberg

---

[11] Quote from Ron Paul via YouTube clip of CSPAN recording of February 17, 2007 Hearing of the U.S. House of Representatives Financial Services Committee.

took control of an idea because he was backed by money.

In the grand scheme of the economy these are small examples. However, Google is *the* search engine, and *the* email outlet, for a dominant part of the internet in the United States and around the world. Same for Facebook.

Consider the effect of this type financial decision-making across the economy. It is mind-opening to consider. Certainly, it does, and has, worked both ways. That conservative ideas got a green light from a conservative banker while a liberal idea was turned away. Progressives would say this of the energy industry and an imbalance in favor of crude oil and fossil fuels.

There is politics in finance.

Thus, it is extremely important to have diverse and broad participation in who decides where the money goes and who gets it first.

It is time for some improvements.

5

INTRODUCTION

TIME FOR A BIG LEAP: BOLDLY TRANSFORMING TO A RADICALLY BETTER ECONOMY

America has been a leader in so much throughout history.

And with respect to an economy and financial system of the future it is the United States of America that is most capable of quickly embracing a bold, new path.

Time and again American ingenuity has led the way in the world. As FDR would say there is nothing to fear but fear itself.[12]

A big leap in how we manage our economy is desperately needed.

**The financial system of the future will be
radically different than the economy we live in today.**

**The questions are only from that premise.
How? Why? What will result? Who will bring it about?**

How long will it take to overhaul our economy? When will it happen? There are so many new and different ideas that already happening. They just haven't 'bubbled up to the surface' yet. Masses of people don't know about the innovative ideas happening in say, urban Berlin. And, it may be difficult in the short-term for these smaller ideas to gain momentum.

---

[12] http://historymatters.gmu.edu/d/5057

Short-term, the current power brokers have a big advantage. They will fund many of the new initiatives to try and steer change that will be 'the more things change the more they stay the same.'

Some of the biggest proposals that get the most media attention, those are not likely to be the fixes that are needed.

Real changes will be fought. Hard. Establishment and entrenched interests will put up a fight when it is truly something they are not controlling.

Real changes will not be part of a flashy political campaign of "Hope and Change." Sorry. That sounded awesome. We know how it turned out. If you are honest with yourself. That was the stuff of Hollywood... and Wall Street.

From the standpoint of those in charge now they want to steer us into a future—that sounds trendy and different—their way. This type of change could come about quickly.

If we aren't careful the future is going to be the same old actors running the show. It is going to sound different, but be more of the same, and worse.

The same old Wall Street bankers will come up with a nice "bipartisan" commission to decide where the money goes. And who could argue with it? They will have the media out there talking about how balanced the plan is and how fair this new concept will be. And then, bam, step 2. Who gets the money they give out? They might say, well look it's not the same old banks, it is going to new "Fair Financial Brokers for the People and Better Society." Seriously. It will be something like that. There might even be several different types of names such as "Fair Finance for our Elderly" and "Fair Finance for the Children." Who is going to be against *that*?

What about the Long-Term? The People Will Win

There is a window of opportunity now. For you. For you to believe. For you to take steps no matter how seemingly small.

Long-term, the future is likely to be forged by entirely new faces.

It will be those that push forward with a) no fear and b) no doubt. No matter what ideas seem to be winning around them, they will keep pushing. And they will ultimately win in creating a better future for all of us.

One giant step for mankind is what is needed.

A radical pace of reform will take hold *one way or another*.

The U.S. cannot stagnate. We cannot tolerate and accept where we are. We must continue to innovate and improve. It starts—at least—with dialogue. And that is what this book aims to do. This book aims to build energy: helping to generate new ideas. There is a very nuanced difference to have it both ways. We need radical change. At the same time, it is not that the U.S. is in some dire, terrible situation. It is not coming out of a view that everything is wrong. Rather, there is so much that is good and positive about America. Can it be both at once? Incremental, but radical changes? How can this be?

How Radical? How Quickly?

We are likely to witness change in radical quickness at times. However, overall, the Japanese concept of "kaizen" is highly relevant. The goal of long-term, radical change must be viewed in this light. That is that incremental improvement (or small changes) over time eventually result in a radically new system or entity. The computer could perhaps be traced to one or two critical moment founders in which what we know as a computer today first came to existence in the mold we are today familiar with. However, the reality is that today's computer is the result of a series of improvements over centuries.[13]

Perhaps the right term is finetuning. With proper discussion and a principal toward continued finetuning we can get there. The term finetuning rather than incremental. Some of the changes need to be bold and direct. Along with willingness to adjust courses. In other words, we can get our sail up just the way we wanted to get it up but what if the wind than changes direction. We did everything correct. However, the outcome of our work turns out to be wrong for the circumstances. So, fine tune. Make a change for the situation.

Ideas and Action

If we don't make bold improvements soon Americans are going to give up. They are going to pull out of the financial system. Some may find an exciting new technology or innovation to do so. Others are just going to stop caring.

Too many Americans are working hard for $10 per hour, and less. Employers are providing jobs that keep them under full-time hours, so they don't receive benefits. All of this is unsustainable.

Meanwhile, there is a total disconnect: top corporations giving some of *their* employees so many perks. Government employees too. Incredible health care. Retirement plans. Huge amounts of vacation time. Raises. Flexible work time. At Intel, employees take lengthy sabbaticals. At Google and Apple employees get to play foos ball in common areas and other absurdities. These

---

[13] *The Innovators*, Walter Isaacson, 2014.

tech companies are building massive new headquarters. Apple. Facebook. Google. Google is building a $1.3 billion "sidescraper" or "groundscaper" that will be longer than a skyscraper is tall. The building is planned to be the "best place to work in the world," featuring basketball courts, rooftop fields and gardens to walk through and an Olympic-size swimming pool.[14]

Facebook is going beyond just an office building to create a "village" neighborhood center, including housing for employees, a grocery store, retail and a visitor center in addition to the office complex.[15]

There must be a system for everyone else, so to speak. Too many people left behind. We must be capable of an economy that can both allow for the ingenuity and profit of a successful entrepreneur. And at the same time, provide a lot more income—or at least financial security—to working classes. How do we do this?

The calls for a better economy have been numerous. Economists such as Joseph Stiglitz have written several books trying to improve. In *Freefall*, Stiglitz outlines a vision "toward a new society." Stiglitz points out that metrics are a large part of moving to a solution: "what you measure is what you value." Conservative David Stockman lamented the "corruption of capitalism in America" in his economic treatise, *The Great Deformation*." And Robert Reich has written several books about improving the economy to help more people. "For the many, not the few" is Reich's subtitle of his 2015 book, *Saving Capitalism*.

What is the right answer?

I don't know the right answer.

I do know something must be done.

---

[14] http://www.dailymail.co.uk/news/article-4562146/Google-unveils-plans-new-1billion-London-HQ.html

[15] http://www.mercurynews.com/2017/07/07/facebook-campus-expansion-includes-offices-retail-grocery-store-housing/#comments

6
FOUR D'S:

FOCUS ON
DIFFERENT OUTCOMES

Different outcomes. Turning our minds to different outcomes. The first of four 'D's to frame a much-improved economy and better financial system: Different Outcomes, Democratization of Finance, Decentralization of Finance, Distribution of Money.

What are we measuring?

Why?'

Could there be new ways of looking at the success of our economy and financial system?

Could we track different outcomes and achieve even better results?

The answer is unequivocally, and emphatically, YES!

Why do we track GDP and run the economy to grow that number?

A big focus for management of our economy is a) to ensure inflation is held in check and b) to keep the unemployment number low. Admirable goals. Hard to argue they are not good goals. However, what they are, is, overly simplistic.

The way we manage our economy does not achieve the outcomes we look and hope for because we don't aim to achieve those objectives?

Why are incomes stagnant for so many?

We don't have any policy in place to care about it.

Quite simply, the reasons incomes do not go up for the population is because we don't try to make them go up. But we could!

We need to focus on different outcomes.
We need to be smart about it.

If we focus on different objectives and goals we will get better results. In some cases, it might not even be aggregate target statistics but tangible, specific goals. Back in the day we built the Interstate Highway System. We can have similar massive visions of large-scale projects that can be a more specific objective that fuels real-world accomplishment and improvement.

Inflation and Wages; and the
Struggle for Many Just to Keep Their Heads Above Water

How come so many Americans feel like they don't have any money left over after paying the bills? We directly feel the effects of what could be called the income/inflation ratio. We don't call it that because it doesn't get reported on.

Consider this. The economy is managed to grow at say 2% per year but what if your wages stay the same? If the inflation target is 2% per year and wages do not increase, then the purchasing power of an employee's earnings has declined to just 82 cents on the dollar a decade later. You can afford 18% less than you could 10 years ago.

Fortunately, we have so much great technology around us and productivity improvements that the 82% that we get is better than what 100% bought 10 years ago. So, we feel a little bit better about it all. But for most Americans, they are not getting ahead.

The margins for error are not there for too many Americans. Too many Americans are unable to save. They are incurring rising credit card debts simply to stay afloat and/or live an otherwise normal, or even meager, life.

We need to focus on different outcomes.

It is the outcomes that ultimately matter.

Opportunity in America

We can talk all day that, for example, capitalism is intended that everybody has their chance and we are capitalist and therefore it falls on individuals to get their own job done. And if they don't, well the system was in place for their success. To a great extent it could be argued that is true. Especially in theory and perhaps, for the most part, in practice too.

As Charles J. Givens said, "The last four letters of American are I CAN." He added, "Everyone can be a winner... You don't need to have big money to make big money."

We could read about Karl Marx or an even better utopian concept of a socialist world that helps the entire population and because we believe in that and are working on a plan that it is all good. We can have the best intentions as the government bureaucrats. We know deep down we are good people doing the right thing. And if it doesn't work out exactly as intended well, it's because not everyone went along; and/or some capitalists mucked up the perfect plan.

Continuous, Critical Evaluation

We don't know what is going to work. We don't know if what worked yesterday is going to continue to work tomorrow.

Our hearts can be in the right place, but unfortunately that is not enough. Our intentions can be pure and noble, but unfortunately that is not enough.

The plan we lay out may be the best plan. We may have numbers to support how well it should work. We can have the best people implementing the plan and all of them can have their hearts, minds and intentions in the right place. None of it is enough.

Continual evaluation is essential.

Critical attention, too, should be welcome. In other words, the ability to accept counter ideas. People that question the track.

The first solution—just because it appears it can help the situation—does not mean it is the best idea. Moreover, too often marketing is used—particularly by establishment and nefarious elements—to promote a "solution."

It Starts with the Actions and the Means

And, a good end is not always achieved by any means. Just because your heart is in the right place and you *want* the right thing to be the result does not mean your actions are moving in that direction.

It starts with the actions and the means.

Thought needs to go into the means to achieve the desired end. If you have a great end in mind and then go out and strive toward the end but haven't thought about the proper means, you are liable to finish at a different end. And if you aren't evaluating along the way, no matter what means you do select, then again you are liable to finish somewhere different from where you intended.

The outcomes we are currently focusing on in society. The reason we haven't really changed is because the outcomes we are aiming toward it's not like they are bad on their surface. For example, keeping the unemployment rate low. The point is we can step up our game.

Improving the Simplistic Unemployment Number

Looking at one government reported overall unemployment rates has not been enough. The measure of the overall unemployment rate is far too simplistic as a number. It doesn't tell us anything about how hard those people that are employed are working and it doesn't tell us anything about whether the money they are earning while working is enough to live. The unemployment rate—as simply a percentage number—is not telling the full story. It isn't working. So, the measure needs to be improved. The outcome we work toward needs to be updated.

At a minimum, we need an updated target that measures unemployment, job quality, time worked and earnings vs the cost of living. With that, we can focus on how do we improve upon that new and improved outcome.

Modify, Evaluate, Improve

What steps do we take so that the numbers head in positive directions?

And, then, continually improve. Review. Modify the approach. Make tweaks and adjustments. Get better at the calculations. Get better at what the goal is. And get better at achieving the goal.

It is imperative that we focus on different outcomes.

The stock market going up. It's helping some, but it is not broad enough.

Same with GDP or inflation. Too abstract.

For the big bankers and bureaucrats running the U.S. economy from Washington, DC and New York City it makes sense, at best. At worst it is a deliberate decoy. A way to say they are doing something.

Is it a giant deception? Growing GDP, making the stock market rise and keeping the unemployment rate low. Is all that merely a way to say they are actually achieving the goals they need to achieve. Yet these metrics are simply not getting the job done. Period.

7
FOUR D'S:

DEMOCRACY IN FINANCE
(DEMOCRATIZATION OF FINANCE)

We tout having "democracy" in voting for our government representatives. Why do we limit democracy to our government representatives?

Should we also have democracy in how we divide up money? Why not democracy for money creation? Why not democracy in determining who is getting the money?

Finance also needs to be democratic.

Call this the "democratization of finance"—a vital step toward having all people as not only participants in their government but as more active participants in the management of the economy and financial system. A more democratic financial system will benefit all among us in the economy.

Our financial system should be democratic. People should have a direct say in the economy they live in!

To effectively run an economy, a financial system should have a democratic foundation.

> The people—all people—should have a more direct say in
> how money is doled out to society.

As a starting point, we can say that civilization has achieved "political democracy". We vote for our political representatives. We have a government that is more-or-less accountable to its citizens (a subject we will return to). But, what of "economic democracy"? Or "financial democracy"? Depending on how we take the discussion, whether it is "economic" or "financial" the question is about money. Who prints the money? Who distributes the money? It is not a democratic system? No, unfortunately.

We do not, in any sense, have economic or financial democracy. Why not?

Democracy in Politics and Government

We have taken a bold step *toward* power to the people in setting up governments such as that of the United States of America.[16] However, what we mean when we say democracy and what we currently actually have are different things. We say we want democracy and that democracy is the ideal. Currently, we have instances of the people voting on issues and we are heading toward more referendums. However, we have these votes—*by the people*—overruled by courts. We have not achieved perfect democracy in our government. Beyond the point that we merely vote for those that represent us, we have so many loopholes if you will in our representative democracy. The rise of the bureaucratic state—Congress ceding more and more authority to the executive. The dominant power of the Supreme Court. None of this is democratic enough.

We have countless instances of modern politicians that say one thing during an election and then govern completely differently. There are huge conflicts of interest due to political campaign donations.

Moreover, we have a much bigger country today than we used to. The House of Representatives we started with had 65 representatives: 1 rep for every 60,000 people. Today there is 1 rep per 740,000 people.[17] Structural reasons why the people continue to lose power.

> **By these measures the sad thing is that**
> **for big money lobbyists this is better and better.**
> **It costs those that can afford to buy influence**
> **relatively less to control more people.**

So, "democracy in finance" must mean more. We need to leapfrog.

---

[16] We do not really have true political democracy. It is representative democracy. We elect those that represent us. That in and of itself is perhaps not democratic enough. True power in the hands of the people may be direct voting on more and more issues—if not all issues—by the people at the ballot box. Akin to referendums. Where the people are asked to vote about an issue, such as government bonds (spending) for a new library or park or school, whether or not to allow abortions or gay marriage.

[17] If today's ratio were the same, there would be 12 U.S. House representatives in your one district! There would be 5,345 representatives in the U.S. House! Perhaps that is excessive.

Democracy in finance should ultimately be more akin to a quantum leap from behind the eight ball to out in front. Changes to our economic mindset and financial systems that move us to an extraordinarily different future compared to what we have now. We need to leapfrog our current form of democracy.

Democracy in Finance

We vote to give people political power.

So, why do 7 unelected people make all the decisions about money, which is arguably the more important thing, or has such a huge impact.

Why is it that we vote about who represents us and we have "democracy" for voting our government representatives? But we don't extend that to the actual printing of money. Who prints the money? Why them? Where does it go? These are the questions to answer now.

In other words, the people can decide.

We have democracy in a lot of areas. We vote for our representatives. We do not have democracy in the printing of money.

Think democracy.

Voting on where the money goes. Voting on who gets the money.

It is time for the "democratization of finance."

Not a brand-new idea. John Taylor on the link of democracy and finance, writing in 1814: "Wealth, like suffrage, must be considerably distributed to sustain a democratic republic; and hence, whatever draws a considerable proportion of either into a few hands, will destroy it. As power follows wealth, the majority must have wealth or lose power."[18]

John Taylor is not a name we study today or even think about in terms of finance.[19] However, he may, in the due course of time be seen as a brilliant economist, many, many years ahead of his time.

Currently, our financial system is for the most part managed through the Federal Reserve. The Federal Reserve is an unaccountable entity. The people don't have much power or control.

This power granted to the Federal Reserve is not unique. A related entity, the Supreme Court, is similarly tightly controlled and removed from the people's oversight. And, oddly so indeed. Neither were part of the original Constitution. But federalist loyalists to the King and used to controlling society would work tirelessly to ensure that the country would eventually be ruled ultimately by a Supreme Court and a Central Bank. Lifetime appointments at for nine justices at the Supreme Court to decide all laws.

---

[18] http://afterthefuture.typepad.com/afterthefuture/2010/09/quote-of-the-day-john-taylor-of-caroline-.html
[19] https://en.wikipedia.org/wiki/John_Taylor_of_Caroline

We need to 'do' democracy a lot better in America. We can start in finance.

8
FOUR D'S:

DECENTRALIZATION OF FINANCE
DECENTRALIZED FINANCE

Beyond democracy and bringing the power of individual voters into the financial system is an interrelated—or perhaps 'instead of/both'—option to focus on decentralization within the financial system. Decentralizing the power and control of our economy.

Call it the "decentralization of finance."

Finance needs to be decentralized.

New York City and Washington, DC dominate our economy from a matter of control over the financial system. That must be spread through the country.

Beyond geographical concentration is power within the hands of too few people and a limited number of institutions. Thus, decentralization to involve more people and processes in managing the economy.

> *Decision-making (in finance and the economy)*
> *must be made throughout the country,*
> *throughout the economy, and*
> *by a far greater number of people.*

This will be the trend of the 21st century. Financial and economic decision-making will be dramatically decentralized in coming years.

Decentralize control a) away from Washington DC and New York City and b) away from too much concentrated decision-making by a select few people.

Beyond New York City and Washington, DC, Finally

Too much control is centered in New York City.

And from Washington, DC a coordination of still more power emanates.

Unfortunately, most ideas and solutions regarding taking power out of the Wall Street power brokers simply switch power to other authoritarian leaders.

That is what we already have. The fox watching the hen house. Washington DC regulating in such a way that New York City banks are the controlling nexus of power in America. For example, the recent creation of the "Consumer Financial Protection Bureau" sounds all great but in reality, is just a way for the banks to watch themselves.

Silicon Valley, California (and Seattle, Washington) seem to be leading the way in shifting the power of gravity to places beyond NYC and DC. Still, the big giants of tech—the so-called "frightful five"[20]—are thus far playing by the same rules when it comes to finance and the economy.

Beyond All-Powerful Government Institutions

Beyond geographical concentration, too much control is in the hands of too few people. A handful of powerful institutions have way too much control over our economy and financial system.

A select handful of bankers and leaders should not be deciding which banks will get the money first, what the interest rates will be, how much money to print and with whom to establish close connections regarding the distribution of money.

There are many ways to look at financial decentralization. The biggest example is "Too Big to Fail" banks. The economy should not be run so predominantly by only a handful of mega banks.

Also, the Federal Reserve—which is the 1 and only central bank for the United States—is far too centralized in how it controls the overall economy.

Why is it that the power in the printing of money is in the hands of so few? We have, in the U.S. at the Federal government level, three branches of government, consisting of $435 + 100 + 9 + 2 = 546$ people.[21] Then we have

---

[20] https://www.nytimes.com/2016/01/21/technology/techs-frightful-5-will-dominate-digital-life-for-foreseeable-future.html

[21] The legislative branch consists of the 435 members of the House of Representatives and 100 Senators; the executive branch consists of the President and Vice President, who is

state governments. And local governments. Meanwhile, the power to print and distribute money exists only at the national level via powerful government interests. The Federal Reserve is the *central* bank of the United States. Today, the creation of money, monitoring of the money supply and decision-making for national financial transactions and monetary policy is entirely too centralized. So, starting with bold changes to the Federal Reserve we may rightfully call changes—the "decentralization of finance."

The Opposite of Socialism or Communism

Decentralization is not necessarily a new concept. However, it has yet to capture the public attention as a definition let alone a movement with a future.

In the 1930's FDR's right-hand man, Louis McHenry Howe envisioned "economic domination out of the hands of financiers (to a future) where the country's economics would be dominated by the producers."

Back in the early 1900's it was *suppose-to* be, first, the progressivism of Teddy Roosevelt and then, second, the New Deal of FDR which would shift the economy in a direction toward better circumstances for all Americans.

When Louis McHenry Howe made his remarks he surely felt he, as part of the newly elected FDR administration was on the way to steering the country along to the progressive ideals of the early 1900's. Ultimately, Howe's vision was not succinct enough to ever become something. And, socialism isn't what Americans wanted then. It is a deeper issue that can be solved other ways.

What is not needed is to romanticize past notions of socialism. Though I do believe that since Americans have shown an incredible ability to do just about anything at exceptional levels. If America wanted to become socialist, we would probably do a bang up successful job at figuring out how to do it right.

However, traditional socialism is largely about placing power in the hands of a powerful government.

Decentralization is a solution in the opposite direction from that centralized control. The main problem is we are *too* centralized as it is.

Decentralization of finance is so radically different from communist and socialist ideals. There should not be a powerful central government making decisions to ensure we are all on the same fair level. *The means are the opposite, while it is the outcomes that could be considered more socialist.* Decision-making needs to be in the hands of everyday people. That is the essence of the principle of decentralization.

We should bring finance down to as many people as possible. Out of the

---

added especially due to the tie-breaking power of the Vice President in the Senate; and the judicial branch consists of the 9 members of the Supreme Court.

banking center of Wall Street. Out of the ivory towers. Out of the centralized control from Washington, DC.

Free Individuals (Not Unregulated, Free Markets)

The point for me is to free individuals. Unleash potential across America. Decentralize—for those capitalists out there—is a step toward pure capitalism.

This is *not* to imply that the concepts here are a secret attempt to have unregulated, free for all markets. That is missing the point.

The point is that control in a handful of banks is not a free market. And all of America—its most socialist elements included—would benefit from freer markets, or truer forms of capitalism.

I want small businesses able to compete with big corporations. Entrepreneurs thriving in town. What policies can help enable small business to thrive? For example, cutting red tape in a way that makes it easy for them to compete while monitoring public safety.

We have become more and more centralized.

Is this populist to decentralize? Is it progressive?

The solutions are as much Trump as they are Elizabeth Warren or Bernie Sanders. Or, rather, what any of these politicians are *in theory* to their supporters.

Truly put the people in power. Put the sources of power much closer to the people. For example, citizen panels could make recommendations regarding potential projects. Thus, instead of much of the economy being run by Wall Street banks, the financial power would reside with the population at large.

Innovation and American ingenuity is very much at the center of this concept. Real world Americans, such as truck drivers and union employees could be at the table discussing the economy at large. In fact, the Federal Reserve Board of Governors could be replaced by citizen decisions. What should the national interest rate be? Well, for one thing, anyone *setting* an interest rate is not free market.

We need radically more decentralization. The answer does not lie in Rockefeller style capitalists like today's Warren Buffett's, Bill Gates and Mark Zuckerberg's. Much better than the Kings and Queens of the past but we are still nowhere close to human potential.

The polar opposite alternative to our current very centralized financial system is to decentralize finance to such an extent as to allow individuals to act like the banks. Let individuals have a Fed discount window to borrow against with no collateral. Can we talk through a thought like that and turn it into some progress?

31

Change to the central bank Federal Reserve system will either come over time through complete political change in Washington where a new bill will be written changing the framework. Or, change will come all-of-a-sudden. As it has to many industries in retail and technology. New concepts and inventions will rapidly leapfrog our current way.

9
FOUR D'S:

THE
DISTRIBUTION OF MONEY

How is money distributed? Two essential perspectives on this one very important word. Over and above, and beyond democracy and decentralization, distribution is perhaps the most important.

The word "distribution" has a couple different meanings. First, in the actual giving out of an item. Second, the resulting spread of that item.

In the case of money. First, who gives the money out. Second, how much do people end up with.

So, who spreads it out? How? And, why?

And then, is the resulting spread of money among the entire population reasonable and just?

And within each meaning is a multitude of factors and connotations.

Distributing Money

Who distributes the money? Who hands out the money? Who gives the money out? How are they doing that? This is one part of the distribution of money. How is the money disbursed; dispensed?

So, on the first question, who is giving the money out?

In the words of Ron Paul, "Law permits this highly secretive, private bank to create credit at will and distribute it as it sees fit."[22]

Paul laments this in his 2009 book, *End the Fed*, that it was Congress that has set up this secretive Federal Reserve and put the power to distribute money into the hands of so few.

Why does the Federal Reserve have exclusive control to print and distribute money? These are questions we, as regular people, are just now starting to ask. The Federal Reserve was formed in 1914, but only now—over 100 years later—are people saying, 'well, why is it that way'.

Murray Rothbard simplifies it "the Fed prints dollars and hands it out."

And, counted as one of Rothbard's Laws: "If you have the power to print money you'll do it." Call that a question of: the ethics of money production.

State governments cannot print money. Why should the federal government? If government must be relied on to print money, then why not place the power at the state level?

Income Distribution

Taking a look at society, what is the end result of that distribution?

Once it is given away, how does it end up from the perspective of each individual person?

How much does each person end up with? How is the money spread out among the people? This is 'distribution' in the sense of 'is the money distributed across the population?' This view of distribution then touches on incomes, income gaps, CEO pay. Inequalities of the resulting distribution are calculated by some as the Lorenz curve.

How is the money spread out among everyone? Is everyone happy with the result? Is money divided up among all of us?

In theory, capitalism is brilliant. Everyone has the same opportunities in a free society to work hard and make something of themselves. Some of us end up with lots of riches. And it is due to their hard work and effort. However, capitalism in theory is not balanced with an objective review of reality.

**Capitalism in theory is not balanced
with an objective review of reality.**

Due to the ridiculously ultra-centralized and undemocratic manner in-which the money is given out, the resulting opportunities are not balanced.

Drastic changes are essential. We must fix the way money is disbursed. And with those changes we will see a much better resulting end distribution.

The goal is not just to give everyone equal amounts of money. The goal is not to fix all imbalances.

---

[22] *End the Fed*, Ron Paul, 2009

One goal however is to take away unfair advantages. We can get money distribution a lot closer to a lot more people. People don't really have enough access to money. Or, more succinctly, it is not really enough *people* that are touched. There are still far too many people that (for lack of a better analogy) fall through the cracks Many more people need access to big time capital.

Fair is Not the Goal

Addressing income distribution disparities does not mean the end goal has to be: "fair."

Among those that have taken on the endeavor to create a better financial system and economy, one that has spent more time and effort than most is John Kenneth Galbraith. His 1996 work on this subject is appropriately named for his goal, *The Good Society*. On his concept, Galbraith said *"The Good Society does not seek equality in the distribution of income. Equality is not consistent with either human nature or the character and motivation of the modern economic system. As all know, people differ radically in their commitment to making money and also in their competence in doing so."*[23]

We are not all the same. We are not all in it for the buck. Some have little desire, care or concern about money. Money is not even important to some people. Other people don't want to work hard. Others don't put the time or effort in to become competent at a skill that can earn them money. Some work hard but just take the money they are given. Some people don't want to, or need to, make that much money.

On the other hand, money is quite important to others. Some will cut corners and do whatever they can to get ahead and/or 'get theirs.'

Still another category of people wants to make the big bucks but just can't quite figure out how, or never seem to get the breaks to get there.

Finally, some could care less about money but end up with a lot of it.

So, what do we do?

Is there a better, or right, answer to what the distribution *should* be?

Galbraith asks "What, then, is the right course as regards the distribution of income?"

"There can be no fixed rule, no acceptable multiple."[24]

Galbraith carves out that it is completely acceptable to both recognize there is a problem that needs to be corrected while at the same time not point fingers or presuming everything should be equal.

To date, in addressing income quality, the typical course taken by government has been to provide a "support system" for the poor, "a better

---

[23] *The Good Society*, John Kenneth Galbraith, 1996, pp 60
[24] *The Good Society*, John Kenneth Galbraith, 1996, pp 63

break for those at the bottom."[25]

Another option that is typically viewed as a major part of the problem is "to address the personal income maximization of corporate management" (such as placing a maximum income multiple relative to the lowest paid employees) as corporations have "become a major cause of socially adverse income distribution."

Penalizing so-called white-collar crime is another method to protect "honesty in financial transactions" including, for example, insider trading and addressing speculative and deviant investment activity.

An effective process of capital allocation is critical to a healthy economy.

How much money should be circulating? How much money should be available? Who should decide?

Radical overhaul is needed, and more people involved in the distribution of money is the long-term answer. Pick the path forward:

Either the people need to be in charge of the money, or the money needs to be distributed by, and to, the people.

Distribution is all a matter of the lack of democracy and the over-centralized management of our economy. In the words of Galbraith, "distribution of income derives ultimately from the distribution of power." Power is "both a cause and a consequence of the way income is shared." The problem perpetuates itself through power.[26]

---

[25] *The Good Society*, John Kenneth Galbraith, 1996, pp 63
[26] *The Good Society*, John Kenneth Galbraith, 1996, pp 65

10
CENTRAL BANKING

BANKING AND MONEY

There are a lot of advantages to why money and finance are the way they are today. When we save money, we want to know it will be safe. Banks provide a place to hold our savings securely.

Your $1,000 is safely tucked away at the vault inside Bank ABC. At home under the mattress, someone might discover it, take it. At the bank? Nope. Safe inside the bank.

Beyond this security is the next benefit of banking. It's almost magical.

The economic principle of "liquidity transformation."[27]

Liquidity transformation. In plain English, you don't have to go to that vault to retrieve the money when you need it. For example, instead of simply cash, we also have a checkbook. Your money is available in other ways then literally the same exact cash.

Back in the Renaissance era financial centers of Europe (such as Milan, Italy) liquidity transformation was one of the most profound breakthroughs. New ways to move money beyond literally and physically taking the money over the hills and through the mountains.

As an aside, I subscribe to the idea that the past is what has gotten us to the ability to do even more amazing things. We can look at, say, crude oil, as evil or you can look at it as an amazing discovery that we have used wonderfully on our way to the next thing. And so, it is with me and the

---

[27] *The Alchemists*, Neil Irwin, 2013. Pp 30

Federal Reserve and our current financial system. Hey, job well done. Now, on to the next.

Beyond the checkbook. The ATM machine is magical. You can go around the world to little kiosks and have access to your saved money.

More... we don't even need to hand the money (or a check, or credit card) to the person receiving it-- such as wiring the money.

**All of this seems basic to us today
but it is part of the amazing advances in money movement
that are a major contributor to our
economic achievements and rising standard of living.**

That is *our* perspective—as a customer of a bank. There is another perspective on the advantages of saving money at a bank: the bank's perspective.

The bank has the $1,000 that you dropped off. What does the bank do with it? They should safely store it for the customer. And for that, as a business, they should earn a fee. They should charge a storage fee. This simple view kind of demystifies the bank to just an everyday business like a restaurant or dry cleaner. Hey, we will save your money right here. When you need it come on back.

Yet, just like other businesses come up with more and more things they can sell. Like gas stations sell soda, bubble gum and beef jerky. Banks charge different fees for checking accounts and ATM withdrawals. Banks have expanded the number of ways to make money off your savings.

And then, real innovation happened by doing something with the money.

Banks lend the money out to other people. It didn't stop there. Banking has gotten more and more complex and increasingly regulated. Banking today is unrecognizable from the simple business it should be. To such an extreme that something will have to change.

One issue is fractional reserve banking.

Fractional reserve banking means that your bank only needs to have a fraction of the money people have saved with them on hand at any time in case of withdrawal. This is what enables lending.

Over time, the fractional reserve ratio has continued to decline. Today, banks need only have 10% on hand of the money you have given them. What if a bunch of the banks customers all wanted their money on the same day?

Trading--even speculative trading-- takes place now, by banks.

All of these are reasons why banks are becoming "too big to fail." Not just because they are too big. But they are too big, don't keep enough money on hand, and they are able to gamble. All these risks are reasons why the banking system has the potential for collapse.

Money

What are the origins of money?

Suffice it to say that money was originally primarily used as a method of exchange. And it was "hard money" or "hard currency." In other words, a physical coin. A coin made from a metal. Originally, bronze, copper or silver. Silver for a long, long time. Eventually gold. And gold became "the standard."

Paper money is relatively new. But it is not as European as might be thought.

Marco Polo was astonished by the amount of paper money in China. The currency was printed by Kublai Khan in the 13th century. Khan paid for everything with paper money. If there is something Khan wanted, he printed the paper money and give it to them. Khan's power and clout meant everyone had to accept the paper money for payment. Then, those receiving the money used it throughout the society. In those days, it was such a new idea. And it fascinated Marco Polo, "with these pieces of paper they can buy anything and pay for anything." One ordinary person would give another person paper money and receive in return nice belts or such. Kublai Khan had succeeded in building trust throughout society to have a piece of paper serve as a medium of exchange.[28] China was the originator of the magic power of money?!

Chinese leaders had been trying paper money under prior governments such as that of the Sung Dynasty. However, those governments continually paid for more and more items and labor with paper and the money quickly would lose its credibility.

It was not until 1648—400 years later—that Europe (and thus Western society) issued such paper money in Sweden.[29]

The U.S. Dollar

The original colonies of the United States—even before the Constitution was established were political entities that issued "bills of credit" as a means to help finance the French and Indian Wars. Paying for wars has historically been a large reason why money is needed. Upon war, there is a sudden and huge need to mobilize troops and weapons. So, money must be printed up.

That is one important point—that the expansion of the supply of money

---

[28] *The Discoverers*, Daniel J. Boorstin, 1983. Pp 502-503

[29] *The Discoverers*, Daniel J. Boorstin, pp 502-504

dollar". Today, simply: "The United States of America.".

And at the bottom of the dollar bill? Today, under the picture of President George Washington, it says "ONE DOLLAR." In 1935. it read "One Dollar in silver is payable to the bearer on demand."

The difference is a change to what is called "fiat money". Fiat is Latin meaning "let it be done" or "it shall be."

Fiat money is not backed by anything. The only thing fiat money is backed by is the government's ability to print more of it. U.S. dollars prior to Sunday August 15, 1971 were backed by a precious metal commodity: gold or silver. From 1933-1971, a one dollar bill could be exchanged for an ounce of gold. Could you imagine? Money actually meant something as recently as 1970! That one-dollar bill in your pocket. Just one dollar bill. It could be exchanged for an ounce of gold. Today it takes over $1,000 to buy an ounce of gold. That is what Ron Paul is talking about when he says that the Federal Reserve has been making our money worthless over time.

The future of the U.S. Dollar

What is the future for the dollar? As a fiat currency, it is subject to all the restraints of history. Well-known interest rate expert James Grant said, "the dollar is faith-based... there's nothing behind it but Congress."[35] Money is based ultimately on trust. And how much you print, affects how safe it is for people to trust it. Too much money printing and you have a problem. How does that happen? It might not happen. It's unpredictable. If or when it does, historian H.W. Brands said, "the next tremor might trigger another tsunami, producing even greater damage than before."[36]

As money and currency evolve it has been a great era the 20th century where the dollar is universally accepted around the world and we can travel anywhere and just about buy anything we want. That does not have to be the case going forward.

The Death of Money, James Rickards, 2014 pp 292 According to U.S. economist and historian, James Rickards, the dollar's demise could happen in 1 of 3 ways. First, world money is created that trumps the need for the U.S. dollar. Rickard's suggests monitoring the development of SDR's. Or, second, a return to the gold standard. Or, third, societal disorder creates a crash in trust of the dollar. A fourth possibility, not mentioned in his book is the action of other countries. In a global economy it is not only what Americans think about the dollar but how other countries choose to accept dollars. What if a country banned the use of dollars? Or gave no value to U.S. dollars? Future wars may be over money (as opposed to traditional causes such as religion or resources or territory).

---

[35] *Greenback Planet*, H.W. Brands, 2011. Pp 121.
[36] *Greenback Planet*, H.W. Brands, 2011. Pp 3.

11
CENTRAL BANKING

WHAT IS A CENTRAL BANK?
WHY IN THE WORLD DO WE HAVE
THEM?

One bank that manages an entire economy.

That is a central bank.

Now, just about every nation on the planet has one.

The oldest central bank in the world? Opened in 1668—350 years ago.

**There are calls to make one
big global central bank overseeing
finance for the entire world.**

In the United States, the Central Bank is called the Federal Reserve.

If the Federal Reserve were proposed today for what it is, the proposal would be laughed off the table immediately.

What free market—free society—would hand control to a secretive, unelected, unaccountable organization to manage the entire economy?

A central bank epitomizes the three problems standing in the way of the future of a better financial system.

1) Central banks are too centralized.
2) Central banks are not democratic.
3) Central banks act as the sole distributor of money.
4) Central banks fix interest rates and interfere in markets

MARCUS R. BOWMAN

In the distribution of money, Central Banks work closely with the biggest banks. It is a process best summarized as legal counterfeiting. Giving money to a handful of big, private banks. All in close cooperation with the government—financing and backing deficit spending.

In the United States, there has always been a struggle over who prints the money. It was among the most distinguishing fights at the founding of the United States of America. Alexander Hamilton and Federalists loyal to the British King pushed hard for centralized control over finance.

Ultimately, America did not want a central bank. A battle was won by Andrew Jackson to halt centralized banking in America.

The First Central Bank

England formed a central bank in 1694. That bank, the Bank of England was established nearly 100 years prior to the U.S. Constitution! King William III oversaw the creation of the Bank of England. And it survives to this day.

The first central bank predated the Bank of England by a few years. Sweden opened the first central bank in the world.

The Sveriges Riksbank, or Riksbanken, was formed in 1668![37] It is Johan Palmstruch who was behind the creation of Sweden's central bank. Palmstruch is also credited with the production of the first paper money in Europe.[38]

Sweden and Britain had the first two central banks. Both of those central banks predate the existence of the United States. Even more interesting, central banks predate the establishment of legislature-style government.

How the U.S. Ended Up with a Central Bank

The roots of a U.S. central bank date back to Alexander Hamilton. He was the first Treasury Secretary in the United States. Hamilton was a big proponent of a Central Bank.[39] By time the U.S. Constitution was being written and ratified, central banking had already been firmly established in Europe. Thus, there were plenty of 'loyalists'—of which Hamilton was one—that were hoping to get a Central Bank in the new country, just like Britain

---

[37] Some believe the Bank of Amsterdam—founded in 1609—was the true precursor to central banking.

[38] https://en.wikipedia.org/wiki/Johan_Palmstruch

[39] http://www.let.rug.nl/usa/essays/general/a-brief-history-of-central-banking/central-banking-in-the-united-states.php

44

already had.[40]

War financing has usually been what gets a central bank over the hump in terms of necessity.[41] According to Alexander Hamilton, "a nation is threatened with war (and) large sums are wanted on a sudden to make the requisite preparations. Taxes are laid for the purpose, but it requires time to obtain… If there be a bank the supply can at once be had."[42]

Today, Hamilton is being recast as a sort of noble, poor man of St. Croix—the ultimate immigrant. However, reality is Hamilton was one of just 600 nobility on an island filled with over 30,000 slaves. Growing up free among so many slaves, he was an automatic aristocrat. As such, in the U.S. he steered the direction of the new country like the kingdom. The people of America ran to get away from the imperialism of Europe; and yet Hamilton was working to reimpose all of it in the new country.

The fight between those wanting a central bank in the U.S.—just like the one England had—versus those that wanted more freedom in America's approach hit a peak with the Presidency of Andrew Jackson. It wasn't until Andrew Jackson, in the 1820's, that freedom in banking was fought for. Up until that time Alexander Hamilton had succeeded in establishing the Bank of the United States which was kind of like a central bank. Jackson shut it down. And the U.S. managed an era of competition in banking (and currencies) for a few decades; up until the Civil War. Which, we likely cannot go into all the history of Abraham Lincoln and the Civil War but suffice it to say here that there were likely more than coincidences going on regarding the "need" for a war at that time and why Lincoln was the one needed and why some very significant changes in money, banking and currency happened around that time, such as the Legal Tender Act of 1862.

A true Central Bank—which is what the Federal Reserve is—was Hamilton's plan from the get-go. America—being so independent—made it more difficult. Ultimately though the central bank was rammed through Congress in 1913… just in time to fund World War I.

Modern Central Banking

---

[40] Ironic here is that Hamilton is the focus of a Broadway show that makes him out to be a wayward, mixed-race immigrant for the masses when the truth is he was among the richest 5% of the population on a Caribbean Island filled with slaves and before long found himself inside George Washington's orbit, defending the interests of the King, and the powerful, of Britain. His history is perhaps nearly opposite of his modern depiction.

[41] Britain beat France in the Napoleonic Wars due to stronger banking. Central bank money printing is what defeated Napoleon.

[42] *Alexander Hamilton, American*. 1999, Richard Brookhiser. Pp 92.

Walter Bagehot is a name that few people know. He wrote a book that is, essentially, the foundation of modern central banking finance. The book certainly did not have a catchy name. Few have heard any word of it.

Bagehot's book is far more relevant to where we are today than Karl Marx. And it rivals Adam Smith. The book, *Lombard Street: A Description of the Money Market*, outlines a period of time in the late 1800's when the Bank of England was hitting its stride and dealing with financial crisis. As Neil Irwin said, "to this day it remains something of a bible for central bankers."[43]

The panic of 1866 is one particular event Bagehot covers in the book. The Bank Governor at the time, Henry Lancelot Holland, captured the negative spiral of a panic: "Banking is a very peculiar business, in that it depends so much upon credit (trust) that the very least bit of suspicion is sufficient to sweep away the harvest of a whole year." And such it was in 1866 that the presumed collapse of one bank led to a spiral of claims for withdrawals across England.

Who would have thought "too big to fail" has roots going back so far?!

The Bank of England made the then unheard of, and extraordinary decision to, in the words of Walter Bagehot, readily extend credit and lend to "this man and that man... by every possible means." With that, central banks became the lender of last resort. The move was blasted at the time as "the most mischievous doctrine ever broached in the monetary or banking world." *The Times* also noted that unworthy firms were saved.[44]

Over the years, central banks have been established in all major countries. For example, the Bank of Japan opened in 1882 and the Bank of Italy in 1893. Today, there are few countries without a central bank: Cuba, North Korea, Iran and Syria, for example. Just over 15 years ago, in 2000, there were some other countries that did not have a central bank. Afghanistan, Sudan, Iraq and Libya. There is an obvious theme.[45]

Central banks, per Bagehot, were established to help solve financial problems. Instead, these central banks have overseen everything from massive hyperinflation in Germany in the early 1920's to a massive deflationary cycle in the Great Depression of the 1930's. A "deflationary cycle that the central bankers allowed to take hold" according to the insightful work of Neil Irwin.[46] Central banks are established for stability and yet yield the exact opposite—as we will go into much more detail later in this book.

What is interesting about these central banks is that they have unelected decision-makers. As the book jacket of Neil Irwin's seminal work on this very subject, *The Alchemists*, says "suddenly, in August 2007, three men who had

---

[43] *Lombard Street: A Description of the Money Market*, 1873. Walter Bagehot. Pp 28

[44] *Lombard Street: A Description of the Money Market*, 1873. Walter Bagehot. Pp 32-34

[45] http://www.univverse.org/politics/only-4-countries-left-without-a-rothschild-central-bank/

[46] *The Alchemists*, 2013. Neil Irwin. Pp 62.

never been elected to public office found themselves the most powerful people in the world." This is especially unfortunate in the case of the Federal Reserve—America's central bank. Founded more recently, in the 20th century, it should have been established in a more democratic fashion.

Future of Central Banking

What is the future of central banking? The Central Banks want a Central Bank for all the Central Banks. They want a Global Central Bank.

This is needed to oversee one global currency. As with the European Union (which was an idea from as early as the 1940's) it takes time for all the pieces to fall into place.

Behind the scenes much of the work has been done. Just a few more things (such as a perfectly timed crisis) and then, voila, a global central bank will be open. James Rickards outlines much of this in *The Death of Money.* Operating behind the scenes of the economy—without much public knowledge or discussion—is the Bank for International Settlements (BIS), a sort of 'shadow operator' for central banks, holding gold and Special Drawing Rights (SDRs).[47] These SDRs are a non-descript way of saying "global currency."

Over 300 years in the making it is time to put the brakes on this trend and the continued dominance of a few over society.

Central banks are an outdated idea.
We can also definitively say it is time—
in the 21st Century—
to branch off to new and better ideas.

Central banks and the Federal Reserve are responsible for monetary policy around the world. In a way, they basically set the amount of money that is in circulation. And then they act as the dispensary, with a "discount window" that is open only to the largest banks in the nation. The notion of *any* centralized authority having such a grip over society is the worst elements of authoritarian, communist government and has no business in the future of a free society. Decentralized, democratic distribution of money must be the future.

---

[47] *The Death of Money,* James Rickards, 2014. Pp 276

12
CENTRAL BANKING

THE
FEDERAL RESERVE

In 1913, the Federal Reserve opened its doors.

By the next summer World War I was underway.

By early 1917, the U.S. entered World War I. The ability to freely print money helped to finance the war effort.

The 1920's saw a spectacular rise in the stock market.

Then, just 16 years after the founding of the Federal Reserve, the most disastrous crash in the history of the U.S. stock market took place.

Right after that (not even 20 years into the Federal Reserve) began the largest, longest and worst recession in U.S. history—the Great Depression.

At the stock market decline bottom the Dow Jones Industrial Average was down 90%. Ninety percent!

1913 Federal Reserve opens
1914 World War I starts
1929 Worst stock market crash in U.S. history
1929-1939 The Great Depression

The Federal Reserve—far from a help to alleviate cyclical booms and busts—became the place to create, control and manage them!

Within two decades of the Federal Reserve opening its doors, the size of the federal government conveniently tripled during the 1930's.

The absurdity of swings in our "markets" *since* the founding of the Federal Reserve would not make sense to anyone that talks about why the Federal

Reserve was allegedly needed in the first place.

Interest rates spiked to over 15% in 1981.

Since then, interest rates have dropped to 1%.

Treasury yields have been declining for 36 straight years!

We no longer have regular economic cycles.

We go from one extreme to the other in a straight line.

Prior to the Federal Reserve we had
swings around a normal.
Consider that for 55 years before the Federal Reserve
rates never dipped much below 3%
and they never went above 10%.

From December 2008 until December 2015 the Federal Reserve kept their target interest rate at 0.25%! And just 30 years early interest rates on U.S. government bonds soared over 15%. We are on a Federal Reserve created roller coaster.

In 2009 Treasury Secretary Tim Geithner said, "interest rates were too low for a long period of time" referring to Greenspan's drop in interest rates from 6.5% in January 2001 to 1% by June 2003 before moving the rates back up. At the time dropping rates to 1% was unprecedented. Now, in early 2015, Geithner's words of 2009 are laughable. The Fed is artificially holding down rates. This unprecedented manipulation is squeezing the life out of any normal cycle and perpetuating a downtrend in rates that begin in 1981.

This is what the Fed does. They oversee sweepingly long cycles. And they take prices to impossible extremes. They always have it under control. *Their* control.

84 consecutive months
the Federal Funds rate was kept at zero.
(December 2008 to December 2015)[48]
No fluctuations. No changes.
That is *not* a market.

We have seen huge cyclical swings in interest rates to see a) a swing in rates down to lows never seen before in the 30's to highs never seen before in the early 80s back down to lows that beat the 30's in the 2010s.

Extreme market volatility the likes that
couldn't happen unless coordinated to happen.
A true market would have natural ways of balancing itself

---

[48] https://en.wikipedia.org/wiki/Federal_funds_rate#Historical_rates

without these huge swings.
Moreover,
The prolonged stability of staying at extremes is
mysterious at best, impossible in a market.

It is not new. From 1989 to 1992 a bizarre string of 24 or so interest rate cuts in a row, 675 basis points dropping rates from 9.75% down to 3%. The Dow spiked up 50% in that time frame.

If your friends are the Federal Reserve, you know what the next move of these central banks is going to be. You know when the change is, or isn't, coming.

And the most recent twenty years?

What have the last 20 years looked like?

Tech bubbles. Housing bubbles.

The great recession and massive declines in stocks in 2008.

Chronic unemployment. People working multiple jobs.

Stagnant incomes!

In *The Death of Money*, James Rickards points out the perpetuated myth of central banking, and the notion of the Fed keeping the economy from going to too wild of swings one way or the other.[49] From the Fed Chairman of 1951-1870, William McChesney Martin, said "I'm the fellow who takes away the punch bowl just when the party is getting good."[50]

Well, how many analogies can we run with from there.

They don't invite everyone to the party. And, even then, not everyone at the party gets the good punch.

You might get the good punch. The Federal Reserve gets you drunk (they got everyone drunk on housing in 2006). Then they steal your wallet when you pass out. Then, in the morning, they are serving you breakfast like you are their best friend. Driving home that afternoon their regulatory buddies pull you over for not having a driver's license. Who bails you out? Your best buddy is there again! That's how we are run by Federal Reserve "punch bowl" shenanigans.

Why a Federal Reserve? What do they do?

Why the Federal Reserve? What does the Fed do?

By various interpretations it could be correct to explain the Federal Reserve in three basic functions. According to the Federal Reserve website,

---

[49] *The Death of Money*, James Rickards, 2014. Pp 242

[50] https://quoteinvestigator.com/2010/10/21/take-punch-bowl/

their responsibilities fall into four general areas,[51] but in terms of main functions it is the following three. First, and most well-known is setting the Federal Funds interest rate. They adjust this rate up or down at _ meetings per year. There is big media attention given to the announcement. The purpose of interest rate changes is to guide the economy to better results during down periods and help to curb enthusiasm when the economy gets too strong. The guidelines are expressed as "the dual mandate." All of this we will examine in greater detail. Second, the Federal Reserve maintains a "Discount Window." This window is open to the largest banks on Wall Street. The banks are allowed to adjust their holding by going to the Federal Reserve to borrow on a short-term basis at the established interest rate via this "discount window." Finally, the Federal Reserve conducts "open market operations." If there was a fourth, I would argue it is the collusion aspects. As a quasi-government institution, the Federal Reserve serves as the chief liaison in the "fox watching the hen house;" closely colluding with Wall Street to coordinate activities within the government to the benefit of the connected banks.

The "Dual Mandate"

The Federal Reserve manages the economy to the accomplishment of two statistics: keeping the unemployment rate low and keeping inflation low.

That is the "dual mandate."

Congress passed the Employment Act of 1946, which sought to address unemployment and price stability with an expressed objective:

**"it is the continuing policy and responsibility
of the federal government
to use all practical means... to promote
maximum employment, production and purchasing power."**

This was the birth of the dual mandate.[52]

In 1977, Congress amended The Federal Reserve Act, more-or-less reiterated these monetary policy objectives of the Federal Reserve. The "dual mandate" is thus reflected in U.S. Code and guides the Fed's decision-making in conducting monetary policy.[53] The Federal Reserve also summarizes the dual mandate on their website as: "Conducting the nation's monetary policy by influencing money and credit conditions in the economy **in pursuit of full employment and stable prices**."[54] (emphasis added)

---

[51] http://www.federalreserve.gov/faqs/about_12594.htm

[52] http://www.institutionalinvestor.com/Article.aspx?ArticleID=3410530

[53] https://www.chicagofed.org/research/dual-mandate/dual-mandate

Those are the *two* things the Federal Reserve considers when adjusting the national interest rates.

With respect to a "dual mandate:"

First, there should be more than 2 mandates. More than only 2 goals. The so-called smartest bankers and policy makers on the planet can only discuss and target 2 simplistic numbers? Millions of Americans juggle a lot more responsibilities in their own daily jobs. Any management of a financial system of the 21st Century ought to be able to handle more objectives.

Second, the targets as stated are not thorough enough. They don't solve any problems. They don't help *people*. We need to drill into the numbers so that the management of the economy is directed toward meaningful targets that actually have a positive effect and outcome that makes a difference.

Third, what are we focusing on? For example, since we are simply satisfied that people have a job the Federal Reserve has no need to focus on the quality of that job. Or the income of that job. What if the economy was managed to focus on growing incomes? Where would we be as a society today?

We are capable of a much more complex operation. The current Federal Reserve is too simplistic in its analysis. The amount of data available. The ways to connect and interpret data are changing. Kindly, we could say that the Federal Reserve is not to blame for the past in the sense that this new perspective is only now available. Now, however, there is no excuse. Take GDP versus the stock market. Overlay that with unemployment and incomes. The Federal Reserve really has zero impact right now on what matters to the masses of population in this country. No doubt trickle-down economics can work. No doubt that at some level of course it even does work. The issue is it does it so poorly. There are better ways. There must be better ways now.

The Discount Window

The Federal Reserve has a "discount window" that a select few banks can turn to for emergency lending whenever they need to balance out their holdings. Who has access to the Discount Window?[55] It is not really known the extent of banks with access; nor how much each of these banks uses the "discount window." This type of thing might come out if we could audit the

---

[54] http://www.federalreserve.gov/faqs/about_12594.htm

[55] The Federal Reserve maintains a list of assets that are acceptable as collateral to get a loan at the discount window. https://www.frbdiscountwindow.org/RightNavPages/Pledging-Collateral.aspx

Fed.

Wouldn't it be nice to have your own "discount window?" Another, opaque and abstract term used to describe an aspect of our economy they don't really want Americans to know too much about. How about a "discount window" that any of *us* could walk up to?

Open Market Operations

This one was invented without enough care to cover up exactly what it does. The Federal Reserve is now authorized to buy and sell in the "open market." And with this, "markets" ceased to be.

The Federal Reserve now conducts "Open Market Operations" as its main influence over the supply of money and the entire U.S. economy. The Discount Window has been superseded in importance. So-called "OMOs" are the "buying and selling of government securities in the open market."

The Federal Reserve Bank of New York manages all this, basically via one person: the Manager of the System Open Market Account (SOMA).[56]

The Federal Open Market Committee (FOMC) was established by Banking Acts of 1933 and 1935 as well as amendments in 1942.[57] The FOMC designated the SOMA to execute OMOs on their behalf. That is rather astonishing really. How far removed this has become from the people?

How did we let this happen? We didn't. Authority to conduct OMOs is granted in Section 14 of the Federal Reserve Act.[58] However, the Federal Reserve then blindly delegated the authority to SOMA. Most of the actions of the SOMA are kept under lock and key. The public is not entitled to see how or why SOMA exists. Or what it is SOMA can and does do.[59] Who is the SOMA *manager?* Good luck finding out. You can read about a lot of it though.[60]

Most of the Federal Reserve activities are purely image. Speeches by the Chair. Meetings. A lot of that is just show. Meanwhile, markets are

---

[56] https://www.newyorkfed.org/aboutthefed/fedpoint/fed32.html

[57] The FOMC was preceded from 1923 to 1930 by the Open Market Investment Committee and from 1930 to 1933 by the Open Market Policy Conference. https://fraser.stlouisfed.org/federalreserve/#18

[58] https://www.federalreserve.gov/monetarypolicy/clbs_soma_201003.htm

[59] http://openjurist.org/443/us/340/federal-open-market-committee-of-federal-reserve-system-v-r-merrill

[60] Read about the System Open Market Account (SOMA) here http://faculty.msmc.edu/hossain/grad_bank_and_money_policy/open%20market%20operation_ny%20fed.pdf and https://www.federalreserve.gov/federal-reserve-banks/fam/chapter-4-system-open-market-account.htm and https://www.federalreserve.gov/monetarypolicy/files/FOMC_RulesAuthPamphlet_201701.pdf

"influenced" by intervening in stock and bonds with buying and selling. What does the Federal Reserve buy and sell? What if you were in charge of the Federal Reserve? What would you buy? That is the point of this book.

Meddling in the "Markets"

Unprecedented market interventions of large magnitudes in short periods of time. And then on the other end of the spectrum, massively drawn out cycles to unimaginable extremes. From one crazy extreme to the other. Look at interest rates changes before the Fed and then after.[61] That is the long-term manipulation. The short-term is harder to know for sure, without auditing and demanding accountability. It is probable the Federal Reserve has spurred speculative booms with buying of S&P futures (most astonishingly, sometimes buying to recover a market from a decline that they, or their bank partners, orchestrated). Also probable, their public announcements are coordinated with corporate earnings reports, corporate stock buybacks. Lots of planned and staged news, often using surprise announcements to move the markets.

Instead of relying on a market we have a Fed that may do this or might do that. A Fed that at any moment can throw anything, any news, any decision, any trade at the market. As Ron Paul put it: markets must guess what the Fed is going to do.[62]

There has been unprecedented volatility under the Federal Reserve system

Since 1913	
1914	World War I starts
1925-1929	Huge stock market run-up then crash
1930's	The Great Depression
1940's	World War II
1973	Dollar Crisis
1979-1981	Oil Shock and Record High Interest Rates
1990's	Stock and tech bubble and then crash
2006-2009	Housing bubble, stock crash, "Great Recession"
2010-2017	Record low interest rates, new stock bubble

[61] Steady range prior to 1913 and then wild moves down to an extreme low in the 1940's, up wildly to an extreme high around 1980 and now back down again to an extreme low. https://www.globalfinancialdata.com/databases/Graphs/US10YearBond.png
[62] *End the Fed*, Ron Paul, 2009.

13
CENTRAL BANKING

"QUANTITATIVE EASING"

In late 2008, the Federal Reserve began a "Quantitative Easing" program as its solution to help grow the economy.

Quantitative Easing (so-called "QE") = buying bonds. Neat that they come up with cute and crafty terms to describe what they are doing. It became "Quantitative Easing 2" ("QE2") and then "QE3."

The Federal Reserve was buying government bonds. The purchases were halted in October 2014. Starting in 2008 the Federal Reserve would make various pronouncements. One day, 'we are going to end quantitative easing soon.' Then a couple weeks later they announce an update to keep the program going 'longer than anticipated.' All of this helps control and manipulate the market to the benefit of big bank partners like Goldman Sachs.

Quantitative Easing

The U.S. Federal Reserve came up with a term most people just gloss over as a complicated financial policy: "Quantitative Easing."

Go ahead Fed, do what you need to do. That's what pretty much most of us think. Sounds important. Sounds like a complex solution to a critical problem.

Quantitative easing is the purchasing of bonds.

In 2008, the Federal Reserve started buying bonds from the biggest banks in the world. Astonishing really. And they made the purchases using money made up out of thin air.

The goal is that buying bonds retires them out of the market, shrinking the supply of bonds.

This pushes bond prices up and the effect of that is interest rates drop.

Quantitative easing thus can help to keep interest rates low which is supposed to spur economic activity. It certainly has worked from the perspective of Wall Street banks and the stock market. Straight up in 2009. And 2010. 2011. 2012. 2013. 2014. 2015. 2016. 2017. Hardly so much as a dip. Nine straight years of partying for owners of stock certificates and bonds!

The Federal Reserve is printing money and giving it to the biggest banks on the planet.

The Fed buys bonds from the banks.

Coincidently, bond prices are the highest they have ever been in history. So, the Fed buys these bonds at the most inflated high prices in history too!

Then they come up with a fancy sounding term for it. The Fed says they are engaging in "quantitative easing."

Long-time market observants of the Federal Reserve and Treasury Secretaries say this is operating in an extremely radical manner. James Grant, in a January 2015 *Financial Times* article said, "the virus of radical monetary intervention has entered the world's political bloodstream." He continued in his article referring to quantitative easing as "the practice of buying bonds with newly minted money" and that, with that, the meaning of money itself is becoming lost.[63]

For much of the "QE" program the Federal Reserve was buying U.S. government debt and GSE debt at a rate of about $1 trillion per year.

Where do they hold these bonds that they buy?

In outer space.

What does the Fed do with these bonds that they buy?

If *you* buy a bond you have a holding in your account.

If the Federal Reserve buys a bond where does it go?

The Fed keeps an account like you do. However…

The issue is that the Federal Reserve balance sheet is accountable to no one.

The Federal Reserve balance sheet exists--for all intents and purposes--in outer space. Completely outside the economy.

$4.5 Trillion Balance Sheet[64]

---

[63] https://www.ft.com/content/14078740-9277-11e4-a1fd-00144feabdc0

[64] https://www.cnbc.com/2016/06/13/12-trillion-of-qe-and-the-lowest-rates-in-5000-years-

Accountable to No One

The Fed doesn't need to sell anything they hold or buy. Just like they didn't need any money to buy them. The Federal Reserve didn't need 1 penny from anyone in order to go about their "quantitative easing."

They can print money. They can spend. It never comes back to hurt.

The Fed buys things but never needs to sell.

It is like the Black Hole of finance, able to help whoever they want, and never lose. They aren't protecting anything. **Their assets sit outside of the markets and outside of this world really**.

They don't have to balance a checkbook. And it is a global coordination; and a global experiment. Before quantitative easing in America it was tested by Japan in 2001.[65] A buddy of Ben Bernanke, Masaru Hayami put the idea of buying bonds through its first test.[66] Once that went off without problems, presumably the big power brokers of Wall Street knew they could create and manage a crisis such as they did in 2007-2008. Bernanke could use the power of buying anything he wanted to recover the markets.

Your Balance Sheet, a Business Balance Sheet...
And then the Fed's Balance Sheet

What is inside at the Federal Reserve?

They do have a balance sheet[67]. That is: an accounting of all their assets and liabilities.

Your balance sheet? Your personal balance sheet consists of your assets (checking account, savings, car, home, etc.) and liabilities (loans, credit cards, other debts). You are accountable for your balance sheet. Banks can hold you liable for your debts.

If you don't have enough money coming in there are consequences. If you don't have enough assets you can't get the loan. You can't buy things when you don't have access to any money or capital.

Same with businesses and corporations. Investors look at their balance sheets. They expect to see cash on hand, strong assets and manageable debt (liabilities).

---

for-this.html

[65]https://en.wikipedia.org/wiki/Quantitative_easing

[66] https://www.japantimes.co.jp/opinion/2016/07/19/commentary/japan-commentary/bojs-perpetual-qe-quandary/#.We1OK9enHIU

[67] https://www.federalreserve.gov/monetarypolicy/bst_fedsbalancesheet.htm

The banks have balance sheets. Accountable like a corporation or business. Banks can go out of business if they are not run properly.

Businesses can go bankrupt when their balance sheet goes wrong. American citizens? Of course, we can go bankrupt.

Well, the Federal Reserve balance sheet?

As it exists somewhere out there in space. The assets it holds can just sit on its balance sheet forever. They could simply be erased.

The balance sheet of the Federal Reserve is, today, massive.

Over $4 trillion.[68] Trillion.

Although, again—and believe it or not—it doesn't matter.

The Federal Reserve balance sheet does not matter.

The whole thing. All $4 trillion could simply be zeroed out tomorrow and no one would be affected. They could just start over.

The Federal Reserve could buy up whatever they want to because it is just money printed out of thin air. They didn't need any collateral or money accumulated to go about buying bonds from banks.

Selling the Bonds

Now, it turns out, the Federal Reserve is saying they may want to sell some of the bonds that they bought.

And, of course, they have a neat, fancy term for it.

The Fed calls selling "Balance Sheet Normalization."

"Quantitative Easing" followed by "Balance Sheet Normalization."

Buy bonds with money printed out of thin air, putting them on a fictitious balance sheet. And then sell the bonds.

All of it… all… so they can manipulate the markets. At times they pick and choose. They know when they will go into the market and buy and sell. Their big bank Wall Street friends know when the Fed will be buying and selling.

All of this is why, later, we will talk about just taking the keys to the car away. It is the only way to put an end to nonsense.

---

[68] https://www.federalreserve.gov/monetarypolicy/bst_recenttrends.htm

14
CENTRAL BANKING

THE FEDERAL RESERVE
CAN BUY ANYTHING

Watching CNBC from time to time and hearing that term "quantitative easing" over and over again. And reading *The Wall Street Journal* too, I started to dwell on this notion and started considering:

What is really going on?

The Federal Reserve is buying bonds.

I was struggling to pay my own bills and watching many of the rest of us across the country struggling to pay bills.

So, it hits me that if the Federal Reserve is taking some money to buy bonds why not buy something else? To me, it was a matter of thinking what is the most efficient way to help the economy? Is buying bonds the best way? If you can buy bonds what else could you buy?

If the Federal Reserve can buy government bonds,
why couldn't it buy
just about anything else that it wants?

The Fed can buy anything. They have paid to buy government bonds from big banks. Why not buy things that help the Main Street economy and real people?

Why not, say, buy homes from people in financial trouble?

59

From there, you start to wonder, why not just give people money?

It can get even more absurd from there. Really.

Frankly, our entire $20 trillion national debt could vanish overnight. All the Federal Reserve needs to do is write one check and buy the debt. Poof: $20 trillion federal debt gone.

The Federal Reserve can do whatever they want.

Who Will They Rescue?

Why does the Federal Reserve have power to print money and buy stuff?

The founders of the Federal Reserve have known from the beginning the magic power of simply printing money out of thin air. The United States was jumped into World War I shortly after the Federal Reserve doors opened.

The Federal Reserve can save who they want to.

In 2008, it was the big banks. Soon it could be state and local governments. Puerto Rico to set the precedent? Then, Illinois, California, Detroit and on and on? They save big business. Big banks. Their friends.

To some, it might even be a deliberate strategy to go bankrupt and start over? Some Democrats have expressed such a perspective. Republicans too. Despite the reputation as better stewards of finances, Republicans from Dick Cheney to Donald Trump have said "deficits don't matter" because "you never have to default because you print the money."[69] Look at all the states and cities that are on the verge of bankruptcy. Bankruptcy doesn't take away what you already have. Bridges. Inflated government salaries and pensions. All of that has already been paid and the advantages of it all, already accumulated to those.

Some seriously don't think we need to pay back our national debt. Some believe the national debt is a good thing. Not a new idea. In fact, it is another of the ideas that goes back to Alexander Hamilton: "A national debt, if it is not excessive, will be to us a national blessing. It will be a powerful cement to our nation. It will also create a necessity for keeping up taxation... which will be a spur to industry."[70]

Governments Don't Even Need Tax Revenue Anymore

Printing money has taken government spending to a whole new level.

---

[69] https://newrepublic.com/article/133431/donald-trump-right-deficits-dont-matter

[70] *Hamilton's Blessing*, John Steele Gordon, 2010

Governments can spend with no limit. A government used to have to collect tax revenue to spend. That isn't necessary anymore. They can deficit spend with bond issues. And backed by "the full faith and credit of the United States" (i.e. money printing of the Federal Reserve) investors believe there is essentially zero risk of default when holding a government bond.

Double the Stock Market Overnight? Give People Money?

When I was thinking about the absurdity of buying bonds, one day another couple ideas popped in my head.

First, the stock market goes up every day. So, I was like 'well why not just double the stock market overnight?' If the goal is to get the stock market to go ever and ever higher why not just skip everything in the middle and get right to the point. Why do we have to wait? Just open the Dow Jones Industrial Average at 50,000 tomorrow morning.

Then another idea hits me. How much money does the Federal Reserve spend on buying bonds? Why not divide that amount among the population?

What would that work out to? Like $10,000 per person?[71] Or, what? Back of the envelope math is that just a small part of the QE could have been at least $3,000 for every person in the United States.[72]

**Just take the money you were going to use
to buy bonds from big rich banks and
give it to the people instead.**

More than $3,000 per person. Just provide people their income without even going to work. The Federal Reserve could just give us all some money.

Believe it or not, it turns out the Federal Reserve is actually discussing giving people money.

The concept is to give each person a basic amount of guaranteed money. They call it helicopter money. Money printed and falling from the sky to everyone. The concept has come to be known now as "Universal Basic Income" (UBI). UBI is basically just giving everyone some money to spend.

Why do they get to print money? Who is it that has that power? Who are they giving that money to?

And what kind of economy and world is possible if we start tinkering with who has the money and where it goes.

---

[71] https://www.cnbc.com/2016/06/13/12-trillion-of-qe-and-the-lowest-rates-in-5000-years-for-this.html
[72] At one point in the 2011 timeframe, the Federal Reserve bought about $1 trillion worth of bonds in little over a year.

15
TURNING POINT

THE
TREASURY SECRETARY

It was February 22 and February 23, 2017 when the mission to complete this book took hold of me. February 23^{rd,} it was statements of the U.S. Treasury Secretary. And we will get to that in a moment.

First, the title hit me. On Wednesday, February 22, as I was on the road, the title of this book. The title hit me as a nice play on words. Maybe a catchy slogan too. And really a goal that maybe a title like this can get a little attention and strike a chord to build a good and large following. Provide some cohesion. Toward achieving improvements to our financial system; even radical changes as soon as possible.

Living in Fairhope, Alabama has been a great transition for me right from the start. I really like where I ended up moving to. The little town of Fairhope is thus always on my mind.

I was driving along and thinking about finance, economics and public policy. As I like to do. Much of what this book contains was stirring in my mind. The substance and material has been gathered over the years, much of the content written and it was taking increasing shape. The title though helped crystalize how to really pull it all together.

Then, Thursday morning February 23, 2017—*the very next day*—put the fire in the belly to get the writing cranking. I had turned the TV to CNBC—the financial markets channel. Again, something I am likely to do. CNBC had interviewed Donald Trump's new Treasury Secretary that morning. The former Goldman Sachs Executive, Steve Mnuchin, had just been appointed to the position.

Mnuchin said a couple things of which CNBC clipped a sound byte or two. And scrolling across the bottom of the TV screen it said something to the effect of "**It'll take time to reach (economic) growth goals.**" He also mumbled something like it "may take until 2018." That set this book in motion.

Of course, it is <u>very</u> reasonable for a new Administration to need time. And it totally makes sense to make a statement like that. No one can be expected to come in as a new Administration and flip a switch to faster economic growth.

But what set me off is the full context of who said it and where we are in time and as a society.

This wasn't just a new Treasury Secretary moving into position. It is another of a familiar line of the same people. Goldman Sachs—the big New York City, Wall Street bank and brokerage—is quite used to having such power in Washington, DC.

It has become typical for these Wall Street titans to cycle in and out of the Federal government.

The U.S. Secretary of the Treasury, as they are officially titled, was Jack Lew right before it was Steve Mnuchin. Lew was a COO at Citigroup. Before that, another key friend of the industry, Timothy Geithner served as Treasury Secretary. And former Goldman Sachs CEO Henry "Hank" Paulson was Treasury Secretary at the tail end of the George W. Bush Presidency. Paulson oversaw the financial bailout.

Wall Street power brokers are used to running the Treasury Department.

So, Steve Mnuchin is not new. Not remotely. He has a cadre of the same old folks whispering in his ear and helping to guide the ship.

How much time did it take Wall Street's biggest banks to recover from 2008?

It didn't take much time for Mnuchin and Goldman Sachs to recover. For Wall Street's biggest banks. And for Steve Mnuchin, our current Treasury Secretary. They were back on their feet in short order. 2009. Eight years ago. Already back on their feet.

Goldman Sachs and the biggest Wall Street banks were the first ones getting big time government cash and assistance. They hardly skipped even a beat. Execs like Mnuchin hardly saw a dip in their mega-million-dollar bonus checks.

Meanwhile, the rest of the country had folks left and right that were losing jobs, losing homes and losing businesses. Many Americans were watching their

own 401k balances' melting away.

So here it was, February 2017. Just about exactly 8 years removed from the worst of the financial storm of 2007-2008. And Goldman Sachs needs more time to figure out how more Americans can be helped? For the previous 8 years Goldman Sachs was front and center inside the Obama White House. Mr. Hope and Change didn't get through to any of them. A guy who campaigned ever so eloquently about helping real people.

So, when I heard the words about it taking time. I knew there wasn't going to be a fix. It was time to start making a difference.

The Treasury Secretary for the United States of Goldman Sachs isn't going to ever make anything better.

In 2003, President George W. Bush appointed John W. Snow to the post of Treasury Secretary. A lot of people dump on George W. Bush, but this one move was a determined effort to put a non-banking, non-Wall Street, private sector businessman in charge at the Treasury Department. Snow was a railroad guy. Former CEO of CSX. He was not from Wall Street.[73]

That certainly had to be the moment Wall Street decided they would have no problem throwing W. under the bus. Snow was pushed out and in the middle of 2006, came Henry (Hank) Paulson. From Goldman Sachs.

The CEO of Goldman Sachs in as Treasury Secretary. Why in the world would the mega-millionaire CEO of the world's biggest bank go in to run the Treasury? The orchestration of the financial crisis was set in motion. Not much more than a year later, Paulson and his boys started their games.

---

[73] Paul O'Neill was George W. Bush's Treasury Secretary just prior to Snow. O'Neill also was not from Wall Street. O'Neill was called on by Bush to replace Lawrence Summers, a Robert Rubin protégé and the ultimate financial globalist and Wall Street insider. Summers was serving as Treasury Secretary the last few years of the Clinton Administration.

16
TURNING POINT
THE 2008 CRISIS

The 2008 economic crisis (mid-2007 to March 2009) was an incredible phenomenon which witnessed countless Americans suffering terrible economic consequences while the largest Wall Street banks were handed big, fat checks from the government.

In hindsight it is surreal. The so-called smartest bankers had to be bailed out. Meanwhile, everyday Americans lost their homes, savings and businesses.

TARP Bailout Vote

Also, we were provided with some clear political distinctions as a result. The TARP "bailout vote" demonstrated Wall Street loyalties cut across the political aisle.

The TARP bailout vote in Congress is one of the few times when the rubber really met the road up on Capitol Hill. The Wall Street loyalists (regardless of whether they were Democrat or Republican) needed to support the bill.

Thus, the result stands as one of the few votes in decades in which there was true bipartisan support. The Wall Street/establishment congress members voted for the bill. The anti-establishment, or representatives that truly support Main Street and the broader citizenry voted no.

The Threat
Never Let a Good Crisis Go to Waste

"Never let a good crisis go to waste." The establishment can create the problem so then they can go solve it with their solution. The Obama Administration was a big proponent of this perverse mentality. [74]Though the concept may have actually started with Winston Churchill.[75] It is a classic refrain of the establishment. A mantra for big government and control. It has become standard operating procedure.

Major pieces of legislation *need* to be enacted immediately following some triggering event. The legislation is usually promoted as "bipartisan" and the name of the bill is most likely going to include something like "for the people." In other words, who could be against it? And it will *need* to be passed right before Congress is adjourning or up against some deadline. Therefore, all the representatives *had to* vote for it. Or else some dire consequence... for all of humanity and all of eternity.

That is exactly how the TARP bailout vote came up. Remember that vote in Congress? Money was needed. A lot of it.

ASAP! Or the world literally was about to come to an end.

Bear Stearns had gone under. Lehman Brothers too. There was AIG. It seemed nearly every week, sometimes every day, there was a bigger and bigger bank or corporate whale that was about to go belly up. It was terrifying.

And so emergency legislation was drafted up for Congress to vote on.

Now hindsight analysis demonstrates the facts that none of us could see in the heat of the moment. First, many of these 'takedowns' were themselves orchestrated. It was the Paulson's and Geithner's of the world calling the shots on many of the decisions that, for example, closed Lehman Brothers.

The drama built to the ultimate storyline: the Dow Jones Industrial Average was going to crash if the TARP Bailout was not passed. Congress members were even threatened that martial law would occur if the vote failed.[76]

The housing crisis was the problem back at this point. And the TARP Bailout legislation was written and originally drafted to fix problems of the housing crisis. That was the main problem leading into the vote.

The legislation was altered at the last minute. The money was not going to go to fixing the housing crisis. Americans suffered in a dull real estate

---

[74] https://www.brainyquote.com/quotes/quotes/r/rahmemanue409199.html

[75] http://freakonomics.com/2009/08/13/quotes-uncovered-who-said-no-crisis-should-go-to-waste/

[76] https://www.youtube.com/watch?v=SHFUa4SpPBU

market for the next several years while a record Wall Street bull market took hold straight out of the gate without a pause from 2009-2017. We know where the money went.

So... the DJIA was going to crash if the TARP bailout bill was not passed.

The initial TARP bailout votes failed, and the mega banks of Wall Street decided to send the ultimate message to Capitol Hill. Better pass the bill! The Dow Jones Industrial Average (DJIA or Dow) had finished the previous week with some nice gains. However, the next week started with a drop of -777.68 points on Monday September 29, 2008. An astonishing 150 points of this loss came in just the last minutes of trading—as if the bankers had picked "Dow down 777 points" before the trading day even started. To setup the needed newspaper headlines to get their money.

The Senate passed TARP two days later. By Friday, a revised bill was passed in the House. President George W Bush signed the bill 10/3/2008 at the end of the week that started with the -778 point message from the bankers.

With the bill now passed did the stock market rally? Ironically, the Dow dropped over 100 points each-and-every trading day the following week. Down 370 points Monday 10/6, down 508 points that Tuesday, down 189 points on Wednesday, down 679 points Thursday and down 128 on Friday 10/10.

The DJIA was at 11,143 the day before the first TARP bailout vote and 10,325 the day it was signed by the President. A week later 8,451. Down almost 20% *after* TARP was passed. And that was just one week later.

The Dow ended up dropping below 6,500. The Dow dropped nearly 40% *after* the bailout was passed! The market was supposed to be saved. The market was supposed to start to recover. The TARP bailout was supposed to save us from the worst. We ended up with a financial Armageddon anyways. Countless small business owners were forced to close their shops. Many people lost their jobs, their homes, their dignity, marriages dissolved amid the financial stress.

The whole point of the bailout was to prevent more chaos in the markets. Ironically, with a safety net coming, Wall Street took the vote as an "all clear" to have maximum fun (for them) and chaos in the markets. Just given plenty of money, they would recover the markets *when they saw fit*. Instead of stabilizing immediately, the bankers did the opposite and created and profited from keeping the crisis going. The low on the Dow Jones Industrial Average would not come for another 5 months, March 9, 2009.

The intraday trading low on the S&P 500 was 666.
One last shot from the bankers.
They were fully in control from start to finish.

Investors saw their 401k's erode. Many, many Americans lost money. And when people were selling in early 2009, the biggest Wall Street banks (flush with all that TARP bailout money) were buying it all. They didn't start buying when they got the money. They let everyone else suffer. And to this day, they haven't cared much of a lick about the rest of the country. If you ask me, these Wall Street banks should be handed heavy penalties. There is no monetary penalty harsh enough really. Shut them down would be fine with me.

Let's Save...
The Smartest People in the Room

There is a lot of blame to go around for the 2007-2008 financial crisis. All of us, regular people too, got caught up and overly optimistic with money. However, much of the blame does fall to the biggest Wall Street banks. The biggest banks—and their revolving door of government appointees—almost willed the entire fiasco into existence. They managed the debacle; step by step.

The key players quickly wrote books[77] afterwards to describe how they 'saved us all' from unforeseen disaster. Writing a book describing how you want everyone to believe the events happened has become a part of the process. Everything they want you to know about is in those books. Paulson and Geithner rushed to get books out, telling us their version of the events.

Paulson's book says "Lloyd (GS) was very afraid that if something wasn't done, Morgan Stanley would fail... And Goldman could be next." The reader is supposed to take that to mean the magnitude of the problem was so great that big steps were needed. But wait, so Paulson used his office to save his former company?! The revolving door must be closed. The fox cannot be watching the hen house any longer. Our financial and political system today is: Heads the big banks win, Tails the people lose.

Heads the big banks win,
Tails the people lose.

When the big banks win it is because of their self-proclaimed brilliance. When these smartest people on the planet lose, well, it's someone else's fault.

Unbelievable. The people's money was used to fix the biggest banks.

---

[77] For example: former Treasury Secretary Henry Paulson, Jr wrote *On the Brink* and his successor Timothy Geithner wrote *Stress Test*.

At a time when the people needed the help more!

We the people paid for *their* losses? These banks are filled with the best and brightest. MIT and Harvard educated superstars. The type of people that a) should face the consequences of the free market they trade in just like anyone else operating a business, working and/or trading in a free market must; and, b) who else is better positioned to handle suffering the consequences? Ultra-rich bankers from MIT and Harvard. That is who can handle losing.

Is America not about getting knocked down and getting back up again? How many small businesses and start-ups fail? So, why can't the smartest, richest people in the country own their losses like anyone else.

Goldman Sachs could have gone bankrupt. At the time the bailout passed the Dow was 11,000. TARP was supposed to save the world. Dow dropped to 6600 anyway—the type of low that would have happened if we would have let the system work its way out naturally with some of those biggest banks busting.

What if we saved the people instead?

August 9th, 2008 the U.S. stock market dropped nearly 400 points. A Federal Reserve statement the following day: "depository institutions may experience unusual funding needs because of dislocations in money and credit markets" and "the Federal Reserve is providing liquidity to facilitate the orderly functioning of financial markets".

The Fed would be helping the banks through the crisis.

What if the Federal Reserve was run for the people?

The Federal Reserve statement could have read "in current circumstances, individuals may experience unusual funding needs... liquidity will be provided to facilitate the orderly functions of day-to-day living, keeping your small business running, and paying your rent and mortgage".

Why do we have a central bank that saves banks?

Why do we have a Congress that votes to save banks?

That is why we need decentralization and democratization of finance.

Dead Wood Legacy

Consider an analogy.

Trees in a forest.

We have propped up the dead trees. These big, tall trees are propped up, so they are crowding out light for the smaller newer trees looking to grow.

In 2007, we had some very big, tall trees up in the forest. They were aging. Beneath their vast canopy were all the smaller trees and the new growth. Little baby trees grabbing what light they could and sprouting up.

What happened in 2008? A couple medium-sized trees were knocked over, like Lehman Brothers, and Bear Stearns. But not the big ones that should have. Not Goldman Sachs, or Bank of America, or Citigroup. Not one of those super big trees was allowed to fall over like it was naturally ready to.

What did we do instead?

We chopped wood from smaller, new trees (the bailout money) and we used that wood to prop up the bigger trees (the mega banks). We nailed fresh wood to the base of the biggest dying trees.

So now we have propped up giants. And we have a lot less fresh energy around in the forest. Those trees we cut down might be much bigger by now.

There were many of the smaller trees (big regional banks and such) that did not get caught up in the excesses of the upside in real estate and stocks in 2006-2007. Plenty of cautious money managers that kept a lot of cash on the sidelines. They were ready to go to work when the inevitable might come.

It would have been those prudent managers that would be leading us today. Instead they never really got a chance to take a bigger role.

Rather the biggest banks have consolidated more power.

They have far more power today than they had before.

We don't have a true capitalist system where failure is allowed for big corporations and big banks. The biggest risk takers have the most access to Washington, DC.

Taxpayers bail out "those that created the crisis, the major financial institutions." Continuing the words of Noam Chomsky, "You wouldn't do that in a capitalist system."

These banks want this bailout way.

They can't play in a real free market any better than most small businesses. So, they use political power and financial clout to get their edge. Fresh innovation is the way of the U.S. We need to keep America bold and dynamic. And all must enjoy the ups and downs of freedom.

A Better Future for All

Real people across America took it on the chin. Sitting at the dining room table… or driving down the road… wondering… what will be next for them.

Losing a business and their dream.

Losing a job and their income.

Losing their houses. Losing their savings.

Meanwhile, these mega bankers are bailing themselves out. Successful "rent seeking." It's disgusting.

So, a totally new system is needed and required. A decentralized economy (economic framework) that works for a much, much broader economy.

There are so many good, honest, hard-working people out there. And they deserve better.

Honesty needs to be rewarded.

Hard work needs to be rewarded.

Who is out there earning it?

Even volunteer work. How many people are out there volunteering their time or working jobs for very little money? They are unsung heroes. How can we reward *them*?

None of this is to say that it could have happened without our own involvement. If all of America was diligently managing its finances and not taking financial shortcuts, the conditions would not have been present for Wall Street to exploit. Many of us took out home loans we shouldn't have. Many of us extended our credit beyond good reason.

Still, even that may not be Americans fault. It can more-or-less be demonstrated now that average Americans were simply following the options presented to them by the big banks who purposely loosened credit standards—letting the flood gates open, perhaps (most disturbingly) all as part of a plan for eventual failure. Many of us were made to feel financially invincible. 'No problem, Mr. American, we have a loan for you.' This is not intended as a one-sided Wall Street bashing session. However, the facts are what they are. These are some of the parts that aren't part of their books.

Time to Take the Keys to the Car Away

The solution is not likely to come from within the current financial power or Wall Street's biggest banks. Of the 2008 crisis, Noam Chomsky recalls, "the people picked to fix the crisis were those that created it." Goldman Sach's CEO Hank Paulson was put in charge of the Treasury Department just in time to orchestrate and oversee the crisis of 2007-2009.

"The rich and powerful, they don't want a capitalist system."[78] They want to protect themselves. Continues Chomsky, it is "the Robert Rubin crowd," "the Goldman Sachs crowd." "When you pick those people... (to

---

[78] *Requiem for the American Dream*, Noam Chomsky, 2017.

create the) economic plan (and fix a crisis they created) ... what do you expect to happen."

"It will just go on and on like this."[79] Today, the powers on Wall Street are that much further ahead of the population based on the distortions of the free market from 2007-2010.

David Stockman noted that the day of the TARP bailout was "a decisive tipping point in American capitalism and democracy." It resulted in "the triumph of crony capitalism," that is what "took place on October 3, 2008."[80]

To right the ship will take some bold action by the people, to adopt seemingly drastic and radical new ways. Our financial system is run by what we could liken to strong willed teenagers that are not just going to politely hand the keys back to mom and dad.

The keys to the car need to be taken away. We most likely will need to literally take the keys of power away.

We will need to lug all the dead wood up and out of the forest, so the new trees can see the light and thrive.

[79] Noam Chomsky, via https://www.alternet.org/books/requiem-american-dream-chomsky-income-inequality
[80] The Great Deformation, David Stockman. 2013. Pp. 3.

17
THE GOOD AND THE BAD

THE GOOD IN OUR SYSTEM

All around us, there are *so many* examples of what we have been able to achieve as a society.

Huge professional sports stadiums.

Hospitals filled with incredibly powerful, new health care technologies. We have new found treatments and pharmaceuticals that save, and extend, lives.

New homes for so many people and families.

Big bridges. Long tunnels. Safer new cars... filled with features.

Mobile phones more powerful than an entire computer.

Our country and economic system has also brought out the best within each of us-- competitions like *America's Got Talent* and *American Idol*. There is a book out too about all the amazing things invented and developed in America.[81]

Simple things too.

The simple and yet profound ability to drive-through at McDonald's, order a super-size value meal and be taking our first bite of food within minutes.

We can get in a car (your own or a rental) and drive to wherever we would like—the beach, the mountains, our friends house, a family gathering at the park. We can walk into Wal-Mart and buy just about anything we need, want and/or desire, for a fantastic, low price.

Why does it cost so little to buy so much? Ever buy things for $1, $5 or thereabouts and wonder: how is it possible that thing could be so cheap? It is like the magic of a postage stamp. There is value in numbers. Scale. For just

---

[81] *America the Ingenious*, Kevin Baker, 2016

49 cents you can put a letter in your mailbox. It will be picked up and delivered across the country for you. By combining and consolidating various processes it is possible for you to buy things that no one in the world could come even close to getting the supplies to build it and deliver it to you.

Milton Friedman pointed out the brilliance of the capitalist system and "the power of the market" in a decades-old post now on YouTube, "I, Pencil."[82]

Looking at technology and advances in manufacturing and other aspects of life, industry and our economy can help frame this discussion. For example, a lot of menial tasks get replaced by computers and robots. Inventions of different appliances and utensils save us time in the kitchen.

Thus, replacing certain jobs is a positive. It is not a bad thing that robots replace jobs. We just need bigger discussions around what can we do now? What big ideas can deliver real work and real rewards for a lot of people?

Take for example central banks.

Central banks were a novel idea in the 1600's. They are not likely to keep the U.S. ahead of the game in the future. They are not the best organizing method for a modern global economy. Central banks have failed to bring up people and left so many going on day after day without hope.

What has worked well in the past is no indicator of success is an ever-changing world.

We can do better.
We will do better.

There are far better ways. Financial power-- for lack of a better word-- needs to be brought to the community level. Financial power needs to be in the hands of the people.

The ultimate, best impacts
of an efficient and successful economy--
next--
need to be squarely felt by different people.
And a lot more of them!

Centralized control of the economy is not the path for the future. Creating the Federal Reserve central bank for America in 1913 has benefited Americans. The middle class of America is the rich Wall Street banker to those living in a third world country. Earn more than $25,000 per year? You are among the richest 10% in the entire world.[83] The Federal Reserve, by

---

[82] http://oll.libertyfund.org/titles/read-i-pencil-my-family-tree-as-told-to-leonard-e-read-dec-1958 and https://www.youtube.com/watch?v=R5Gppi-O3a8

virtue of being in the U.S., has benefited the U.S. to the detriment of the rest of the world. There are 6 billion people in the world. So, you might not know who owns and controls the Fed. You might consider yourself quite removed from the banking executives that have direct access to near free money from the Federal Reserve.

However, relative to someone in, say, rural India or Zimbabwe, you are really close to the Fed. All of us in America benefit from this contrived scheme to print money.

There is a lot of amazing greatness that has been going on, and is currently going on, in the U.S. There are ridiculous amounts of good in our current financial system. It is easy to say we live in a better world. Safer. Cleaner. Our financial structure has resulted in a lot of improvement.

So, this book isn't a rant on how bad things are.

The question is:
What now? What from here?

Our economy can be better. The point is it must be better. We can make it better.

We continually make new versions of phones. Every year computers are getting a little bit faster. And both computers and phones have more and more memory each year.

We make everything better.
So… why are we not taking what is already great
about our financial system and economy
and making it ten times better?

Not only do we improve the mobile phones we have. Think back to the radical game changer or the very first mobile phone.

That.. is the vision for changing our economy.

How can we take an economy that is like a static, landline telephone (the brilliant and amazing invention that it was) and revolutionize it into an economy that goes with you, anywhere? So to speak. And then keep improving *that*.

---

83 https://irememberthepoor.org/3-2/

18
THE GOOD AND THE BAD

WHERE DID WE GO WRONG?

We *do* have so much good in the country and so many more ridiculously great ideas. Yet we are stuck stagnating in a boring economy that is not embracing the biggest opportunities right in front of us.

We stare at our smart phones.

We drive past the same busted windows and dormant buildings.

We see the same people struggling and not utilizing their unique talents.

Where did we go wrong?

The U.S. economy is not what it should be. And it is not what it *can* be. A lot of people are left out. Struggling. Just getting by. Government reported unemployment rates have become fabrications to present an overly positive frame for the economy. Moreover, traditional statistics and reporting on jobs and income simply do not reflect the experience of many Americans.

Where Did We Go Wrong?

Each of us has our own versions of what the problem is.

Is it too much government regulation?

Or an out-of-control, unregulated free-market?

Is it so-called "Crony capitalism?" Some call it "corporatocracy."

There isn't really one right answer. Your answers are as equally correct as mine. We are all products of our own experiences.

And another thing: We can't take back the past. Where we are today is where we are. Spending time complaining about the past and all the errors and wrongdoing will accomplish nothing to make the world better *in the future.*

The point of exploring problems (of the now and past) is A) to help us learn from mistakes and identify areas we can improve upon, and B) for those from outside industries to read this as an idea generator—where your brain fires with new ideas like 'why don't we ___' instead.

Leap beyond too. It will be pointless to fixate on trying to correct any one imbalance or another. Read this complete list of problems simply to always remember it is time to keep the sleeves rolled up and get down to business. Not to fix this problem or that problem, but as an overall reminder.

There is room for improvement. It *is* a little bit of these and other problems that we can make better.

So… where *did* we go wrong?

Was it Reagan?

Was it President Ronald Reagan and plans like "supply-side economics?" Was it the Reagan years when the financial system really started to favor Wall Street instead of the people? Did we start to export America beginning with Reagan? Outsourcing jobs? Consider the "balance of payments" statistics which had pretty much always been positive, or at least neutral up until the 1980's. A big change started under Reagan. And now we have a structurally negative trade imbalance.[84] John Perkins wrote that sometime about the 1970's began a return, on a "global level" of the "robber baron" economics of the John D. Rockefeller days of the late 1800's. The people have failed, "we have allowed corporations to co-opt the democratic process." Instead of "government of, for, and by the people" we have a "corporatocracy."[85]

Was it "Trickle Down Economics"?

The theory of "trickle-down economics" is that money in the hands of the rich benefits all of society because the rich buy things and make improvements. Builders are needed to construct their mansion. Workers build the fancy cars and things the rich buy. Waiters and bartenders get bigger tips when wealthy people come in and spend. The money of the rich "trickles down" and out throughout the economy.

Trickle down? First, what is the definition of 'trickle?' No solution in

---

[84] http://www.worldfuturefund.org/Charts/Economy/tradecrisis.htm

[85] *Hoodwinked*, John Perkins, 2009. Pp 141, 143. Which, by the way, I believe John Perkins is himself "hoodwinked." His book goes on and on about George W. Bush and Republicans. Your average conservative is much more willing to see both parties as a problem. The grassroots support of the Republican Party is just as skeptical of establishment Republicans as they are Democrats. And vice versa in the Republican Party as the establishment only likes its own candidates. Democrats on the other hand are usually all very loyal. And most progressives do not see their own party as a problem. My two cents!

America should be about a "trickle" of anything. We think big and we dream big in America. If it must flow from the top, better to be more like a waterfall.

Second, "down?" Or course the richest and most connected are going to like this idea. Give the money first to the rich and it will find its way "down" to you. That is not the way of the future.

Big Government:
Too many government programs and too much government waste?

In the words of Milton Friedman, "Special interests that benefit from specific programs press for their expansion—foremost among them the massive bureaucracy spawned by the programs."[86] Ronald Reagan famously said, "Nothing lasts longer than a temporary government program."[87] Reagan has a slew of famous slogans about the size of government.

"Government is not the solution to our problem,
government is the problem."[88]

"A government bureau is the nearest thing to
eternal life we'll ever see on this earth."[89]

"No government ever voluntarily reduces itself in size."[90]

"Outside of its legitimate function, government does nothing as well or as
economically as the private sector."[91]

Do we have too many entitlement programs? Is welfare helping at all? President Clinton reformed welfare but many problems still exist. Some form of safety net is perhaps inescapable. But do we have too many entitlements? Is too much given away and expected? "Undocumented immigrants" come here without following the legal process and yet we give them benefits paid for with taxpayer money.

Reagan on providing assistance said,
"Welfare's purpose should be to eliminate, as far as possible,
the need for its own existence."[92]

---

[86] *Free to Choose*, Milton & Rose Friedman, 1979. Pp 97.

[87] http://www.goodreads.com/quotes/540552-nothing-lasts-longer-than-a-temporary-government-program and
https://www.barrypopik.com/index.php/new_york_city/entry/nothing_is_so_permanent_as_a_temporary_government_program

[88] 1981 Inaugural speech http://www.presidency.ucsb.edu/ws/?pid=43130

[89] http://www.presidency.ucsb.edu/ws/index.php?pid=76121

[90] https://www.brainyquote.com/quotes/quotes/r/ronaldreag147680.html

[91] http://www.let.rug.nl/usa/presidents/ronald-wilson-reagan/the-1964-speech.php

[92] From a 1970 interview with *Los Angeles Times*, according to PBS.

And this is the small stuff. Many government agencies and much government spending benefits big powerful industries. Healthcare. Defense. What about the size of major government agencies such as the Department of Energy (didn't even have one up until 1977 and now has a $28 billion budget) and Department of Education (didn't even have one up until 1979 and now has a $68 billion budget)? Are they really necessary? Or, at least do they need to always expand? These questions should be asked.

Burdensome Government:
Too Many Rules, Regulations and Meddling from Government?

Another perspective on where we have gone wrong is to say there has been an expansion of too much government.

Too many rules and regulations!

How many pages and pages of U.S. Code are there? Several estimates in the 1970's placed it around 27,000 pages and now over 74,000.[93] CCH is a firm that has analyzed the federal tax code since 1913. The *tax* code is now over 74,000 pages and 187 times longer than just 100 years ago.[94]

Bureaucracy and ever-expanding government is a problem difficult to restrain. Once established there are negative implications to any changes. And so, the rules and laws have to stay in place in order not to negatively impact anyone.

There has been too much government meddling. We have global government starting. We have federal control of education starting and being implemented faster and faster via programs like "common core." More and more people have government-supported healthcare. Energy and EPA regulations affecting businesses. Banks and corporations burdened with trying to understand all kinds of laws and requirements. Companies have staff time dedicated to complying with government regulations. This has an impact on our global competitiveness. If companies cannot focus on their core competency but must also spend countless hours discussing compliance. Regulation is important. And crony capitalists and corporations must be monitored and accountable. We just need to be a lot smarter about it.

---

https://www.deseretnews.com/top/2866/4/Government-is-the-problem-21-of-the-most-iconic-Ronald-Reagan-quotes-.html

[93] Cfr code of federal regulations us code the official compilation and codification of the general and permanent federal statutes of the United States. there are over 74,000 pages in the federal tax code. As recently as 1913 it was under 1,000 pages. It was under 27,000 pages in 1984. http://www.washingtonexaminer.com/look-at-how-many-pages-are-in-the-federal-tax-code/article/2563032

[94] http://www.washingtonexaminer.com/look-at-how-many-pages-are-in-the-federal-tax-code/article/2563032

Capitalism Itself? Crony Capitalism?

Is capitalism itself the problem? We are so selfish. We aim for short-term corporate profits. Companies and individuals feel the only thing that matters is we are all trying to pursue making money. Do we have too little regulation of our markets? So many elite billionaire bankers seem to get whatever they want out of our economy and Washington, DC. Is this "crony capitalism" the problem? Politicians and government bureaucrats exchange their power for favors. Crony capitalism is the resulting corruption and unfair advantages that are gained by political and government access.

Innovation is lost

We are losing freedom

And we are getting behind in innovation

Small businesses, individuals and entrepreneurs cannot compete with the big corporations that are able to write the rules in Washington DC. Big business literally writes their competition out of business

It is in industry after industry. Truck driving rules. Banking regulations, etc.

Thus, entrepreneurship is lost, and we don't have enough of the big new ideas breaking through. No competition to rail, roads and airplanes in part because we have to keep the status quo. Netflix broke through and took out a dinosaur in Blockbuster. But the real big changes, they get held up and blocked.

Wasteful Spending

Wars and the military industrial complex. Wasteful spending at the Pentagon and throughout government. The Pentagon charged the armed forces excessive amounts for fuel in order to create a slush fund of money to be spent on programs and projects for which Congress would not provide funding. That is the audacity of those in government. Government overcharging another part of government and they both end up with higher budgets! If taxpayers and Congress don't give them the money they desire, then the government bureaucracy just finds other ways to come up with the money and do the projects anyways.[95] Theoretically, because the armed forces are so large and use so much fuel their combined purchasing power would mean lower prices for fuel not higher. Instead the Pentagon receives a markup of at least 20% on average over the years. And, during a stretch in 2015-2016 the Pentagon raised over $6 billion via overly excessive fuel charges![96]

---

[95] https://www.washingtonpost.com/investigations/at-the-pentagon-overpriced-fuel-sparks-allegations--and-denials--of-a-slush-fund/2017/05/20/c5ff4bf4-31b2-11e7-9dec-764dc781686f_story.html?utm_term=.b1a7d48b43c2

[96] https://img.washingtonpost.com/rf/image_1484w/2010-

Spending by government tends to expand in democracies because politicians wish to satisfy voters demand for more programs. Politicians in democracies "seek to alleviate nearly every imaginable 'misery' of their citizens." Thus, "at the behest of voters, democratically elected governments pay for medical care, housing, education, food, entertainment, parks, pools, and sundry other goods and services for voters." In the United States the result is annual budget deficits every year amounting now to a cumulative federal debt of nearly $20 trillion.[97]

Money is also wasted in the stock market. Companies buy back shares of their stock. This makes stock prices go up, but it is a total waste of money in the long-term. It distorts the short-term stock market valuation and the money is gone. Money that could have been used to invest in the company and workers. Instead corporate profits are used to buy paper stock certificates in the market. Really, only to benefit the board members and executives calling for the share purchases. It helps their stock options. Selfish behavior at best. And robbing our present and our future.

The Federal Debt

All the government spending on defense, welfare, social security. We keep spending and spending. And we are racking up federal debt. We have a huge accumulated deficit.

The US government is more than $20 trillion in debt, with actual unfunded liabilities pushing far higher. Meanwhile, American families have amassed more than $1 trillion in credit card debt alone.

The amount of government spending is determined in large part by the Legislative Branch (Congress) and the Executive Branch (President). Still, the Federal Reserve as a lender of last resort backstops the relentless spending campaigns. No one—not Republicans or Democrats—wants to tackle this problem. For some, racking up a huge debt is a deliberate strategy. If a state like Illinois or a city like Detroit goes bankrupt guess what doesn't get taken away? The huge construction projects and the schools, bridges and hospitals that are now built cannot be taken away. Money put in the pockets of government employees--whether salary, benefits, pensions—it's all there for them. Go bankrupt. And then you can do it all over again. It is called "moral hazard" to deliberately engage in this practice. It is the secret of the Washington DC establishment why the biggest insiders are not worried about

2019/WashingtonPost/2017/05/17/Investigative/Graphics/2300-pentagon-fuel-0517.jpg?uuid=1N8eAjsREeelmybgRRqW_Q

[97] Raymond Niles in The Objective Standard writing a review of The Political Economy of Public Debt: Three Centuries of Theory and Evidence, Richard M. Salsman, 2017. https://www.theobjectivestandard.com/issues/2017-fall/the-political-economy-of-public-debt-by-richard-m-salsman/

the national debt. We don't have to pay it back. It is just fictitious money.

Consumerism

Too much consumption. Our economy revolves around buying things.

So, we build strip malls and big box stores. Retail stores. Minimum wage jobs to buy low priced goods from China. Everything is about consumption.

How much can we turn into consumption? Everything? The engagement ring wasn't always what it has become.

Christmas gifts.

Black Friday. Cyber Monday.

Singles Day—a Chinese holiday in which Alibaba broke records for online shopping.[98]

Easter. Halloween. Birthday's. Mother's Day. Father's Day.

Commercials. The 1950's. The TV itself.

With all the consumption comes so much waste. So much waste in production. And waste generated throughout the chain. Boxes to ship things, bags for our McDonald's in the garbage minutes later.

Inflation:
Prices of Goods Rise, but not Incomes

Prices of everything go up year after year. Meanwhile wages are stagnant. The Federal Reserve targets keeping inflation of about 2%. Every year. Every year prices up 2%. And wages for most people? Stagnant.

Today we are rolling out 40-year mortgages and longer.

We have 8-year and longer car loans.

We used to own things faster. We used to earn more for our work. Many families had moms that could stay at home with their babies because their husband earned enough for the family.[99]

You may be doing well but there are too many stuck in perpetual mud.

Technology Replacing Jobs

Is it simply technology? Over the period of several decades. Technology and global trade.

Manufacturing jobs disappearing. Some moving to Mexico. Moving to China. Some replaced by computers. And robots.

The change has been rather dramatic. As recently as 1980, 20% of the economy was manufacturing jobs, but by 2010 it was just 11.5%.[100] Bad trade agreements?

Martin Ford wrote in *Rise of the Robots* discusses a "new economic

---

[98] https://www.cnet.com/news/over-25b-generated-on-chinas-singles-day-alibaba/
[99] http://www.zerohedge.com/news/2015-08-10/escaping-serfdom
[100] *Freefall*, Joseph Stiglitz. Pp 65.

paradigm." Politicians usually try to create more education and training programs. But the world is changing so fast. Ford also stated we have "diminishing returns to education."

We are rapidly adopting new technology and rolling over. Without a plan B for the people left behind. It has an impact. It is bubbling under the surface. And we will need to address it. Either head on. Or by getting hit over the head.

What Else?

Was it the New Deal? LBJ and Medicare and welfare?

A loss of work ethic?

Are we not capitalist enough? Are taxes too high for corporations?

Fill in *your* blank. It is all the reason. The reason we need to improve for the future.

The past cannot be changed.

The point to me is building on where we are and making it better. To me, radical ideas and changes are what can truly make us way better. We are capable of that. We should presume we can make big bold moves with successful outcomes.

If anyone can succeed at an ambitious project, it is the people of the United States! As Charles J. Givens said, "The last four letters of American are I CAN."

What if the answer is that we have never had it right? It is what we know. It has been an amazing ride. But should we be going down a completely different track? Time to carry our bags over the mountain and get on the right track?

19
THE GOOD AND THE BAD

PROBLEMS TO FIX

As much good as there is, we have so many problems in our economy. Too many to list. We shouldn't have this many problems. Some might not be a problem to you, but they are to others. Cumulatively, putting some of this on paper helps determine where we can improve. Then the conversation can start for how. Make the economy, our country and our world a better place.

As the saying goes, 'if we can send a man to the moon…' we should be able to solve some of these problems.

Point them out, and then start working at their solution.

Poverty

Why do we still have so much poverty? Why are there so many poor in the U.S. and around the world?

Amid so much wealth? We have so much poverty.

We need to really stop and think about our priorities.

This is a problem we can fix. And we need to fix.

Why does widespread poverty persist amid continued, ongoing, unparalleled increases in wealth?

Some estimates are that the U.S. government has spent over $20 trillion in the last 50 years on social welfare programs.

In the words of George Weigel what are we (as a society) to do about "the scandal of poverty amidst vast wealth"?[101]

---

[101] Article "Ryan invites a social doctrine conversation" in *The Catholic Week*, September

Many of us take the easy way out and want the government to solve all problems. So long as a politician comes on stage and says they are going to help the poor and talk about a government program, if we support that politician we are a part of that solution. Then, we can rest assured that the problem is now out of site and out of mind for us. Back to your regularly scheduled business and pleasure. The politicians and the government got this! In 1931 Pope Pius XI rejected this mentality calling for decision-making to be left at the lowest possible level in society.[102]

The Wage gap: CEO pay vs minimum wages and income stagnation

The wage gap is perhaps one of the most obvious issues understood by all throughout the economy. In terms of income stagnation, from 1973 to 2013 hourly compensation for the average worker rose just 9% overall. In 30 years![103] That is the equivalent of a $10/hour pay going up to $10.90/hour pay over 30 years. A raise of 3 pennies an hour per year. CEO pay bears little reality to the rest of the economy: 0.003% per year.

Meanwhile, a recent calculation had CEO pay at 271 times the average worker.[104]

271 times higher than the average worker
That is based on a $57,000 per year income!
How many Americans would dream of $57K per year.

There are different categories of CEO. If, in your head, you are picturing the person that invented the idea and built the business from scratch that is different from CEOs of mega-corporations that give themselves huge paydays. If you ask 5 people to divide up the money of a major corporation, how will they divide it up? That is the problem in a nutshell. Our biggest corporations have a handful of people at the top that divide the profits—to themselves.

Pensions

It is going to be difficult to fund all the pensions.

Many, many big pension systems are grossly "underfunded." Meaning they have not put enough aside to pay out all the promises made. Some pension plans are more-or-less total Ponzi schemes.

The people that worked years and years to earn those pensions are going

---

15, 2017. Pp 4.

[102] Quadragesimo Anno (On Reconstruction of the Social Order), Pope Pius XI, 5/15/1931 http://www.ewtn.com/library/encyc/p11quadr.htm

[103] http://www.epi.org/publication/charting-wage-stagnation/

[104] http://fortune.com/2017/07/20/ceo-pay-ratio-2016/

to take it very personal and feel incredibly 'wronged' if they do not receive their pensions.

What are we going to do? Bailout all the underfunded pensions?

At the same time, is the solution to take tax money from people that have also worked hard over the years but didn't get to work one of the 'good' jobs that accumulate these pensions? So, we take tax money from workers that don't even have a pension and use it to pay someone else's pension?

Social security

Social Security is a similar problem. Underfunded at best. Social Security, when initially started had roughly 10 workers paying in for every 1 worker drawing benefits. The program is not viable over the long-term.

Selfish Mindset

We have become a selfish-oriented society. We are told that it is through our own hard work and effort that we either do (or do not) become something in America. It is through your own brilliance and hard work that you are successful. Or it is your own fault that you are not successful.

And yet that misses so much of the structure of our economy and financial system. The closer you are to the bankers the better you are going to be doing.

Manipulated Government Statistics

First, we aren't even monitoring the problems that actually need to be addressed. Second, the statistics that we *do* monitor, are manipulated.

The numbers published by the government are massively manipulated. The Obama Administration consistently decreased the labor participation number so that the unemployment rate would steadily decline.[105] This type of manipulation takes place across Administrations and in all kinds of government statistics. The Trump Administration seems to also have gotten creative in manipulating the numbers. In the summer of 2017 they adjusted the birth-death factor. In August of 2017 this slight-of-hand adjustment added over 100,000 new jobs to the employment figure.[106]

The Federal Reserve manages the economy in part based on the employment rate. A lot of people can be counted to *have* a job. The problem is they may have 2 or even 3 jobs to make ends meet. Their jobs are not paying enough money. Proposals to increase the minimum wage are reflections of the reality beyond just reporting an unemployment report. Many Americans are underemployed. They have college degrees, masters degrees and even PhDs

---

[105] https://www.usnews.com/news/the-report/articles/2015/07/16/unemployment-is-low-but-more-workers-are-leaving-the-workforce

[106] https://www.barrons.com/articles/the-job-the-federal-reserve-cant-get-done-1504321061 and http://thehill.com/opinion/finance/358905-dont-be-fooled-by-low-unemployment-figures

but are working at parking garages and Starbucks. The number of Americans on disability has also skyrocketed. And that is not counted as unemployed.

Much work needs to be done on transparency of government reporting as well as identifying the right statistics to track and guide policy decision-making.

The 'Americanization of the World' and Growth of the "Middle Class"

With more and more people around the world gaining access to money, we will be using more and more of earth's resources. The middle class in America is like 200 million people. Imagine another 2 *billion* people that are middle class.

Some call this over-population.

What will *our* solution be for *them?*

Liberals are going to want to protect the environment and restrict what *they* do Things we have done. To sustain the planet, protect the earth and preserve resources we would put limits on their and our consumption; and limits on their and our movement. These are issues we need to talk about now because one day something *will* need to be done. For example, ow many tourists can go to this or that beach, or this or that National Park? Do we make some wildlife areas totally restricted to any human access? I believe these types of proposals will be coming.

Many in America that think they are poor are so rich. Water whenever we need it. Electricity. Healthcare. Education. Relative to the rest of the world we all have it very good.[107] So, fixes to the economy go beyond just taking on the 1%. Doesn't take anything away from the need to reign in crony capitalism. It just means the problems run deeper. And the solutions too, require deeper conversation.

Divided Economic Experiences

There is definitely a 'haves' and 'have nots.'

Many of us have new cars, new houses. Others have all that plus great jobs and high incomes. Some have all the above plus amazing benefits (awesome healthcare coverage, pensions, retirement contributions, stock options).

We have, in effect, "parallel economies" (or parallel realities). On the one hand the 'well off:' those with benefits and great jobs (such as government positions that you can't get fired from and have so much vacation time off, etc.; landing work in the IPO, high-tech industry; and corporate management) contrasted against those in the retail economy and small businesses that do not receive benefits and are paid very low.

Reality is too many people are left out of the excitement (so to speak) of capitalism!

---

[107] https://www.facebook.com/turningpointusa/videos/1502713653110679/

It is like a couple different parallel economies.

Good times for:

Federal government employees;

Intel, Cisco, Google and Facebook employees; and,

Wall Street bankers and those working for big corporations.

What about the many out there struggling?

It is going to take some big changes. BIG changes to make the type of difference that is needed.

More... Brainstorming

Fill in your own blank. The list of complaints spans a broad spectrum.

Some hard-working business owners will say it is simply laziness. There are plenty of positions they could hire for if only there were skilled and/or motivated workers out there. On the other 'extreme' perspective is talk of reparations. For native American Indians?[108]

Do we not have enough freedom?

Do we need regular people (like truck drivers and retail workers) helping to make big picture economic decisions?

Environmentalists will say the planet is at risk. What is the maximum sustainable population? Is planet earth at risk?

On the flip side you could take this conversation of uncovering problems to fix in so many different directions. Could there be an unspoken deliberate strategy by powerful interests to keep wages low to keep population down? The population would grow with higher wages.

Back to brainstorming...

Do we waste a lot of time and energy on building things and buying things with little meaning? Are we working on the 'right things'? Are we just working to work? Are we creating only to make money? Do we need more purpose?

And we run around. There is not enough time. Most people don't have the money, and don't have the time to tithe, give to charity and/or volunteer.

Stagnant for too Long
Time to Innovate!

More than any of the above is simply fighting stagnation.

We need to innovate!

We all experience time going by so rapidly, right?

It is the year 2017.

Since the 2008 financial crisis, these tech firms-- in combination with their

---

[108] https://archive.org/stream/indiansourwildth00dodgrich/indiansourwildth00dodgrich_djvu.txt

proximity to the Wall Street banks-- have consolidated power within the technology space and even beyond. Google, Facebook, Apple and Amazon in particular are taking new ideas from start-ups as well as branching into completely different businesses (such as self-driving cars). The scary effect is that they are literally driving out all competition and innovation. Entrepreneurs have no opening and thus the number of small businesses has declined substantially in the last decade.[109]

Some of the battles for the economy go all the way back to Andrew Jackson and the founding of the country... Alexander Hamilton.

Regarding Wall Street, the existing building for the New York Stock Exchange (NYSE) was opened in 1903, rebuilding from 1865. Trading on Wall Street and the NYSE dates to 1792! That is when the famous "Buttonwood Agreement" was signed.

The current system of finance, founded before the U.S., has largely been in place for 300+ years. The London Stock Exchange dates to 1571— established in England under the rule of Elizabeth I. And that Royal Exchange was itself modeled off a stock exchange opened prior to that in Belgium. We know central banking in Europe dates to 1648.

**Capitalism—as marked by these entities—is
rather an old way of doing business.**

New organizations and brand-new models of "business" (for lack of a better term) are quite possible. It is time to begin to envision that tomorrow's economic future may look entirely different from today's financial system.

It is time to embrace a bold new future.

---

[109] https://www.theguardian.com/technology/2017/oct/20/tech-startups-facebook-amazon-google-apple

20
THE GOOD AND THE BAD

INCOME INEQUALITY AND THE WEALTH GAP

Income inequality is among the biggest challenges facing society.

I call it an "**income imbalance.**"

The average CEO earned $15,600,000 in 2016. That calculated as 271 times the average income of Americans.[110]

There is an enormous disparity in incomes.

Earning a lot of money, that can be respected. That is freedom.

I definitely believe in the fundamental capitalist values of working hard, making your own choices and having a free society that rewards innovation.

The bigger problem in the gap between wealthy and not-wealthy is that hard work is not so much connected any more to how you are rewarded. You can work your tail off in America and not make much progress.

Hard Work is No Longer Correlating with Pay

It is not as easy as casting the blame on others for not working as hard.

The disparity in income has been persistent—going on for a long time.

Why is it not addressed?

Why don't we try to solve this problem? This gap in income is left continually unresolved in our current economic structure and financial system.

---

[110] http://fortune.com/2017/07/20/ceo-pay-ratio-2016/

It is not tracked or monitored.
Hence, solving it is never discussed.

Income inequality is not calculated by the Federal Reserve. It is not considered by the Federal Reserve. All they track is a basic employment statistic. One Federal Reserve Board member to another:

Do people have a job?
Ok, great, job done, time to go home.
They don't discuss job *quality*... or pay!

Thus, income inequality is certainly an issue within the United States.

It is definitely a major concern in other parts of the world as well.

And, over and above within a country we also need to stop to consider the pay gap of an average American relative to the rest of the world.

Average Americans can point to the CEO easily. And yet, around the world, people living in many other countries can point to the average American as the absurdly rich one. The average American makes 10 times as much as an average person in India.

Looking at statistics as either the "average" (mean) or "median" can twist conversations about income in different directions. Because of the high extremes, the averages are higher than the median.[111] The median is calculated as half of the people are above and half of the people are below. In the U.S., *more than half* the people make less than the average.

Income inequality is certainly exacerbated in the current U.S. economy in large part due to the increasing power of corporations, the rise of the stock market, and the insane levels of pay to CEO's and managers. Professional sports stars as well. They are making big time moola these days. Huge contracts approaching $50 million per year for the top athletes. Thus, we have massive income imbalances in the U.S. Critics like to blame capitalism but communist countries such as China or Russia also have extreme income inequality. The poor in those countries are that much poorer. In contrast, the rich class (synonymous a lot of times with 'ruling class'), use their government connections to have extraordinary wealth. In the words of Milton Friedman, "Nowhere is the gap between rich and poor wider, nowhere are the rich richer and the poor poorer, than in those societies that do not permit the free market." It is not free markets that are the problem as much as it is corruption—crony capitalism.

---

[111] https://qz.com/260269/painfully-american-families-are-learning-the-difference-between-median-and-mean/

Income Imbalance

Is there a better term for the income gap?

Inequality?

Equality is certainly not a goal of mine. I do not believe everything needs to be fair and equal.

It is an "imbalance" in wealth and income.

We are only scratching the surface both in terms of a) understanding the ins-and-outs of income inequality and b) implementing solutions. Prior to implementing solutions there needs to be a lot of brainstorming ideas and dialogue and discussion about the proposed solutions.

Income equality is essentially a look at who has the money at a snapshot in time. And the disparity between individuals. There are of course several other problems that are either or both contributors, or related, to income inequality.

- Wage rates (value of an hour worked and minimum wage)
- Stagnant incomes
- Income from labor vs income from capital
- Access Advantage (being closer to who creates money)
- Asset advantage (using assets to get a loan; stock options and corporate structure; making money off assets such as interest on bonds or even being able to Uber or Airbnb because you own a car/house)
- Geographical disparities (rural vs urban and first world to third world)
- Wealth disparities and the so-called "1 percent"

From this list, perhaps the focus on a better future would best focus on addressing the "Access Advantage:" the use of access (connections/proximity/ control) to get money. John Taylor called this "patronage gained by banking" and equating it with money and power "obtained by conquest."[112] Adding that "enormous wealth invariably accumulates enormous political power."

Income inequality leads to large disparities in the amount of wealth held. And disparities in wealth exaggerate and perpetuate economic inequality.

Wealth Gap, Wealth Imbalance

There is a substantial gap not only in annual income but in accumulated

---

[112] https://fee.org/articles/the-political-economy-of-john-taylor-of-caroline/

holdings of wealth. By some calculations, 8 people hold as much wealth as the bottom half of the rest of the world. This according to Oxfam research on "extreme inequality."[113]

Bill Gates ($75 billion)
Armancio Ortega ($67 billion)
Warren Buffett ($61 billion)
Carlos Slim ($50 billion)
Jeff Bezos ($45 billion)
Mark Zuckerberg ($45 billion)
Lawrence Ellison ($44 billion)
Michael Bloomberg ($40 billion)

Put another way, each of these ultrarich mega-billionaires holds as much wealth as about 750 million other people in the world.[114] This has been called "socioeconomic segregation."[115]

What is interesting is the play on statistics here. Because it is generally calculated that there is over $200 trillion in wealth on the planet. $241 trillion to be exact.[116] By this calculation, the richest 8 on the planet own less than 1% of the total wealth in the world. All 8 do not add to even half a trillion dollars. So, their combined $427 billion into $241 *trillion* is just 0.18% of all global wealth. Less than 1% of all wealth. To put this another way, there are approximately 74 million homes in America. The average price of a home is $189,000. The richest 8 could trade in all their wealth and buy 2.3 million homes in America. That is just 3.1% of all American homes. Not to mention the rest of the world. Not to mention land. Not to mention cars, stocks and all the other ways people own wealth.[117]

The median wealth of a person in America is calculated as $45,000.[118] The richest 8 people on earth hold as much wealth as 10 million average Americans.

You can look at these statistics so many ways.

You can look at *any* statistics many ways. So, how can we keep sharpening our focus? How can we better understand the issue to increase our

---

[113] https://www.oxfam.org/en/pressroom/pressreleases/2017-01-16/just-8-men-own-same-wealth-half-world via http://fortune.com/2017/08/01/wealth-gap-america/

[114] https://www.commondreams.org/views/2017/06/12/now-just-five-men-own-almost-much-wealth-half-worlds-population

[115] https://www.nytimes.com/2017/07/11/opinion/how-we-are-ruining-america.html

[116] http://www.businessinsider.com/the-combined-wealth-of-everyone-in-the-entire-world-2016-9

[117] Author calculations using figures in the articles/reports in the associated footnotes.

[118] http://money.cnn.com/2014/06/11/news/economy/middle-class-wealth/index.html

knowledge?

On the one hand, the richest 8 can't buy *that many* homes and other things. On the other hand, the average American can hardly by anything. Half of Americans don't have enough wealth to buy more than two $20,000 cars. Meanwhile, the richest 8 could buy 21 million cars.

Here is another way to look at the wealth gap.

$$53,375,000,000$$
$$45,000$$

Average wealth held by 1 of the richest 8. And the average wealth held by an average 10 million Americans.

We could go on and on with statistical comparisons where it does seem huge and then doesn't seem that bad.[119]

Where it really is different is at the long tail of the curve of wealth held.

In other words, it takes the combined wealth of *a lot* of people at the bottom to add up to the wealth held by the richest 8. It would be difficult to work out the exact calculation. For example, there are about 325 million people in the U.S. However, say about 240 million of them are old enough to work. Roughly 20 million of those over 16 are in high school or college so you are looking at about 220 million people to earn wealth in America. Pulling a number out of a hat it is probably safe to say the richest 8 holds as much wealth as the bottom 80 million workers. 80,000,000 people to 8.

So, the number of people that have relatively little purchasing power in America is staggering as compared to how the richest 8 can spend in society.

Economist Joseph Stiglitz calculated that the top 1% of Americans control 40% of the nation's wealth.[120] However, these economists are provided money for projects, like his book, that end up directing people's focus on a goose chase. Stiglitz writes about giving more people a chance at becoming the 1%. Admirable and hard to argue; but the problems are deeper than that.

The 1%

It is not wrong to be rich. And 1% of the population should not just be singled out as automatically wrong. At the same time, there definitely are problems in society due to over concentration of wealth. Some people do have far too much money. To some extent it may not matter how great that person is and how nice they are, it is still too much money. However, that

---

[119] Here is more on comparisons of the wealth gap http://www.businessinsider.com/the-combined-wealth-of-everyone-in-the-entire-world-2016-9

[120] *The Price of Inequality*, Joseph Stiglitz, 2012.

doesn't mean we should engage in violence. It doesn't mean we should just presume that 1% of the population is wrong just for getting out of bed. In the words of Alan Kahan, "The existence of vile capitalists did not necessarily demonstrate that capitalism was evil."[121] Today being rich has become "inherently wrong."

The wealth gap gets exaggerated by the fact that money earns money.

Once you own some money you can earn interest on that money and/or invest the money and increase your wealth even more.

You could simply live off the wealth you accumulated. If you accumulated $1,000,000 and put it in the bank earning a relatively modest 3% interest rate. You could take out $30,000 per year every single year.

The issue here is that the wealthy make money just sitting there.

French economist and author Thomas Piketty is among the best at statistically demonstrating the magnitude of this problem. It is not income inequality alone that is a major disparity for society to understand and address. However, Piketty in making many good points is among many astute economists and highly-regarded researchers that are missing bigger points.

Capital/Income

In, *Capital*, Piketty discusses the impact of a higher rate of return on capital versus growth rates. When the rate of return on capital is higher than the growth rate (as it has typically been throughout history) those who are rich and flush with capital earn interest that pulls them further and further ahead of the rest of the population. Earnings from the interest on their savings grows faster than the income of the population. A rich capitalist earning interest is making money while laying poolside. Piketty does a great job analyzing capital/income and capital/labor ratios and why they are both important.

However, ultimately (similar to Occupy Wall Street), Piketty misses the nuance of making a difference. To such an extent that a skeptic such as myself wonders if his book was funded to the benefit of the world's biggest bankers?

According to one review of Piketty's book, *Capital in the Twenty-First Century*, "there are two types of wealth: Income, earned as wages; and the capital built from assets and land. If your wealth comes only from income, you're the loser. The ruling class makes sure its wealth is generated from assets and land." This, according to Piketty division is nearly "the entirety of the basis of inequality in the 21st Century."[122]

[121] *Mind vs. Money*, Alan S. Kahan, 2010.

[122] http://www.businessinsider.com/best-ever-classic-non-fiction-business-books-2017-5/#capital-in-the-twenty-first-century-2013-thomas-pikettys-masterpiece-on-the-roots-of-

What Piketty does not cover is the actual distribution of money in the first place. That is why his book is pushed to the masses. As thought-provoking as it is; as deep as the thinking gets, he glosses over the real root causes. Just the kind of thing establishment interests want the public to read.

Picketty does make poignant points such as drawing the distinction of income versus wealth. He helps his readers grasp why seemingly small distinctions are keys to finding the most valid solutions. Income is what each person earns a year. How does a person earn their income? Are they earning it through work and labor? Or are they earning it because they already own capital? In other words, they have money already and they earn interest income on that money and/or they own the factory and equipment and thus earn money from the labor of others using their machines and buildings? *That* is the importance of delving into differences of wealth (ownership; and counting up what you have *now*—at this moment in time) and income (what you will go out and earn this next week—and in the *future*; and... *how*).

21

THE GOOD AND THE BAD

CAPITAL VS. MONEY

Money facilitates transactions as a medium of exchange. Capital is muck more than that. Capital includes money but is also everything more: access to money (credit), borrowed money (loans/debt), assets (such as land and cars), machinery, tools and the so-called 'means of production.' Capital allows for the storage of money as well. And capital is now also the earning of more money simply by having money (interest).

Capitalism is associated with freedom and free markets but really it is a completely separate thing.

Capitalism is called capitalism because of... capital.

Interest, credit, loans, assets, machinery.

Money is separated out of this.

Free markets and freedom is different too.

Hernando de Soto succinctly says, "capital is now confused with money... the mind (understands) 'money' more easily."[123] In other words, we call things money or associate them with money, but they are really capital.

And capital, a lot of the aspects of capitalism, do not have any intrinsic value. To 18th century French economist Jean-Baptiste Say "capital is always immaterial by nature since it is not matter which makes capital but the value of that matter, value has nothing corporeal about it"

Capital and money are thus totally different. In fact, capital doesn't really exist. It literally is simply a number assigned to something.

To understand capital and money turning to Ayn Rand can help. Rand is

---

[123] *The Mystery of Capital*, Hernando de Soto, 2000. Pp 43

considered one of the titans of capitalist intellectualism. Rand's popularity emanated from her 1943 novel, *The Fountainhead* and is best-known for her lengthy 1957 novel, *Atlas Shrugged.*

The fundamental message of *Fountainhead* is that individualism is better than collectivism. *Atlas Shrugged* features an impassioned defense of money by a billionaire in the novel, Francisco d'Anconia. Rand not only strongly dispels the idea that money is the "root of all evil," she goes on to exalt money as "men's protection" and "the basis of a moral existence."[124] These bold statements are why Rand (1905-1982) is considered today as one of the key 20th century supporters of capitalism, even regarded as a "radical for capitalism." However, philosophically, Rand supported freedom. Her defense of money is based on a medium of exchange and it is unclear what her position would be with respect to delving into whether capital is essential to the freedom she supported.

Capital and Labor

Capital is, to be fair, quite miraculous. Capital is, in many of its forms, the granting of power out of thin air. Print a little money for someone and you have just given that person power. Also, clearly a problem. Capital is easily manipulated. Capital has too much potential to bear little resemblance to the work or contribution of those that may have it.

What then of *labor*?

One downside of the modern capitalist system is that capital is becoming increasingly detached from labor. One's ability to borrow money that they do not have can give them an advantage over the work of any other individual.

The question of the meaning of labor is perhaps at the baseline of all future economic planning. Peter Drucker equated labor to capital by posing a question of each. Drucker asks that we need to identify "the future role and function of labor" *and* "the future role and function of money capital."[125] The essence.

Capital and Production

The dictionary definition of capitalism is "private or corporate ownership" of "capital goods." Who are the owners? And what are the "capital goods" they own? There are two types of goods: capital and consumer.[126] A candy bar

---

[124] http://www.capitalismmagazine.com/2002/08/franciscos-money-speech/
[125] *Post-Capitalist Society*, 1994, Peter Drucker. Pp 69.

is a consumer good. The materials used to produce the candy bar are capital goods.

Now the discussion for this can get technical; and even philosophical and deep. For example, while a candy bar might be truly thought of as only a consumer good, consider a bicycle. A bicycle, even one bought only for personal use does at least have the *potential* to be used as a capital good. For example, one can use a bicycle to deliver newspapers. Same with the microwave oven. The microwave is by and large simply an appliance for your kitchen. A classic consumer good. However, it *could* be used to make cookies that are sold at the local store. Therefore, the owner of the microwave could use it as a capital good. Even a book. The book is merely a consumer good purchased by a consumer, correct? What if the book is used to gain understanding and knowledge that is used in another context.

Raw materials could be considered a classic capital good. And ownership of the means to transport raw materials is also a capital good. The manufacturing facility that the raw materials are dropped off at and then delivered to is also a capital good.

Things start to get interesting from there. Some goods produced at the manufacturing facility—"manufactured goods"—are consumer goods while some are capital goods. Some manufactured goods are produced to be used to manufacture other goods. For example, making a machine.

This is where some definitions of capitalism will divide society into only two classes: the capitalist class and the working class.[127] The capitalist owns the machine. He hires workers. The workers operate the machine to produce the product. The capitalist earns the profit from the consumer good.

The owner of a capital good has an advantage in the system in that they can use the capital good to make and sell consumer goods, thereby earning their living merely by ownership of the asset.

There is no "middle class" according to this perspective. Capital kind of created the "middle class." Money earned, and work used to be more synonymous. There are now "white-collar" jobs and so many ways to make money that are not traditional work. The lines are blurring. Is knowledge capital? Traditional economics looks at terms such as "capital," "labor," "land," "interest," and "rent." The future is likely to skip right over these terms. Either as new ways are simply developed without anyone even putting a mind to the past. As well as by those delving into the weeds of these terms and parsing through to clarify a more efficient, better way.

---

[126] This is only a subset of robust economic breakdowns of a what a "good" is. With respect to this illustration, who owns how a 'consumed good' is put together? It can get quite complex and philosophical. Here, we start at a simple level to begin delving into the subject. https://en.wikipedia.org/wiki/Capital_good#Differences_between_capital_and_consumer_goods

[127] http://www.worldsocialism.org/english/what-capitalism

22
THE GOOD AND THE BAD

NO MORE CASH!?
BITCOIN, AND THE
END OF FINANCIAL FREEDOM

We are a society that functions, more-or-less, on money. We exchange money for what we would like to buy. We exchange our time and effort in labor to earn money.

We *think* of money as something in our pocket.

Just a hundred years ago or so *it was*. Coins.

Before that it was physical gold.

Today?

Today, we are on the verge of a cashless society.

The ramifications could be greater-- and far more negative-- than we think.

Many of the implications are cool and convenient. For example, not having to carry around cash and credit cards in a wallet. Plus, apps on our phone that have our credit card loaded to scan at a store register, such as Apple Pay. This is the easy, visible part of this change.

Bitcoin is the fun, new alternative part of moving to a cashless society.

What will bitcoin mean?

Interestingly, the media initially portrayed bitcoin as an anonymous form of payment for hackers and drug pushers.

What is an anonymous form of money?
The ten-dollar bill in your pocket.

A ten-dollar bill terrifies the government and the establishment.

Why?

Because you are free to do what you want with that paper money.

You can give that ten-dollar bill to a friend in exchange for things the government cannot track, monitor, regulate and tax.

If all money is on a computer than the government will be able to tax and track all the movements of money.

That is what we are heading toward.

That is what bitcoin will inevitably be.

Bitcoin will be regulated to be completely trackable and bitcoin will also be used as the reason to make cash illegal.

The ten-dollar bill in your pocket. Soon it could be illegal to use.

The push to digital money and a cashless society will be sold to us for our own safety and security. And to eliminate unlawful activity. Terrorists can use cash. Drug pushers use cash. So, every transaction needs to be on a computer.

It will be a loss of freedom for all of us.

Bigger businesses will be able to use a cashless society to implement rules limiting the movement of money to their competitors. No joke.

There is a laundry list of transactions
that some online payment systems
(such as Stripe) will not allow.

The government will be able to control whether-or-not your business activity is deemed justifiable. The government will be able to control whether you are permitted to make a transaction. Are you on a corporate-controlled version of something? Good, they will say. That is allowed. Are you on a mom-and-pop website version of the same thing? That is not doing it right. Transactions to that website will be restricted. It is happening already.

Outlawing Cash

The ability to use cash is being taken away from us. We hardly realize how quickly, and definitively, it is happening.

Cashless is already a trend. In just 10 years, Sweden has seen money in circulation decline more than 40% from its peak in 2007. The pace of technology adoption in Sweden (such as via Ericsson mobile phones) has been a big part of the transition. Also, recall that Sweden has the world's oldest central bank. Sweden has a history of leading economic innovation and being willing to push into new frontiers.[128]

---

[128] Read more at, for example, https://www.theguardian.com/business/2016/jun/04/sweden-

A cashless society is a new goal of government. That way, government can monitor all transactions. With all money activity going through government-approved, government-regulated and government-monitored websites they can ensure no one is able to buy products from "the wrong" businesses.

The government is already working hard to eliminate anonymous transactions. Pre-paid credit cards, gift cards and such ways of paying for things that the government cannot monitor are under regulatory review. Banks are already required to fill out "Suspicious Activity Reports" about their customers. [129]In other words, banks are already government-approved spies on their own customers—private U.S. citizens. Make no mistake, finding ways to uncover true crime, especially terrorism, is extremely important. However, the goals and uses of these regulations will impact us far beyond those needs.

Critics of the rise of government power in outlawing transactions call this "Civil Asset Forfeiture." The proposed laws are called things like "Combating Money Laundering, Terrorist Financing, and Counterfeiting Act"[130] but will end up regulating all kinds of businesses and transactions.[131]

Cash is increasingly being watched, monitored and banned. The end of money as we know it could come soon. The end of hard cash could come by 2019-2020. It all could come about very quickly, either via regulatory changes and/or certainly spurred by new technology.

Bitcoin

Bitcoin is a merger of two trends: moving away from cash and onto computers as well as a move to a global currency. Far from being some alternative new idea, Bitcoin is the planned culmination of these two establishment goals.

Bitcoin eliminates cash and puts all monetary transactions on a computer. And Bitcoin is the first global currency. Any computer you use, located anywhere in the world, when you log on for Bitcoin you will see the same price. It is a global, cashless currency.

On Wikipedia you will find that bitcoin was invented by someone in Japan, Satashi Nakamoto. No one has ever seen or heard from him. How quaint. Make no mistake, Bitcoin is a direct creation of the Goldman Sachs banking network.

When I first went in to buy Bitcoin it was supposed to be the wild west and that is what I expected. I quickly discovered there was only one way in to

---

cashless-society-cards-phone-apps-leading-europe
[129] http://money.cnn.com/2006/08/09/news/economy/banks_secrecy/
[130] https://www.congress.gov/bill/115th-congress/senate-bill/1241/all-info
[131] https://redoubtnews.com/2017/06/civil-asset-forfeiture-rises-new-level/

this new cryptocurrency marketplace. Coinbase. There was no back door. Coinbase wanted more information than a bank might ask for to open a checking account: social security number, address, bank account Literally everything. That was the start of me understanding the fix was in.

Initially, Bitcoin headlines touted how it was anonymous. However, that is not the case trying to buy it. And then the fact is, any transaction occurring on the internet has a trail right back to you. Every IP address, every key stroke, can be monitored. If you want an anonymous currency transaction, take a $5 bill and hand it to a friend in your back yard. That is not the case with digital money. And that is why we are seeing digital money. The government. And the financial establishment. They want a hand in every transaction. They want that level of control.

Many of these new digital coins hype how they have built-in ways to make your online transaction anonymous. For example, spin-off cryptocurrencies such as Darkcoin, and others. This is not how regulatory agencies will ultimately approve bitcoin as a mainstream currency. It will be done in a way that, at the end of the day, hand your computer to an expert: they go back through your key strokes. They discover the site you went to, what transaction you made and combine that with review of the servers for the digital currencies and they know where all the money is going. That is the hacker level overview of Bitcoin. The point is that having transactions online, the government will be able to monitor and tax more.

The financial establishment is trying to take control of the transition. Innovations such as Bitcoin have the potential to be a decentralized, financial revolution—or a large part of it. However, to date, Bitcoin seems mostly just a controlled initiative of the very financial establishment it is purported to dismantle. And let's go through that. Technically, the bitcoin network is decentralized. However, centralized control of a decentralized computer network is not decentralized finance. Bitcoin is, and will be, centrally controlled.

23
CRONY CAPITALISM

THE RISE OF FIAT MONEY: DECLINE OF GOLD, AND THE MOVE TO GLOBAL CURRENCY

Unlike anytime in the history of human civilization we are seeing the triumph of fiat currency today. Money has historically had its own intrinsic value. Initial forms of money were coins. They had a value. Even when paper money came about it has historically been tied to a metal, such as silver, or gold. The U.S. used to have a "gold standard" in which the value of a dollar was exchangeable for gold. That standard was abandoned in stages until fiat currency emerged in 1971.

Some would like to see a return to the gold standard.[132] However, a return to the gold standard is not necessarily the answer. Gold does have characteristics for which it is easy to see how it became both a store of value as well as a medium of exchange for so long. Gold has a high value in a small amount of weight. It has a uniform quality. It's durable; easily portable. And it is divisible.

However, it was another metal, silver (which had similar characteristics to gold) that U.S. monetary stability was also based on. Throughout the 1800's silver was demonized in stages, with big changes in 1873.[133] The government

---

[132] For example, James Rickards, who wrote "Anyone who rejects gold as money must feel possessed of greater wisdom that the Bible, antiquity, and the Founding Fathers combined" in his book, *The Death of Money*, 2014. Pp 217

[133] https://www.usmint.gov/news/inside-the-mint/mint-history-crime-of-1873

was moving away from silver and only to gold.

The issue of whether to use only silver, only gold, or a combination of gold and silver to back money was coming to a head in the 1890's when a National Silver political party was formed in 1896. Money issues were a big deal back then. For the new political movement, the "paramount issue at this time in the U.S. is indisputably the money question. It is between the gold standard, gold bonds, and bank currency on the one side, and the bimetallic standard, no bonds, and government currency on the other."[134]

In the late 1800's it was apparent to many concerned Americans that gold alone as a standard was a part of the problem. "We are in favor of restoring the time-honored money of the Constitution-- gold and silver, not one, but both."[135]

Another political movement of that time, the People's Party of 1896 was just as unequivocal; and also referencing a difference between bank-issued money and government-issued money. "We demand a National money, safe and sound, issued by the General Government only, without the intervention of banks of issue" as well as "a just, equitable, and efficient means of distribution, direct to the people."[136]

So interesting the depths of the debate about money back then!

These counter movements actually preferred a government currency because it couldn't be abused by the banks. Little did they know that within two decades the banks would just become the government; and issue the money to themselves via the Federal Reserve.

Proponents of a return to the gold standard, such as Ron Paul are concerned about the ability of the people to have money that has a distinct value. Paper money can vanish. Before Alan Greenspan became the problem as Federal Reserve Chair at the turn of the century, he espoused gold. Writing in 1966, Greenspan said "in the absence of the gold standard there is no way to protect savings from confiscation through inflation. There is no safe store of value" without a gold standard.[137]

Richard Nixon formally took the United States off the gold standard just a handful of years later. In August 1971, Nixon closed the gold window and instituted wage and price controls. The move, in part, "unshackled the central banks in a manner never previously experienced in modern financial history."[138]

Fiat money was born.

---

[134] *The Parties and the Men: Or, Political Issues of 1896*, John Wesley Hanson (Jr.), Stanley Waterloo. 1896. Pp 541

[135] *The Parties and the Men: Or, Political Issues of 1896*, John Wesley Hanson (Jr.), Stanley Waterloo. 1896.

[136] *National Party Platforms 1840-1964*, Kirk H. Porter and Donald Bruce Johnson, 1956

[137] http://www.321gold.com/fed/greenspan/1966.html and
http://www.constitution.org/mon/greenspan_gold.htm

[138] *The Great Deformation*, David Stockman. 2013. Pp. 110.

What is fiat money? Just a piece of paper. It has no intrinsic value. Put another way, prior to 1973 the government had to have a stock of gold available to convert your paper money to that gold in the case you would want to do so. Today, the government can print money and it does not have to have any gold—or any other collateral. Fiat means "let it be done." The government just issues a declaration that the piece of paper is money and voila, "done."

Global Currency

We are, more slowly, losing currencies around the world. The Euro has been the most prolific step toward globalization of money. The Euro turned around 20 currencies into one overnight.[139] An additional 22 currencies are now said to be pegged to (moving in lock-step with)[140] the Euro.[141]

There are still about 165 different currencies in the world. However, 90% of currency in circulation in the world is from the top 10% of those. In other words, about 15 currencies handle virtually all commerce in the world.

At the same time, the remaining currencies are, more-or-less, converging over time. The U.S. dollar to Japanese Yen exchange rate has oscillated above and below 100-1 for several years. And, the Eurodollar to U.S. dollar has oscillated above and below 1 for several years. The establishment calls this "harmonization" and it is a movement in global laws as well. Trying to converge everything into one global government platform—laws, money etc.

However, the U.S. does have to keep it together. The U.S. dollar is globally susceptible for a number of reasons.[142] But, then again, so is the Yen and a lot of other currencies. The value of any of these currencies could dilute rather rapidly—like airline frequent flier miles.

Long-term the push is toward turning the International Monetary Fund (IMF) into a Global Central Bank. For decades they have developed an alternative to the U.S. dollar known as Special Drawing Rights (SDRs). In some respects, it isn't in the U.S. interest to have so many other countries using, and holding in reserve, U.S. dollars.[143] The SDRs are almost a global

---

[139] Depending on your history and counting, between 19 and 22 countries officially became the start of the Euro currency

[140] Another 20 or so currencies are pegged to the Euro—meaning their exchange rate is one-and-the-same with the Euro so even though the currencies are called something different they may as well just be Euros.

[141] https://en.wikipedia.org/wiki/Euro

[142] https://www.forbes.com/sites/ralphbenko/2017/02/25/president-trump-replace-the-dollar-with-gold-as-the-global-currency-to-make-america-great-again/#2bc479554d54

[143] https://www.forbes.com/sites/ralphbenko/2017/02/25/president-trump-replace-the-dollar-

currency unto themselves; though now only used by the biggest banks.[144]

Will we have a global currency as soon as 2018? The Economist magazine says so… in a 1988 cover story![145]

Is it Bitcoin?

Up until this year, Bitcoin was rogue. Alternative. Exciting and fun.

Bitcoin is global. Get on the internet and anyone in the world is seeing the same exact prices. Any of us can make an exchange of bitcoin, quickly and easily over the internet to anyone else, anywhere in the world.

Bitcoin wasn't developed by a random guy in Japan. Bitcoin is intended as a global currency and it is the work of the establishment United Nations and banks such as Goldman Sachs.

So far, the objective is to pull in participants. Beta-mode. Testing. Working out the bugs in the new technology. Is it ready for primetime? That is the stage we are at right now. Testing it in a variety of circumstances. Work it up to scale.

If a new form of money came along that was truly different it would be shut down in a New York minute. Every effort would be made to ban it.[146] If you invent a coin or some form of money it will have to tuck 'the right way' inside the government/Goldman Sachs controlled bitcoin blockchain system. Or it will be shutdown. Fast!

With bitcoin it has been aided and abetted from the get-go. Plenty of media coverage. Well-funded to expand. Not one attempt to reign it in.

In September 2009, the United Nations issued a report outlining their support for the world to move toward a "global currency."[147] Once the idiosyncrasies and kinks have been worked out on Bitcoin and its equivalents then the move will be on to rapidly move in that direction. Already the United Nations has been pilot testing the use of these digital coins; with a focus only on Bitcoin and Ethreum.[148]

Eventually, 2018 or whenever, Congress will have to get involved for some reason and it will be recognized and legitimized. Probably called a "coin" because, conveniently, that is one word that is actually in the Constitution.

---

with-gold-as-the-global-currency-to-make-america-great-again/#2bc479554d54

[144] http://www.imf.org/en/About/Factsheets/Sheets/2016/08/01/14/51/Special-Drawing-Right-SDR

[145] http://www.coverbrowser.com/covers/economist/34#i1678

[146] https://www.marketwatch.com/story/sec-forces-halt-of-initial-coin-offering-2017-12-11?mod=bnbh

[147] https://www.cbsnews.com/news/united-nations-proposes-new-global-currency/

[148] https://www.coindesk.com/the-united-nations-wants-to-accept-ethereum-and-bitcoin-and-soon/

24
CRONY CAPITALISM

WHAT FREE MARKET?

We call our financial system and economy, "free market capitalism."

In theory, I support free market capitalism. The best outcomes seem to arise out of the freedom of individuals. And it is best for all of us as individuals too.

However, we do not have "free market capitalism." And we have many acting in very detrimental ways. And even freedom has been twisted. I don't support the type of freedom that is selfish and takes advantage of any opportunity to get more money under the protection of slogans like "you eat what you kill." That is a terrible guiding philosophy. On every level.

So, what is our society? It is not "free market" and it is not a pure, theoretical "capitalism."

What is our economy really?

If you look at this list of issues: "crony capitalism."

1. Market manipulation by the Federal Reserve via the Bank of New York Open Market Operations (SOMA) of which no Americans are provided *any* transparency about their involvement in stock and bond markets.
2. Electronic trading and front-running of trades in the stock market by large banks
3. Massive banking groups placing their top bankers in positions of power watching their own companies.
4. Quantitative Easing: Federal Reserve buying bonds from big banks.
5. The Federal Reserve setting interest rates. There is nothing "free

market" about fixing an interest rate.

6. Corporations buying influence in Washington DC, writing the laws, setting rules and regulations; crowding out smaller businesses, innovation and competition

7. Federal Reserve "discount window" where a select few banks are allowed to borrow money (at advantageous rates) whenever they need to, or would just like to.

8. Government announcements (statistics, interest rate decisions) of which allies within the financial system know the news before it is made public.

Whether you believe markets are "too free" or "not free enough," both sides are likely to see all of this list as a problem. That is where progress could be made.

As hard as it can be to believe: we simply do not have free markets in the United States. Surely, some of our markets and pricing is fluctuating as markets are supposed to. However, the overall financial system is gamed and rigged by a handful of select bankers. *They know* when they are going to change the prices, i.e. change the interest rates. When they make their decisions behind closed doors everyone else will find out days or weeks later.

It is not a free market. We operate under the illusion of free markets in America.

We Don't Really Have a Free Market

This question of "what free market" is loaded.

"What free market?" can certainly span the political spectrum depending on your perspective.

Our markets are *too* free already. *That* is the problem. Many would contend this. That is a matter of definitions, perception and perspective. It is true that our markets are too free if you call corporate interference in Washington and powerful people using access to gain more money as "free markets."

Thus, many would contend the problem is that our markets are too free?

According to this view of the world, we have a runaway, run-amok "hyper capitalism" or "extreme" capitalism-- and it needs to be reined in and restrained. This perspective is that capitalism has gotten too extreme causing many of the problems in society; even believing the free market is in itself bad.[149]

The corporate-run media feeds this narrative.

---

[149] *One Market Under God: Extreme Capitalism, Market Populism and the End of Economic Democracy*, 2000, Thomas Frank

The U.S.A. mantra is that we have free markets. The symbols we routinely associate with this notion of free markets are our big corporations like Wal-Mart, McDonald's, Microsoft and Apple. And the free market is also symbolized by Wall Street stock market prices and the New York Stock Exchange, NASDAQ and the futures and options trading of the Chicago Mercantile Exchange.

Opponents of the excesses of capitalism would say that if only we regulated the markets more and managed them carefully we wouldn't have disparities of income and we wouldn't have wild swings such as the 2008 crisis.

The problem is in ends and means.

The end is we need to reign it in and regulate it.

The means ends up being Washington crony-insiders writing the laws and making up regulations with the right words and sound bites.

Liberals end up supporting "financial reform" and "protections" that do nothing. In the aggregate I would mostly agree with the pleas of liberals and progressives; but whether I could get a conversation going past the first few words is another matter. People hang on *their own* definition and interpretation. We need to dig deeper.

On the other hand, most of the people that might read this far into this book, may already be inclined to recognize or even know that free markets are an illusion in America.

We don't really have truly free markets in the United States.

Big corporations are not a symbol of a free market. Their collusion with big government perpetuates "crony capitalism" in America. We have unprecedented meddling in the markets. Government comes out with arbitrary announcements. And Washington, DC pushes more rules and regulations that sound like they are reigning in out-of-control capitalism when in reality they are securing the gains for the largest corporations. And banks. That was the case with Dodd-Frank. That bill locked in more power for the dominant Wall Street banks by creating too much paperwork for their smaller competitor banks to keep up with.

Government *is* the Big Banks and Big Corporations

The idea that government can reign in the big corporations and big banks is wrong. The big banks and corporations use liberals and progressives. They use and abuse the media and they use the government. They perpetuate their own control and dominance.

One takeaway is that there is a difference between big established banks and corporations with tight connections to Washington, DC and smaller companies without those connections. You could call it crony capitalism and free enterprise. This distinction needs to become understood by the population.

Also, capitalism does not mean "free markets." That is an essential defining element of this book.

We might associate what we have with free market. We might like what we have. We might be comfortable with what we have. But it is not a free market.

We can do better and yet we are stuck in crony corruption. Capitalists "too often attempt to use the power of government to their advantage" through lobbying and bribing government for favorable treatment.[150]

And we need a lot more freedom if a capitalist-oriented (truly free, dynamic and innovative) America is going to continue to thrive.

---

[150] *A World of Wealth*, Thomas G. Donlan, 2008, Pp 200

25
CRONY CAPITALISM

THE FOX WATCHING
THE HEN HOUSE

Corruption between government officials in Washington, DC and Wall Street power brokers in New York City is a major problem.

The names of the big banks change. But the leaders of the main government agencies largely end up being former big wigs of one bank or the other.

Goldman Sachs

Citigroup.

Robert Rubin. Gabillionaire (my new term I guess).

Hank Paulson. Gazillionaire (what we are used to hearing).

The former, Citigroup. The latter, Goldman Sachs. They both took their turn to oversee our "markets" as a Treasury Secretary government official.

That is crony capitalism.

**The fox saying 'no worries at all, yes, I got this.
I will be watching these sweet little hens.'**

Exploiting positions of power for massive amounts of money.

**The Revolving Door of Wall Street Execs to
Washington DC Big Government Posts
Must Be Reined In.**

Pretty much, these mega-millionaire titans get away with it. Some might call it "white collar crime." You will hear "regulatory capture," or my preferred descriptor: "the fox watching the hen house."

Mainstream economists lump this type of government-business wrongdoing into something they call "rent-seeking." Why do they call this "rent-seeking?"

Because your average Joe, such as me starting out talking about economics and policy issues, has no idea what that term means. If you are reading a book or a news article and you see "rent-seeking" you'd likely just pass over it. Seeing the word "rent-seeking" is not going to make you think anything is wrong. Hearing the words "rent-seeking" is not going to get anyone's blood boiling.

Looking up the definition will do it.

> Rent-seeking: *the fact or practice of manipulating public policy or economic conditions as a strategy for increasing profits; engaging in or involving the manipulation of public policy or economic conditions as a strategy for increasing profits.*

Politely, rent-seeking could essentially be reduced to lobbying. And lobbying is legal. It's regulated. And I am certainly of the opinion that *anyone* should be able to make their case to government.

However, there is a fine line between making the case versus being part of the government and directing the government to your own benefit and protection. Even worse when it comes to Paulson and the 2007-2008 economic crisis they used their positions of power to orchestrate it all!

Lobbying and influence should never result in crony capitalists writing themselves checks through legislative shenanigans.

It has become entirely too easy. It is a culture onto itself. Disconnected.

Fox Watching the Hen House

"Don't worry" says the fox, "I got this all under control here. Have a great day! Catch you later. I will be right here watching over your sweet little hens!"

We let the fox watch the hen house in the financial industry.

And the celebrities of changing this are not really the answer either.

Elizabeth Warren. Says many positive things with respect to shaking things up. Puts forth the persona of a revolutionary. Reality is likely more like a placeholder for perpetuating a complacent population.

Ron Paul? Rand Paul? Audit the Fed? That is not going to make a difference. That is simply buying time to perpetuate the status quo. We need major change.

Fix the problem?

We are doing the opposite. We have institutionalized problems.

The Federal Reserve fixes problems that they create. The bankers are happy because instead of natural economic cycles just happening whenever they would, the bankers can kind of open and close the floodgates at the times they choose. A time convenient to them. A time *they* are prepared for. Do they want to hold the water back? Or are they ready to flood downstream a little? Well, they are right there in charge. And they pull the levers when they want to.

Per legendary libertarian economist Murray Rothbard, "What we are seeing is the old ploy by the robber who starts shouting "Stop, thief!" and runs down the street pointing ahead at others."[151] The finger gets pointed the other way. Hank Paulson writes a book explaining how he saved the economy. Bernie Madoff. "Made off." I mean you couldn't make this stuff up and have it be believable. Truth is stranger than fiction.

History of the Revolving Door

Give 'em credit for being 3 steps ahead of the population at large. There is a level of brilliance, I guess, in manipulating the public and maintaining the grip on power they have.

There is the SEC that most people know. The powerhouse football conference. And then there is the SEC that oversees the financial system: the U.S. Securities and Exchange Commission (SEC).

The government SEC was established in 1934.

The first Chairman named to run the organization? Joseph P. Kennedy, Sr.—JFK's father. It was President Roosevelt (FDR) who appointed Joseph P. Kennedy, Sr., in 1934, to serve as the first Chairman of the SEC.

Another early leader of the SEC was William J. Casey. Chairman Casey graduated from the world of finance to later head the CIA (Central Intelligence Agency) under President Ronald Reagan.

This isn't meant to branch off into conspiracy theories, but the internet *has* made it easier to connect dots. Not faulting them for their ability to get power and keep it. But we can out-game their games. Firewalls need to be established.

Ending the revolving door of Wall Street and government is a major problem to address for a new financial system.

Those looking to exploit the system of capitalism stop at nothing. They do not just 'buy' one political party. They buy both. They buy access to

---

[151] *The Case Against the Fed*, 1994. Murray N. Rothbard, Pp 11.

government. They use government. For their own advantage. They can dress up their actions with new laws that sound all wonderful. They can put lovely sounding people on the TV and have glowingly positive articles written in the newspapers and magazines.

Punish White Collar Crime

There need to be penalties. It is a revolving door between Wall Street and the Washington, DC bureaucracies. Too much insider access. Too much manipulation of the markets. And far too much secretive information sharing with government announcements and transactions to the benefit of Wall Street's biggest banks.

The biggest banks and those controlling the SEC/Fed and Congress can rewrite the rules and change the game whenever however they want. Therefore, broader involvement is needed in regulating. It is no longer acceptable for the fox to watch the henhouse. If they want to close the market they can/will. If they need to change accounting rules they can/will. In fact, they have. In 2009, with little fanfare. Who gets to meet with the President? You? Me? Ha. Corporate CEOs get one-on-one time. Goldman Sachs was one of many corporations that received subsidies in "fiscal cliff" legislation.[152]

As Milton Friedman wrote in *Free to Choose* in 1980, the problem with communist countries such as China and then-U.S.S.R. is "access to government determines position" in society. Surprisingly like modern-day America!

The government is the problem
"one set of rules for the rich" and another for the poor
for the poor market principles are allowed to prevail[153]

"Capitalism cannot work in a society dominated by theft." That according to Lester Thurow who continues that capitalism "needs a legal system guaranteeing the existence of private property and the enforcement of contracts." Thurow sees this as the weakness of a libertarian free market view toward less government. Government is not only needed as a protection to restrain capitalism from unlawful advantage, but it is needed by true capitalists to protect their work.[154]

There needs to be a watcher. It is just that the watcher needs to be completely outside Wall Street. And there needs to be punishment of so-called

---

[152] http://www.huffingtonpost.com/matt-stoller/eight-corporate-subsidies_b_2396559.html
[153] *Free to Choose*, Milton Friedman, Pp 146.
[154] *The Future of Capitalism*. Lester C. Thurow. 1996. Pp 274

"white collar crime." We are locking away people who engaged in relatively small-scale drug trading. And we are penalizing the wrong people in the markets. There are sacrificial lambs, so-to-speak, that are hit hard by financial regulators. Meanwhile, the biggest abusers of the system, such as the top dogs of Goldman Sachs, are zipping across the country to their multiple homes and yachts aboard private jets. So, the calls for "criminal justice" reform ought to include penalizing those that never get caught and believe they are above the law. The whole point of "criminal justice reform" is that far too many citizens are facing disproportionate penalties for minor crimes. At the same time, the major crimes committed at the highest financial levels go unpunished.

There is a level of white collar executive crime in this country that is unparalleled. I doubt very few of the executives either a) think anything they are doing is wrong and/or b) believe there is a chance they will even be noticed for it, let alone c) face penalties and/or charges let alone d) be found guilty and serve jail time and/or pay hefty fees.

It is ridiculous to see regular employees of Wells Fargo all fired while the CEO and management continue about their much more sinister ways. The CEO of Wells Fargo is raking in millions and millions of dollars as this all happens. It is WRONG. Wrong. Wrong. And all the while we see Martha Stewart and Bernie Madoff. Distractions from much bigger crimes that happen right in front of us. How do we turn it around?

Corporations Crowd Out
Small Business Competition

Big corporations have teams of lobbyists working for them in Washington, DC creating regulations and fighting regulations. They create regulations that help protect their business. For example, they create costs of entry for any would be competitors. For example, in the Dodd-Frank financial reform the bigger banks benefit from the mountains of paperwork filings that are necessary. Smaller banks cannot afford to hire all the staff necessary to file all that paperwork. The result is less competition for the biggest banks. And all under a nicely worded term like "Financial Reform". Same thing with the airline industry. They merge and swallow up competition and the U.S. Federal government looks the other way by saying that overall the airlines all have competitive percentages of the overall market. For example, United say is 20% of the U.S. market, and American is around 20% and Delta is around 20%, etc. However, under that surface, Delta controls Atlanta. American controls DFW. And so, they get localized control that helps them keep higher prices while hiding under the umbrella of overall competition. All condoned by their friends in Washington, DC and aided by their lobbyist capabilities. Ordinary businesses and new businesses don't always have that ability. And so, the companies that do find a way to get into an industry anymore, kind of have to game plan from day 1 a government facilitated strategy. JetBlue is an example of a start-up that had government help. In another industry that is Tesla.

These giant corporations work day and night to keep new competition at bay. Smaller businesses, small banks and entrepreneurs are not able to compete against all the rules and regulations. Smaller banks and small businesses are grappling against the power of much larger entities. They don't have the power.

26
CRONY CAPITALISM

RIGGING THE "MARKETS"

Are the markets "rigged" and manipulated? Yes, they are.

Is it a vast conspiracy? No. The point, however, is there is *a lot* of 'white collar crime.' With the same vigor that police investigate inner city drug dealings, we need to investigate Wall Street, the government financial agencies and corporate/banker frauds.

There must be rules and regulations against their illegal behaviors. And there must be punishment.

As I like to say, the only way to put an end to all of this is to 'take away the keys to the car.' They are playing with other people's money. They oversee themselves (and, in the case of the Federal Reserve they aren't even accountable to anyone).

Government Announcements as Intervention

The highest profile economic number for Wall Street is the monthly employment report.

The so-called "jobs number" is released on the first Friday of every month. The number is released at 8:30 a.m. Eastern Time—an hour before the U.S. stock market opens.

Who prepares the number? It is prepared by the Labor Department. When do they know the number? Believe it or not they brief the President on the number a couple days before. So, who knows the number before it is released?

Top brass at Goldman Sachs sure as heck do.

The most frustrating thing about 2008-2009 was so much of it was government decisions. As an investor and trader, I didn't have any idea when they were going to come out with another big decision. When would they declare Lehman Brothers or Bear Stearns out of business? They knew when.

The power of government and the power of the fattest cats within capitalism are the biggest danger to our freedoms and the reason our economy does not thrive for all in the ways that it is capable of.

The Federal Reserve uses "emergency meetings" to surprise the markets at the time they know about as opposed to the regularly scheduled meetings that the rest of the population expect.

Government should not be used by the banks to impact market direction.

Fixing Interest Rates

The Federal Reserve arbitrarily held interest rates near zero for 7 years. Seven straight years of keeping the interest rate at the same level.

First, if anyone is setting an interest rate at a fixed level, that is not a free market. The mere act of *anyone* setting the interest rates is, by itself, not a free market. You don't fix the price of anything in a free market.

Second, the fact that U.S. interest rates are set by a small handful of people meeting a few times a year is absurd. Do we ever stop to think about this? That is communism. It is not a free market or any kind of normal when a small handful of people at the Federal Reserve are in charge of setting the interest rate.

Third, keeping interest rates fixed for 7 straight years is not a free market.[155] That is manipulation. It is not only not a free market, but it is truly anti-market behavior. And it is done for nefarious purposes of rigging their own continued gravy train of power and profits. It is reflective of the reality of too much control by too few people.

Fixing interest rates and holding them at a level for that long is not a free market. Having a small group of 10 or 12 people setting interest rates for everyone is neither a free market or democratic.

Front Running the Stock Market

Just about every trade that goes through the exchange there is a Wall Street bank taking a cut. It happens in a millisecond. The house must get their share.

Worse than that your own brokerage firm will also play with your order when they can.

They might make just a penny or even a fraction of a penny off your trade. Cumulatively, it adds up and makes a big difference.

The fact the take is so small on an individual trade. And the fact it happens in less than the blink of an eye is why no attention is given to this subject.

---

[155] Interest rates in the United States were set at 1% from 2009 until 2017. Set by the Federal Reserve.

Day traders understand this. Day traders experience it and see it happen. The house takes a share. Just like a casino.

Electronic trading on Wall Street has increasingly tilted the playing field against *all investors*. A few major banks handle most of trades. Their computers process every trade being made. They frontline every trade and skim off the top. And they fade trades too. This is bigger money. They make this off higher value trades. A large hedge fund seeking to sell thousands of shares and the big bank handling the trade will get out in front of that.

They have full regulatory capture. So, this isn't going to change anytime soon. Their buddies at the SEC write the rules and enforce the rules.

The problem has become worse with technology. It all happens so fast. And there has been an ongoing race to get trading servers as close to the exchange servers as possible.

It is known as "High Frequency Trading" (HFT). They measure the speed of placing a trade in milliseconds. The ultimate is co-location of HFT servers in the same building that the exchange computers are set-up.[156] The reason "front running" is not illegal is because:

Why would Wall Street regulate away their own profit gravy train?

Famed author Michael Lewis details much of the manipulation of markets in his books. Most relevant is his 2014 *Flash Boys*. Wall Street tries to wash over the public with examples of how HFT is necessary and beneficial. Those that are deep in the weeds of these issues know the difference between legitimate market making that uses HFT from "predatory strategies"[157] that seek only to skim off the top. These are big problems. And, I believe, as the tide of awareness grows, some truly breakthrough innovative solutions are possible. The establishment is *not* going to like playing in 'real, free' markets. They like having all the control setting rules for what they don't like while allowing the processes that give them an advantage.

So, we need new regulators that are not the banks.

Plus, common sense rules that ban front running.

Then, enforcement of the rules by organizations that are not the large banks.

Mutual Funds Skimming Investors

It isn't just trading among the largest banks.

---

[156] https://www.investopedia.com/articles/active-trading/042414/youd-better-know-your-highfrequency-trading-terminology.asp
[157] https://www.reuters.com/article/us-usa-trading-iex-group/flash-boys-exchange-iex-aims-to-price-out-predatory-traders-idUSKBN1AR2CH

Mutual funds engage in tactics that are taking money out of the economy. U.S. Senator Peter Fitzgerald has called mutual funds "the world's largest skimming operation." Mutual funds have grown from just $115 billion in 1980 to over $10 trillion today.[158] So, there is tons of money in the mutual fund industry.

Fees charged by the funds have also gone up.

Fitzgerald takes the common-sense position that with economies of scale mutual funds should be operating more efficiently now. So, fees (charged as a percentage of mutual fund investments) should be going down, not up![159]

Mutual funds are essentially like their own casino. The mutual fund management company (the house) takes a percentage fee off the top and then your left-over money is left to ride the ups and downs of the market.[160] It's all great while the market is going up.

"Open Market" Interventions

The Federal Open Market Committee (FOMC). Talk about an oxymoron! A federal government agency running an "open market committee" that trades in our "markets." The FOMC meets and puts forth a nice public front. These are the friendly interest rate meetings and announcements.

Behind the FOMC is the SOMA. The System Open Market Account (SOMA) is the federal government operation carrying out "open market operations" in the foreign exchange (currency), interest rates (bond) and stock markets. SOMA is managed at the Federal Reserve Bank of New York.

Convenient when you locate the federal government agency right down the street from the exchanges and banks. Makes the insider trading scheme easier.

Just like the creation of the Federal Reserve legalized counterfeiting money for the bankers, their subsequent invention of the SOMA has enabled legalized insider trading. It is brilliant. For them.

When came 1987, the stock market crash was the opportunity for Greenspan and the Fed to expand open market operations from government bonds to stocks. And this set the stage for the late 1990s stock market boom, protected and guided higher by Greenspan and Rubin. The establishment likes to say, 'never let a good crisis go to waste.'[161] When there is a crisis you can jam through legislation and other power grabs while the population has its

[158] https://www.vanguard.com/bogle_site/sp20031103_2.html and
https://www.forbes.com/sites/billharris/2012/08/08/the-10-biggest-mutual-funds-are-they-really-worth-your-money/#1d3669c4f3cf
[159] http://www.wealthmanagement.com/archive/worlds-largest-skimming-operation
[160] http://www.marketwatch.com/story/mutual-fund-casinos-still-skimming-billions-2012-10-12
[161] https://www.youtube.com/watch?v=Pb-YuhFWCr4 and
https://www.youtube.com/watch?v=B62igfNu-T0

head spinning. A ruthless philosophy!

The 29% one day drop in the S&P 500 futures on October 19, 1987 was an excellent excuse for the Federal Reserve (Greenspan had recently become Chair). They *had* to buy stock futures.

All economic indicators were fine going into the stock market crash of 1987. The economy at that time was not in danger, nor overheating. Fed dramatists made it appear as such. One-day drop of 29%! Permission to go into fire mode.

On Tuesday October 20, 1987 the markets suddenly turned around remarkably. The "Greenspan Put" was born. Within months of Greenspan being in charge the market is falling apart. And then bam an immaculate recovery of stock prices. Once a total free market economist Greenspan loved the power of Washington, DC; changed, and threw away everything from his past that people thought they knew about him.

To this day, a rising stock market is viewed as the barometer of success for the Federal Reserve.

Especially in the last 10 years there is no self-correction in any markets. No longer do we have any real, true price discovery. Sadly, if there ever becomes a time to 'save the markets' again you can safely conclude that what will be saved will be the world's biggest banks. Unless... we begin to change oversight and change these exchanges and the entire system.

Just as Greenspan manipulated the 1987 debacle and miracle recovery, the Federal Reserve can take normal markets and just run them up and down based on an announcement. In 1997, Greenspan made his now-famous "irrational exuberance" comment. He signaled to traders that the market was overvalued. Traders and investors believed him. Instead it was a set-up. Some investors sold too early. Other traders shorted the overvalued market. Instead, stock prices went into overdrive. The "market" rocketed 60% higher in short order.

Then, the Federal Reserve had a nice crisis waiting. The Fed had to rescue Long Term Capital Markets in 1998. With prices already way above "irrational exuberance" they intervened on behalf of LTCM. Then the "market" made a parabolic ramp higher into 2000. The tech bubble.

In 2009, there were several unexplainable sharp rallies. The "market" went incredibly straight up an unbelievable number of points in very short times. The government was gaming our markets again. Those of us invested in the markets love the good times and why wouldn't you want the Fed saving the markets and making them go up?

Amid the 2008 crisis, George W. Bush justified his own decisions to allow interference in the markets by saying: you have to save the market to have a market![162] Really? For most of these central bankers they really believe they

[162] https://thinkprogress.org/bush-ive-abandoned-free-market-principles-to-save-the-free-

are saving the markets from themselves. GM, Chrysler, Bear Stearns, Fannie Mae, Freddie Mac. The government swept in with announcements that would wipeout entire companies overnight.

Many people become collateral damage in the process.

Sheila Bair recalls working at the FDIC amid the crisis. She would have to implement dramatic actions on behalf of superiors that would only say "You have to do this or the system will go down." Of those orders she says it just happened over and over: "If I heard that once, I heard it a thousand times." She said there was never any analysis or discussion.[163]

The bankers are so excited about a rising stock market. they really work hard at it.[164] They coordinate with other central banks like China. They coordinate with corporations like GE. Well timed announcements by corporations (such as an earnings report that is, itself, manipulated to be positive) and bam the stock market is back on track. That is their only focus.

November 30, 2011, amid the Greek the stock markets around the world went up 4% in one day. That is not healthy. That is not normal. That is the degree of manipulation that has been going on. The keys to the car need to be taken away. The day before the central bankers were to make the decision to buy the bonds of Greece in the open market, the U.S. market did its infamous "flash crash" dropping to a low of down over 1,000 points on the Dow Jones Industrial Average in the middle of a trading day.

While U.S. analysts tried to figure out what the cause was, the real purpose was used in Europe. As a scare tactic. Europe needed to act fast to approve buying bonds. Thereby granting central banks even more power than they already have. In addition, the bankers benefited by wiping out short-term traders before the news they were sure would make the markets keep going up.

We Need True Free Markets

We desperately need less meddling, especially by nefarious interests.

Reasons you might believe our capitalist society is "too much free market" are basically the same reasons I view the economy as "not free enough."

**If only we just let markets move freely up and down
then all of society would naturally act to
smooth out the fluctuations.**

---

market-system-eef736df2aff/

[163] http://www.nytimes.com/2011/07/10/magazine/sheila-bairs-exit-interview.html

[164] http://www.zerohedge.com/news/2017-06-26/central-banks-buying-stocks-have-rigged-us-stock-market-beyond-recovery

True markets are "chaotic and unpredictable" and "orderly trading suddenly becomes disorderly, even panicky, on the upside or the downside (every now and then)." And this is how markets *should* behave. They self-correct.

Free markets are admittedly hard to define. It is even reasonable to argue that a truly free market is perhaps all but impossible.

However, economists do make a valid point—to me anyways—in arguing the aggregate. That, the bigger the number of people involved the more of a true market it can become.

Critics of free markets point to a crisis like the 2008 meltdown in the markets and believe markets clearly do not work all the time. However, in my opinion, demonstrated through research here, 2008 was a manufactured crisis. It was not as much a failure of markets as it was a failure in regulating out crony capitalists.

The market, left to itself; and the economy-- left to itself-- is indeed a far better direction than most any possible economic system.

F.A. Hayek wrote that "The fact that much more knowledge contributes to form the order of a market economy than can be known to any one mind ... is the decisive reason why a market economy is more effective than any known type of economic order."[165]

Most people are inherently good. Most people work hard and give their best effort. We just need a system that protects the freedom of everyone to innovate and compete without nefarious interests dominating the economy.

Economists struggle with the definition of what a market really is. And then economists really struggle with the definition of capitalism. One view of capitalism could be that it is a society filled with a combination of many free markets. The fact we have markets that are not truly free within our current economy is a breakdown of this definition of capitalism. Another view of capitalism revolves around the "invisible hand" described by Adam Smith in 1776.[166] The baker prepares the cake because he wants to sell it to make money. And the person buying it earning money elsewhere and needs a cake. Neither much has an interest in the other beyond their own self-interest. And yet through the actions of free individuals in a free society it all seems to work, as if by magic... an "invisible hand." Milton Friedman described free markets and capitalism a few times. One, a famous discussion of greed in a famous 1979 interview on the Phil Donahue show:[167] "Einstein didn't construct his theory under order from a (government) bureaucrat. Henry Ford

---

[165] *Individualism and Economic Order*, Friedrich (F.A.) Hayek, 1948

[166] *An Inquiry into the Nature and Causes of the Wealth of Nations* (more simply known as *The Wealth of Nations*), Adam Smith, 1776.

[167] https://www.youtube.com/watch?v=RWsx1X8PV_A

didn't revolutionize the automobile industry that way." The great achievements of civilization are "individuals pursuing their best interest." In another, quite interesting and persuasive YouTube video, Milton Friedman uses a pencil to describe the mysterious "power of the market." Thousands of people from around the world are all needed for little portions of making a pencil and getting it to a store where you can buy it.[168]

---

[168] https://www.youtube.com/watch?v=R5Gppi-O3a8

27
CRONY CAPITALISM

SPECULATION ECONOMY: THE CASINOS OF WALL STREET

Speculation can be a good thing. Necessary, perhaps, to any functioning market. Speculation is a hope and a belief. A hunch. An idea.

Speculative traders are needed to take the other side of a transaction.

In July, a farmer wants to lock in prices for his crop of corn before harvesting the crop in October. He is nervous that prices will decline a lot by time October comes. He can sell the rights to his crop in the futures market.

Who does he sell to? Sometimes it could be to a producer of cereal that has the opposite fear. The cereal producer is concerned prices of corn will rise come October and that would impact their profitability. So, they go to the futures market to lock in the price today for what they need to buy in October.

Speculators come in when there is only one side of this transaction present. A speculator can fill the void to enable the farmer or the cereal producer to offset their fears and risks.

Let's say the farmer wants to sell but the cereal producer is not in an itch to buy. There may be a trader willing to buy what the farmer is offering. That trader has no crop and no interest in receiving the corn. The trader does, however, believe the price of corn is going to rise between July and October.

That is a speculator. And that is speculative trading.

It can, and does, truly serve a valuable purpose and role.

We do need to have a free country and free markets.

128

So, people—any of us—should be able to speculate.

Speculation is making a trade in the markets purely because you believe the market will go up or down. For no real reason. For reasons of your own. With your own money. Just trading.

Speculation in and of itself is healthy.

Some view speculation as a large part of the problem.

It is reasonable to say markets should be left to those that have a legitimate stake in the trading activity they are undergoing. Such as long-term investing, or protecting your crop by selling your corn at an advantageous price. These types of concerns become front-and-center when a lot of speculators are perceived to be impacting prices. For example, oil prices rose a ton in 2008 on a speculative run-up. That caused the price of a gallon of gasoline to skyrocket. Not a good part of having free markets. However, there is evidence that Goldman Sachs ran prices up to bankrupt another firm. And as soon as that firm was bankrupt the prices crashed back down in a hurry.[169]

If the stock market were to drop a lot... there could be speculative short sellers making big profits. Short sellers speculate that stock prices will drop by selling stock first and buying it back later; they borrow the stock from their brokerage thereby owning the stock to sell it, then they must buy it back later, hopefully, in their case, at a lower price. Naturally, short sellers get much of the blame in a down stock market. The truth is these traders a) will not be the reason for the decline, b) in the aggregate have a very tiny influence on the overall market, and c) someone who is short has to buy, meaning in a falling market often times the *only people* that will be there *buying* amid panic selling are short sellers. They *have to* buy at some point. Thus, when it really gets to be no one wanting to buy stocks it is a very valuable thing to have short sellers in the market. They *will* buy (buy back the shares they sold higher) when no one else wants to. It is like the earlier story of the farmer and the cereal producer. When either one of them isn't around it is good to have a speculator to help the one or the other that wants to make a transaction.

But good luck having this common-sense understanding cut through the fog in a down market. I suspect the government and big banks have some nefarious plans with respect to taking advantage of people amid the next down market.

Is Greed Good?

---

[169] Semgroup filed for bankruptcy July 22, 2008. Crude oil prices peaked at nearly $150 per barrel that same month. https://www.forbes.com/forbes/2009/0413/096-sachs-semgroup-goldman-goose-oil.html#6a65aab39f20

Was Michael Douglas spot on when he said, as Gordon Gekko in the 1987 film *Wall Street*, "Ladies and gentlemen, greed—for lack of a better word—is good. Greed is right. Greed works... Greed, in all its forms—greed for life, for money, for love, knowledge—has marked the upward surge of mankind." Bold words.

How often do we ever consider the words of raw capitalists?

It simply is not a part of modern culture.

You won't find these types of thought-provoking notions debated in schools or college campuses.

Too radical right?

Yet, if we can swallow it up; pause and reflect: Gekko's is an interesting notion.

Greed for knowledge? The laboratory scientist that desperately wants to find the answer... the cure. The mathematician that stays up late and wakes up early, determined to make a breakthrough. The A+ student that wants to be class Valedictorian and then goes on to do great things in their career. Are any of these examples different from the type of greed that goes around on Wall Street? Sure, it is. But, could it only be because of the stakes? There is just a heck of a ton of money at stake on Wall Street.

Is the problem only, and specifically, that there is too much money swirling around on Wall Street? And with that, then greed really isn't the problem? If there were no money to pull out of these markets, there would be none of the excessive abuses of power.

Thus... more than this, might we dare to consider that perhaps greed is the solution? Gekko continued, "Greed—you can mark my words—will not only save Teldar Paper, but that other malfunctioning corporation called the USA."

A great concept. Almost a page from a Ronald Reagan speech-- that capitalism and freedom and smaller government can lead to the best future for the United States of America. Can the size of government be reduced? Elections shouldn't matter so much. Too much concentrated decisions with huge ramifications. Less power in government means less to worry about what these politicians can do that impacts your own worldview.

What if Wall Street (stock markets, corporations and all of it) could be tweaked such that the same greed that motivates the laboratory scientist, mathematician and valedictorian student could motivate corporate leaders and Wall Street bankers *to the legitimate benefit of all people in society*?

When Speculation Really Becomes a Problem

The futures and options markets include a lot of trading that is leveraged. It is called "margin" trading. When you trade on margin you are trading with more money than you actually have. For example, you might be able to trade with 10-1 margin or 20-1 margin. So, if you have $100,000 in your trading account than you could buy and sell $1,000,000 worth of stock at 10-1 margin.

This is a very simple example of the types of leveraged trading taking place in the U.S. and global financial system.

It is called derivatives trading.

Today, there are big, big banks placing outlandishly sized trades (bets) on direction. Estimates (by Newsweek and Business Insider) of the size of the derivatives market is $500 trillion to $600 trillion.[170]

Global Derivatives Market
$500 trillion to $600 trillion
Trillion.

Due to the leverage of the types of trades that are made in the derivatives market these numbers represent the risk exposure. There is no way to prepare for the type of disruption that is possible in a market this extreme.

The fact that markets have been relatively tranquil for the last several years will make any future irregular moves in the market could have incalculable impacts.

This is the concept of Too Big to Fail (TBTF). The big banks take on much of this leverage because they feel they have nothing to fear. They are so important to the financial system that if anything goes wrong we will *have to* bail them out.

A related problem is when speculative trading becomes too much of the trading activity. So, in the corn example above it is one thing if an occasional speculator is filling the place in the market for the corn producer or farmer. It becomes a concern when it is the producer or farmer that is the unusual participant. If one speculator thinks prices are going up and another thinks they are going down and on and on you have those types of "one speculator to another speculator" trades than the market becomes more like a casino.

Where we are today in the markets is that they are becoming more and more purely speculative. Massive hedge funds and big banks chasing profits. Everyone is smart enough to handle what they are doing. Until they aren't.

Financial Services and End of Glass-Steagall

Beginning in the 1970's, the invention of financial services and financial speculation were introduced to the economy.

---

[170] http://www.businessinsider.com/new-york-fed-derivatives-500-trillion-market-2017-5 and http://www.newsweek.com/600-trillion-derivatives-market-92275

As the biggest, major corporations reached maximum growth and could no longer grow organically new ways of making money were needed. They had lowered costs as much as possible. And maximized their market share in the economy. Corporations like General Electric. So, they became financial companies. Making as much or more money off from credit cards and financing for people to buy their products. Noam Chomsky[171] calls this "financialization of the economy."

Simultaneously the banks, facing this new competition, looked to the markets to make money. They introduced speculative trading and worked to get into the speculative trading business themselves. This spurred the introduction of financial derivatives and futures. Glass-Steagall was repealed allowing banks to trade in the markets. The biggest banks started making trading profits.

Rather than simply run a market by connecting buyers and sellers the banks and collecting a trading fee, now they could trade along with their customers. The biggest banks—Goldman Sachs, Citibank, JPMorgan—they now trade stocks. And instead of merely facilitating farmers hedging their corn supplies or oil companies hedging on crude oil prices. They themselves speculate. And the rise of speculation has been enormous. Believe it or not, they are now a competitor and really an enemy of their own customers![172]

In the words of Jay Leno, "the United States has developed a new weapon that destroys people, but it leaves buildings standing. It's called the stock market."[173]

Alongside our stock markets, has been the rise of derivatives. Leveraged trading, or so-called "margin trading." With just $1,000 you could buy the equivalent of $50,000 worth of stock. Say what?! Initial margin requirements were 2% meaning 50-1 leverage. That is the way of some of the futures markets, such as the Chicago Mercantile Exchange.

Running the Stock Market Casino

---

[171] A word about Noam Chomsky: I refer to him a few times in this book. Ideologically, Chomsky is very similar to me in identifying the problems. However, in my humble opinion, Chomsky focuses on the wrong solutions. Chomsky argues for expansion of a welfare-based state as he relies on an Aristotelian-solution to the problem of how to restrain the ultra-rich (That Dangerous Radical Aristotle, Chomsky https://chomsky.info/commongood02/). Thus, Chomsky talks about expanding social security. Another pet issue, Chomsky talks a lot about free school and no student debt (presumably because his life and industry was spent so close to public universities). These are narrow-minded solutions. My view is far more radical than a Chomsky mindset. In fact, one might contend Chomsky is just part of the problem by focusing his followers on such narrow objects.

[172] http://www.businessinsider.com/goldman-sachs-trades-against-clients-2011

[173] https://www.forbes.com/sites/timothyspangler/2014/01/24/11-great-quotes-about-life-on-wall-street/#10d9925a144f

An even bigger problem now is Wall Street's largest banks taking a cut.

Today we basically have "casino managers" that oversee the trading and take their cut just like a casino.

They take a tiny piece of
every single trade made by the public!

Big bank trading has gotten so crazy and the manipulating moves of the government, Treasury and Federal Reserve so extreme and ongoing that at some point you just wonder: **why have a market at all?**

If the Federal Reserve really wants the stock market to keep going up, how about just open the market tomorrow at twice the level it is today? Why not? What does any of it matter? If the Fed can make the market go up a little bit one day, or 4% in a day; why not 100% in a day? Why not just double the stock market overnight?

If the stock market going up is so important for all of us
Why do we need to wait?
Just double the price of the exchange in the morning

Until the 2017 Trump rally, the biggest bull market runs have been while Democrats are President. Theories behind that? Republican Congress at the same time is one. Helping pensions is another. Democrats have a huge interest in protecting big pensions (unions, Ivy League universities, CalPERS). Where is the power base of the Democratic Party? The northeast... New York City: Wall Street. Silicon Valley, another new liberal bastion. They all love the stock market running higher. And then they use the media to point at "Country-club Republicans." Nice.

28
CRONY CAPITALISM

MANIPULATED
ECONOMIC CYCLES

The Panic of 1907 was a key factor in passing legislation to create the Federal Reserve in 1913. For decades the New York banks were scheming to get centralized banking institutionalized in America. Competition from banks around the rest of the country was one concern. New York City didn't want to lose its power. The Gilded Age millionaires such as J.P. Morgan wanted to ensure control over the government and financial system as well.[174]

Ending the chance of future panics such as that of 1907 was thus a major rationale put forward by the proponents. Pass the Federal Reserve Act or risk another panic.[175] In 1914 the Comptroller of the Currency, said of the legislation "under the operation of this law such financial and commercial crises and panics (of the past) seem to now be mathematically impossible."[176]

Has the Fed curbed such panics? Um, no. By 1921 GDP dropped 25%. The next eight years the stock market was rampaging higher amid the optimism of the "Roaring Twenties." we had the greatest stock market crash in the history of the country. Never surpassed before. And after that, did the

---

[174] The Men Who Built America, History Channel TV Series
http://www.history.com/shows/men-who-built-america and specifically
http://www.history.com/shows/men-who-built-america/videos/presidential-election-of-1896?playlist_slug=men-who-built-america-season-1-curated-list
[175] https://www.washingtonpost.com/news/wonk/wp/2013/12/21/the-federal-reserve-was-created-100-years-ago-this-is-how-it-happened/?utm_term=.5b864d6aa49b
[176] *End the Fed*, Ron Paul, 2009.

Federal Reserve quickly address the situation and keep the U.S. economy humming along? No. The stock market subsequently declined 90%! *While* we had a Federal Reserve! The stock market dropped 90% in a couple years. On came "The Great Depression." Unemployment rose over 25%. Banks across the country went out of business.

All of this in the first 20 years of the Fed. A total roller coaster. And... come to think of it... what have the last 20 years looked like? Tech bubbles. Housing bubbles. The great recession. Massive declines in stocks in 2001 and 2008. Chronic unemployment. People working multiple jobs. Stagnant incomes!

The Federal Reserve does not help with any of this. Worse, it can largely be shown the Federal Reserve actually has a part in *creating* these economic swings.

It gets worse. Right out of the gate after opening its doors in 1913, the Federal Reserve helped to finance World War I.

What happened during the Great Depression? Several acts of legislation that worked only to grant the Federal Reserve even more power. The country was left languishing so that the legislation to keep empowering the Federal Reserve was more and more necessary. Unbelievable really.

Milton Friedman, in his famous book *Free to Choose*: the Great Depression "was produced by a failure of government, not of private enterprise."

Vast, Nearly Impossible Economic Cycles

Since the Great Depression, we have seen the Federal Reserve navigate the country to massive extremes in interest rates and stock market prices. We had the currency crisis of the *early* 1970's. Then the inflation crisis of the *late* 1970's. Record high interest rates at the start of the 1980's. Now, record low interest rates by 2012. Housing bubbles. Stock market bubbles.

The sad reality is the Federal Reserve engineers our "free markets" into wild ups and downs so extreme no truly free market would ever have it.

Before the Federal Reserve the United States never saw such extremes and wild moves—especially when it comes to interest rates.

Stability would have been interest rates
ranging between 3 to 7% such as they did
for the 55 years prior to the Federal Reserve.

Rates spiked to over 15% in 1981.
Now they have dropped to 1%.
Treasury yields have been declining for 33 consecutive years![177]

We go from one extreme to the other in a straight line. Over an impossibly long-time frame. The Federal Reserve oversees markets that go to massive extremes. Our markets are not random.

We no longer have regular economic cycles.

We no longer have any price discovery or markets.

What we have is basically calculated and controlled movements from the Federal Reserve. It is unprecedented control of the markets. It allows no 'normal' to develop. It is designed to break the back of any competition. No one can predict the absurdity of these "markets."

Since the Federal Reserve we no longer have a free moving market keeping rates in a normal range. Rather we have seen huge cyclical swings in interest rates that last for abnormally long times and have gone to extremes never seen prior to the creation of the Federal Reserve.[178]

Since 1913: a) a quick spike up in the 1920's; followed by b) a long drop to below 2% (a low level never seen before); then followed by c) an over 30-year long continuous cycle higher in interest rates. Topping out at the massive extremes seen in the chart in the footnote link. Over 15% interest rates in the early 1980's! And since then d) a very orderly and continuous drop that has now gone on for over 30 years; of which has included e) interest rates staying at near zero for seven straight years.

Extreme market volatility the likes that couldn't happen unless coordinated to happen. A true market would have natural ways of balancing itself without these huge (and prolonged) swings. The prolonged stability of staying at extremes is mysterious at best.

These are coordinated hack jobs that distort true pricing and help to minimize and eliminate all competition.

Other examples of crazy Federal Reserve policy? From 1989-1992 a bizarre string of 24 interest rate cuts in a row, dropping rates 675 basis points from 9.75% down to 3%. Also, the stock market spiked up 50% in that time frame.

This is the story of the Federal Reserve in a nutshell. Unprecedented market interventions of large magnitudes in short periods of time. And then on the other end of the spectrum, massively drawn out cycles to unimaginable extremes. From one crazy extreme to the other.

You have a microcosm of the century swings over the past 10 years with the straight down dump out of 2007 to early 2009 and then straight up since then—hitting extreme lows and highs in the stock market.

A normally functioning, true market would not perform this way. It is

---

[177] Ten-year bond yields for U.S. government from 1790-2010
https://www.globalfinancialdata.com/databases/Graphs/US10YearBond.png
[178] https://www.globalfinancialdata.com/databases/Graphs/US10YearBond.png

having terrible consequences for the broader economy.

The low of the S&P 500 in 2009? 666.[179] That was to send a message to traders of the level of control they have over the markets. Around that time, at a March 3, 2009 press conference, President Obama said, "profit and earnings ratios" are at a point where "buying stocks is a potentially good deal."[180] Fans of Obama take this as a sign of his brilliance. Calling the low just about to the day! Rather it was like the mafia, Goldman Sachs, sending their ring man Obama out to give an "all clear" for speculation to ramp back up. The market never looked back after the 666 low a couple days later. And the largest banks made a trading profit every single day for weeks around this time. No joke.[181]

"Markets" Priced According to Expectations of Government Actions

Traders and investors now must follow and predict what the government is going to do. In effect then, the market is priced by the government. Priced, by all of us, according to collective expectations and projections of government interventions. What will the government announce? When? What will the government purchase or sell? The fundamental value of any company stock or security is becoming an after-thought to the central bank interventions. The worst part is that *they know*. They know what they will be doing, and when.

Markets left to their own devices occasionally cycle into booms and busts. John Kenneth Galbraith said that this "recurrent descent into insanity is not a wholly attractive feature of capitalism."[182] However, what free cycles bring is freshness to the economy. The old guard could get wiped out. I subscribe to the views of Thomas G. Donlan that "when governments fight economic cycles, they usually make them worse;" that "busts create the conditions for future booms" and that the balance of an approach should error toward the notion that "government's job is to stay out of the way of natural economic cycles and let markets work."[183]

This is **not** to say there is no role for government. It is important to read

---

179 March 6, 2009 intraday low of the S&P 500 index
https://finance.yahoo.com/quote/%5EGSPC/history?period1=1236232800&period2=123657
4800&interval=1d&filter=history&frequency=1d
180 http://money.cnn.com/2015/03/09/investing/president-obama-stocks-market-march/index.html
181 http://www.nytimes.com/2010/05/12/business/12bank.html
182 *A World of Wealth*, Thomas G. Donlan. 2008. Pp 199
183 *A World of Wealth*, Thomas G. Donlan, 2008, Pp 199

the quote for what it is. The point is we cannot presume that government is benevolent. This is how we look at bills like "Dodd-Frank" that are sold to us as solutions.

29
CRONY CAPITALISM

CONTROLLING THE GLOBE

Via a handful of institutions, managed by a revolving door of talent from a select few universities we have a world that is increasingly controlled top-down.

In a of 7 billion people this doesn't have to delve into conspiracy. It is matter of fact, a narrow few that are the ones eating caviar and drinking champagne staying at the world's best hotels and sitting in the best corporate board rooms. All the while guiding our economy to their benefit.

The push is on to maintain, and expand, this grip on governments around the world as well as the global financial system. They sincerely are trying to do good for everyone. And they believe they really are. They live in their own bubble. To themselves, brilliantly managing the economy exactly to the meaningless economic targets they set for themselves.

Our economy continues to be increasingly managed to the benefit of less and less people. Nothing gets done about it however.

We feel the effects are not right and yet we

a) can't quite put our finger on exactly what the problem is
(especially without sounding like a conspiracy nut)**, and,**

b) have no alternative ideas in mind
of what to do about the problem.

It happens slowly and methodically. We are like frogs in a pot that will soon be boiling. We feel and know it's getting hotter. But it is just happening in a way that none of us are jumping out of the water.

Power is continually consolidated at a global level.

And power increasingly becomes more and more centralized.

What is happening is the opposite of the vision of this book: we have continued centralization, when we need decentralization of finance.

We see, in votes for independence and votes such as "Brexit" to leave the European Union that the people are not quite on board with this continued march to global power. Again, we notice the problem. We just are not able to get out from under. This book hopefully helps spur new ideas and action.

To date, any rebellion is quickly snuffed out. Brexit. Quebec. Scotland. Catalonia. When will the people win? When will the people sense, and figure out, they are ultimately in control? *The people* ultimately *are* in control. When will the balance shift in the other direction.? It is not likely to change easily.

Global Institutions and Coordinated Central Banks

In 1945, the United Nations opened its doors. At the end of World War II such an international organization was rightfully justified as a means for dialogue among nations such that another conflict could be prevented.

However, that same year, the World Bank was established. Why? Well, much of the world needed to be reconstructed due to damage from the war. So, a big bank was needed to ensure that mission could be completed. In fact, several global financial institutions were established at that time. Born out of the Bretton Woods conference. Among them, the International Monetary Fund (IMF). Together, these institutions have overseen a push for greater and greater power over the entire globe. For example, they are able to work in every country through central banks.

The issue today is not just the U.S. central bank. Central banks are acting in coordination. Japan, or European, central banks can make announcements to stir markets in one direction of another, helping the major banks such as Goldman Sachs manipulate prices up and down to their advantage.

The United Nations said in 2009 that they would like to see the creation of a Global Central Bank, a global equivalent of the Federal Reserve.[184]

Global Currency

The United Nations has been publicly calling for a global currency at least since 2009.[185] Timothy Geithner, President Obama's treasury secretary said

---

[184] https://www.cbsnews.com/news/united-nations-proposes-new-global-currency/
[185] https://www.cbsnews.com/news/united-nations-proposes-new-global-currency/

the plan is "to increase the use of the IMF's Special Drawing Rights (SDRs)."

Geithner—and the Goldman Sachs, Wall Street, globalist, insider controlling crowd—would like to see the IMF managing these SDR's in a way that they are actually the replacement to the dollar. A so-called "international reserve currency." A reserve currency idea that even China has said it supports.[186] Nobel Prize winning economist Robert Mundell first discussed "Optimum Currency Areas" (so-called OCAs) in 1961. In a 1997 speech he updated his position to remark that "the optimum currency area is the world."[187] A global currency is coming soon. I suspect it will be digital and that Bitcoin has been a globalist plan all along.

Friendly Global Power Brokers

The central bankers have no problem saying one thing and not even two weeks later go and implement the opposite. In 2008, Newsweek pointed out the dominant power and connection of less than a handful of central bank leaders: Trichet, Bernanke and Masaaki Shirakawa.[188]

Henry "Hank" Paulson left CEO of Goldman Sachs (1999-2006) to become Treasury Secretary July 10,2006. He came in to create and manage the financial crisis. At the first moment he could after the plan was executed, he was out the door in January 2009, and back to the big bucks. Timothy Geithner who was over at the Federal Reserve Bank of New York managing the insider trading aspect (Open Market Operations) to keep the crisis swinging in their favor took over for Paulson. Geithner had long been in the insider orbit, groomed for the post under Treasury Secretary Robert Rubin.[189]

Ben Bernanke took over at the Federal Reserve for Greenspan on February 1, 2006. Bernanke attended Harvard University, where he lived in Winthrop House. So, did the future and current CEO of Goldman Sachs, Lloyd Blankfein.

People across the country took the pain on the chin and in the pocketbook during 2007-2009. Directly. There was no central bank saving many individuals across the country. Why did so many people have to suffer and fail? Meanwhile, the biggest banks saved themselves. They saved each other. Their friends.

---

[186] https://www.cbsnews.com/news/geithner-appears-to-flip-flop-on-support-for-us-dollar/

[187] http://www.columbia.edu/~ram15/eOCATAviv4.html

[188] http://www.newsweek.com/newsweek-50-bernanke-trichet-shirakawa-83099

[189] Robert Rubin oversaw the biggest bubble in U.S. stocks as Treasury Secretary under Clinton from 1995-1999. To thank him for all his work, megabank Citigroup called on him as Chairman. He oversaw Citigroup at the height of the financial crisis setting parts of it in motion. In between that, Rubin was at Harvard.

Mervyn King was Governor of the Bank of England during the crisis. King shared an office suite with Bernanke when he was at MIT. One of the biggest power brokers in China, Gao Xiqing went to Duke, then worked at Richard Nixon's law firm.[190]

And so it goes like this. It needs to change. It will.

Legacy Rothschild Financial Order

The Rothschild family dominated global finance in the 1800's.

And the legacy of the financial system they helped create and solidify—basically, stock and bond market capitalism as we know it—still thrives to this day.

Back in the 1850's the Rothschild's had five major locations for their trading operations. The biggest 3 of those were in the big cities of the day: London, Paris and Frankfurt. That is the part that still thrives today. The banking centers that were a big part of the Rothschild's business are still major banking centers today. The biggest one popped up later down the road. New York City. However, that one of course was firmly of the same mold.

Fast forward to the 21st Century.

Controlling finance in the 21st Century is no longer about a handful of big cities. It is indeed quite remarkable that the Rothschild framework of finance still exists at all today. It is a testament of the dominance of what was established. This is not necessarily in any conspiracy matter of way. This is not to set-up as a conspiracy. This is an analysis of facts.

Does the Rothschild family somehow control the entire financial globe? *Still*? Not really. However, it is equally ludicrous to laugh off a review of history. It would be naive to not delve into the history. The current financial system has deep roots and remains the dominate financial order.

Going forward, I would believe it could be pretty easy to state that the existing order is going to have an ever increasingly difficult time maintaining the current financial framework.

Global Control Ultimately Will Give Way

Either a new idea—quite simply—will take hold. This could be called the 'Rothschild 2.0' scenario. Before the Rothschild's, *they* were once the outsiders with a new idea. The Rothschild's latched on to the ideas of stocks and bonds and fostered the concept into financial domination in the 1800's. The system

---

[190] *Greenback Planet*, H.W. Brand, 2011. Pp 122 and
https://en.wikipedia.org/wiki/Gao_Xiqing

could change through new ideas from new places. Much the same as say Google came out of nowhere to now dominate search or Facebook dominates online social networks.

A new idea could sprout up from right across the street from the Rothschild's—i.e. in London, or Frankfurt, or New York City. A new idea and stellar implementation and gone is today's system as a new way of finance takes off.

The other scenario is based on the title of the chapter.

It is impossible to control a globe. It has been a great run.

This isn't just Frankfurt, London and Paris anymore.

You have Tokyo. Shanghai. Singapore. Moscow. Mumbai. Dubai. Rio de Janeiro. Mexico City. San Francisco.

There are so many more big cities. So many countries now with their own ideas. Not to mention an overall world population that is so much larger today than it was in the 1800's.

It can be confidently said that there is no way that one global system will come to dominate the globe.

It would take unprecedented control.

Sadly, that is the reason for this chapter. There are efforts to indeed try to maintain a grip on the entire world. Keeping one, new world order.

So, while trying to control an entire world is not going to ultimately work-- it is being tried.

Harvard, Oxford and MIT educated economists span all the central banks that have been established in countries all around the world. The United Nations, World Bank, IMF and all such organizations serve as meeting grounds for global bureaucrats to hash out how to keep power and maintain the financial order.

Again, this is not in a conspiracy sense. It is just a fact of which I am trying to point out an alternative is needed. And the alternative will pop up and win the day.

The alternative is institutions that are not global. The alternative is power vested outside of global institutions.

It is just simply unrealistic to believe that this existing financial order is going to satisfy all governments and people everywhere on the planet Earth.

Finally, I will state the case here that even if one financial system could dominate the globe. And even if there were all sorts of reasons why it should. For monopoly reasons, I don't think it is a good idea. In fact, for monopoly reasons the case could be made to stop such globalist notions, fantasies, projects and operations now and today, right in their tracks.

Could the new world order end up being a *new* world order?

30
BOLD STEPS

ADDRESSING STAGNANT WAGES; MINIMUM WAGES

Can we (and/or should we) pay people more for their work?

Should we just give people money?

One is an ongoing structural issue for the economy. How do we get wages to go up?

The other, Universal Basic Income (UBI), is a new idea gaining attention.

Giving people money was first introduced in a previous chapter, 'The Fed Can Buy Anything.'

Whatever the solution-- and whatever the merits of various proposals-- the end goals must be kept in mind. We *do* need to do something about:

Poverty, the Income Imbalance,
Unexpected Life Events,
Opportunity

Among the bigger problems today in society is the income imbalance. Part of this problem spurs poverty for which-- despite ongoing efforts-- people do not have enough money for a basic standard of living.

While many of us make decent money, there are so many more out there that struggle every day, week after week and year after year, and. never. get. ahead.

Sometimes it is health or unavoidable circumstances that cause people to slip through the cracks in the economy. Other times it is simply a lack of opportunity not spreading broadly to more people.

One solution outside of money is to create more opportunity. Can we think big and start creating a lot more higher quality jobs?

Minimum Wage

Too many low income jobs out there.

Too many retail jobs. Strip malls and big box stores continue to be a lot of what we create in this economy.

Jobs in retail are inherently low pay. Too many retail jobs is a large reason why the minimum wage is even an issue.

So many people are—for lack of a better word—stuck, in retail jobs.

Retail jobs pay enough for a first job. High school and college students looking to make a little money of their own and gain real world work experience benefit from retail jobs. Usually, they are living with their parents, receiving money for school. Therefore, they can get by on the wages that a retail job pays.

However, since there is both a lack of more opportunities in the economy and a plethora of retail jobs available we have some of our brightest Americans working minimum wage jobs.

Many in the U.S. work two or more jobs trying to pull it together. There are always success cases to point to. People who were once working two jobs or a low-paying job and tough circumstances and then they break through with huge books, or a music album or such.

As a free market, small government libertarian do I support increasing a minimum wage? No. Should we even have a minimum wage? In an efficient free market? No, I don't think it is necessary.

We have too many distortions in our current economy.

We are on a broken-down bus.

It is going to take a while to fix the bus. And until then we need to plug in the generator and keep the A/C (or heat up north) running for folks.

Until we reinvent our retail economy we may need a minimum wage.

The actual details can get very complex. And hardline supporters of a minimum wage increase need to stop protesting long enough to listen so that a truly good solution can move forward. For example, what does not need to happen is more solutions that benefit only big corporations. If small business owners are forced to pay huge minimum wages they aren't going to have the resources of their larger competitors. Somehow, this minimum wage fix needs to hit corporations harder. There is plenty of money to go around in a lot of these big companies. If it lowers earnings numbers and is a hit to Wall Street, well, as we will cover in a chapter soon, that is a hit to our economy that can help level out income gaps.

Corporations claim there are not enough workers. The fact is, in the words of James Allsup, they simply don't want to pay people enough money.[191]

**It is a major problem that an
"earnings announcement" for Wall Street
is more important than
wages for the people.**

There are lots of ways to fund higher incomes for employees. Taxing corporate earnings and closing their loopholes and actually collecting the tax money. Taxes on all the stock they issue and sell. Brainstorming actual solutions is what is needed.

Inflation Impact on Wages

People working low income jobs are being hit on multiple sides. Their pay is low. Wages are not increasing. In addition, the prices of everything go up each year.

The Federal Reserve has a goal to have inflation every year.

So, the prices of everything are supposed to, on average, go up every single year.

The Federal Reserve should have a goal to make wages go up every year.

Incomes are not going up, but the cost to buy necessities increases.

Rent, increasing. Groceries, increasing. The electricity bill. Going up.

Wages? Stagnant.

So, for this reason as well, wages need to be increased. If it takes a steep minimum wage, it is essential we take that step.

Corporations Can Pay the Price and
Easily Keep on Ticking

Maybe we doubly hit big businesses—such as with both a higher minimum wage and an extra tax hit. Then take the taxes and apply them to pay for smaller businesses to handle the higher minimum wages. It will take some creativity. And it will take noise and power of the people to start calling spades, spades. Big corporations need no more advantages. There needs to be a shakeup, that can and will begin balancing the economy. Corporations will use the idealism of capitalism to push back. However, the fleecing of America needs to end. Corporations will be fine. Totally fine. Any shake-up such as

---

[191] https://twitter.com/realJamesAllsup/status/892915821596426240

these proposals would have a miniscule impact on their gravy train profits.

It is for more reasons than one to start with corporations. They have so much money that it spreads through Washington, DC and builds their power ever more, overfilling their pockets and breeding an ongoing cycle of more and more dominance.

In the words of John Kenneth Galbraith, the connection to solving income imbalances is recognizing the direct relation of power to income.

"Power serves the acquisition of income; income accords power over the pecuniary reward of others."[192]

In other words, the rich—who already have power in Washington as well as income—are not really the people that need to be deciding how to balance income and financial rewards for work, including the minimum wage. Galbraith believes it is "absolute(ly) essential," to have a "socially adequate minimum wage."[193]

However, it is not as simple as just slapping up a higher number.

Again, that is the liberal/progressive 'end by any means' knee-jerk reaction. On many issues (environment, wages) I sincerely believe liberals are co-opted into a meaningless solution. The focus needs to be beyond the end.

Many prominent economists, including Milton Friedman, have pointed out that a minimum wage is likely to negatively affect the people it is designed to help. And there is reason—theoretical and actual—to back up the claims.

As with most ideas and potential solutions, the issues are usually a little more complex than a simple implementation. More dialogue is needed to really get to the bottom of making the right decisions for the best outcomes.

Consider Seattle, Washington. Seattle has the highest minimum wage in the nation. However, according to a study by economists at the University of Washington the increase in the minimum wage actually impacted low-wage workers negatively as employers cut back hours and cut back the number of employees.[194] For one thing, technology (such as computers to take orders at fast food restaurants, or even burger flipping robots[195]) can be used to replace workers.

The University of Washington study delved deeper to find some ways that a minimum wage can be implemented with better results. For example, moderate increases in the minimum wage and increases starting from a low

---

[192] *The Good Society*, John Kenneth Galbraith, 1996, pp 165

[193] *The Good Society*, John Kenneth Galbraith, 1996, pp 67

[194] https://fivethirtyeight-com.cdn.ampproject.org/c/s/fivethirtyeight.com/features/seattles-minimum-wage-hike-may-have-gone-too-far/amp/

[195] http://sacramento.cbslocal.com/2017/09/13/robot-fast-food-burger/

level can have their intended effect (more money in the pockets of a lot of low-income earners). If the increase is too substantial it fuels business to make immediate changes to avoid the negative impact.

However, Galbraith dismisses "out of hand" these types of complaints. Galbraith says, "even were it a cost to the employment of the few, it would still be justified as the protection of the many."

A minimum wage increase helps employees that do not have bargaining protection. Retail jobs do not have union protections.

What about those that don't even have a job?

How does an increase in the minimum wage help people without a job? How do we help *them*? Too many people struggle to find meaningful, steady employment.

Wages are stagnant. People are working multiple jobs to try and make it. So, our problems run deeper than merely addressing wages. We need to think big and come up with a lot more meaningful work to do.

One benefit of wage increases is that wages are given because of actual work. In the poignant words of Henry George, "labor always precedes wages." Continuing, "wages come from the fruits of labor."[196]

---

[196] *Progress and Poverty*, Henry George, 1879. Pp 31.

31
BOLD STEPS

UNIVERSAL BASIC INCOME (UBI)

Should we just give people money? We have previously introduced the idea of giving people money in our chapter on 'The Fed Can Buy Anything.'

Universal Basic Income

The idea of providing "universal basic income (UBI)" is popping up more and more in mainstream publications.

UBI is monthly payments from the government, whether you are working or not. It is a "no strings attached" base level of income so every individual knows that no matter what happens they are going to have a base level of money coming in the door. No need to go to the unemployment office or such.

The Federal Reserve buys bonds from big banks
So, why not just give people money?

Why give it to bankers through "quantitative easing"? Instead, give money to the people. Could you really print money and just give it to people?

When I was first understanding the idea that the Federal Reserve was buying bonds from banks so if they could buy bonds why not buy something else? Run your imagination. It was at that point—out of absurdity—that I wondered about just giving people money. And low and behold, I ended up discovering the Federal Reserve was literally already considering the idea.

Crazy.

Not a new idea either. Thomas Paine wrote *Agrarian Justice* in 1795 as he was shocked that upon the founding of the United States—a civilized society—there still persisted "extremes of wretchedness" and that side-by-side "most affluent and the most miserable of the human race are to be found."

Paine came to believe that poverty was actually caused by the existence of the state. Paine believed "the condition of every person born into the world, after a state of civilization commences, ought not to be worse than if he had been born before that period."[197] He went on to describe a fund that more or less is among the first proposals of a universal basic income.

Perhaps even more surprising then the mention of UBI as far back as 1795 is that it there is already a UBI-type scheme in operation in the U.S. today!

Everyone in Alaska receives an annual check, including children. It is Alaska's Permanent Fund Dividend. Even children get the money. The check amounts to a payment of around $2,000 to every person, every year. Just for living in Alaska.

From Thomas Paine in 1795,
to Alaska today,
UBI is not a new idea

Both liberal progressives as well as libertarian conservative economist have their reasons for supporting UBI.

On the liberal end of the spectrum, Facebook founder Mark Zuckerberg places a UBI at the center of a "new social contract." He views UBI as a safety net providing people a "cushion to try new ideas." In other words, if a poor person doesn't need to worry about their bills they could more freely pursue the work that fits them. A related progressive perspective, from venture capitalist Sam Altman says of UBI, "everyone should have enough money to meet their basic needs--no matter what." Altman believes technology is going to decrease the cost of living.[198] One reason Altman talks positively about UBI is because Altman owns a non-profit organization that receives government money to run pilot studies on how the UBI would work in practice. The media sides with liberals and progressive ideas and it is sad we get neither the truth or the frank dialogue this country needs.

Anyway, prominent liberals such as Mark Zuckerberg supporting UBI is not so surprising. What *is* different is that it is not so much only, or perhaps even, a socialist/liberal idea.

Free market economist Milton Friedman was a proponent of UBI in

---

[197] http://www.constitution.org/tp/agjustice.htm
[198] https://www.cnbc.com/2017/05/25/mark-zuckerberg-calls-for-universal-basic-income-at-harvard-speech.html

concept. Friedman comes at UBI from a completely different mindset. Friedman, and libertarians like him that support UBI do so because they want to streamline all the welfare payments and simplify government. They see UBI as reducing the size of government by consolidating several different welfare programs. And at the same time, helping to reduce and eliminate poverty.

UBI could eliminate "welfare, food stamps, housing subsidies, the earned income tax credit, social security, Medicare and Medicaid" according to Charles Murray of the American Enterprise Institute[199] That is where the streamlining and simplification of government comes in.

UBI would eliminate the need for government to manage so many different programs: welfare, food stamps, housing subsidies, income credits, social security, Medicare, Medicaid, etc.

Everyone gets the same basic amount. It doesn't matter what circumstance needs to be fixed.

That is how UBI eliminates a lot of bureaucratic overlap and simplifies government. The U.S. federal government spends about $80 billion per year on food stamps (Supplemental Nutrition Assistance Program, referred to as SNAP). And about $60 billion on the Earned Income Tax Credit (EITC). EITC was first started by the U.S. federal government in 1975. The federal government program has continually been expanded to help in alleviating poverty. Now, many states also have state-EITCs. The relative size of these programs is miniscule. Calling it a combined $150 billion, these poverty reduction programs represent just 4% of the annual federal budget. The U.S. spends 4 times as much on the military and over 6 times as much on Medicare.[200]

Another free market economist, Friedrich Hayek, also discussed the "assurance of a certain minimum income for everyone, or a sort of floor below which nobody need fall" as a "wholly legitimate protection." Hayek said that "a society that has reached a certain level of wealth can afford to provide for all."[201] Martin Ford explains the conservative rationale for a Universal Basic Income that it "provides a safety net coupled with individual freedom of choice." As such, people still have every incentive to make their life situation better but at least if they fail and/or get hurt there is a safety net

---

[199] http://www.sfchronicle.com/aboutsfgate/article/Why-universal-basic-income-is-gaining-support-11290211.php

[200] https://www.nationalpriorities.org/budget-basics/federal-budget-101/spending/

[201] Quotes drawn from *Rise of the Robots*, Martin Ford who was referencing and quoting *Law, Legislation and Liberty*, F.A. Hayek.

to protect us all. Ford continues that "incentives matter." UBI must have the right incentives in place "without creating disincentive to a) work and b) to be as productive as possible." As Joseph Stiglitz pointed out "many of the unemployed chose to go on disability—which pays better and for longer."[202]

How would or could UBI be Implemented?

There are two primary ways to implement UBI.
A simple way is everyone is just given the designated minimum amount.
Or,
People report their income and the government provides the difference for those not earning the minimum.

Basically, below a specified minimum income level, instead of paying taxes the government would pay the citizen the difference of how far below the minimum their income is. This interpretation of UBI is called a Negative Income Tax (NIT). NIT is a concept most associated with Friedman as well as fellow Brit Juliet Rhys-Williams.

Where does the money come from?

Well, we could try to fund the money through this or that method.

However, the absurdity is that, well, technically the Federal Reserve could print the money right up out of thin air.

UBI: Analyzing the Good and Bad

The good? UBI helps to solve unemployment by paying the minimum for those times people lose jobs. UBI also solves income volatility—jobs with paychecks that ebb and flow. For example, commission-only sales jobs and/or seasonal work. When times are good some jobs roll in a lot of money in short periods of time but then work sometimes dries up. So, UBI helps smooth out "income volatility" and also gives workers protection and comfort knowing that if a hard time comes they, and their family, will have a way to keep moving forward. If something unexpected goes wrong most Americans don't have money saved up. Over 1/3rd of households in California could not live at the poverty level for even 3 months.[203] Nationally, 44% of households made no addition to their savings in 2016. UBI is a short-term fix for the U.S. and its very low savings rate. It fits any scenario that comes up providing to those

---

[202] *Freefall*, Joseph Stiglitz, pp 65.
[203] http://www.pasadenastarnews.com/social-affairs/20170725/more-than-a-third-of-california-households-have-virtually-no-savings-are-at-risk-of-financial-ruin-report-says

that have virtually no cushion.

More good? Some see the UBI as a panacea for the next stage of humanity. Essentially, all the positive energy I am trying to portray in this entire book about what the economy could be in the future gets summed up in some interpretations of UBI.

To Michael Laitman, UBI will "release us from the constant concern about making a living" which will enable "personal, social and spiritual development" to the happiness and betterment of society.[204]

So, what could go wrong?

Well, we already have a major problem with a lack of personal responsibility in America. The experience of several decades of entitlement programs is that they just keep expanding and don't seem to make the situation better for any individuals or for society as a whole.

There is also a major problem of UBI in that there is no labor in just giving people money. This is a moral question on multiple levels.

Sadly, to rich capitalists such as the Federal Reserve and big bankers let's not kid ourselves part of the reason for the UBI is just to "buy the little pests away."

**The establishment rich would like to
go about their Ivory Tower existence with
nice houses, fancy cars, travel to exotic locations, 5-star meals
and if that means giving a bunch of money
to lower income people so
they won't complain or rock the boat
then they are all for the UBI.**

And, with a UBI it is not unreasonable to see a larger segment of the population want to try it out. For leisure.

Plenty of people would be more than content to pick up a 6-pack of beer and take that to a tent at the beach, to a city park, or up a trail into the mountains. Plenty more people would be fine watching Netflix and Snapchat all day.

**A lot of people are likely to be quite fine having
only a little money
but a lot of free time.**

They will not need to work. And that brings up a moral question of the value of work. There is more to our existence. And we demand more of

---

[204] http://laitman.com/2016/12/ynet-is-there-a-future-for-capitalism/

ourselves. There is no labor in just getting money.

Guaranteed Work and Jobs,
not Guaranteed Money

Just as there are both progressives and liberals in support of UBI. There is bipartisan opposition. Even former Obama Administration officials question UBI.

No labor in just giving people money is where the ideas of Jared Bernstein, now a senior fellow at the Center on Budget and Policy Priorities (and former Obama Administration economist), can come in.

Bernstein believes a better solution is not guaranteed income but rather a guaranteed job.[205]

UBI is "giving up on work and giving up on people. I'm not prepared to do that,"[206] said Jason Furman who chaired the Council of Economic Advisers under President Obama.

People deserve to be respected more than the "just give them cake" mentality. UBI is as bad as Marie Antoinette's plea amid the French Revolution.

But do we have enough jobs?

Zuckerberg and Silicon Valley are concerned technology is going to replace so many jobs. Therefore, the need for UBI is only going to grow.

On the other hand, Furman's perspective is that we are only limited by our imagination. There is so much more that people can work on. We just need to put more thought into job creation.

The rich want to take the easy way out. Essentially, the rich are just like, deliver what I need with a drone and give everyone else money so they don't bother me.

People should take pride in their work and creations.

As Emma Goldman has pointed out, we are being robbed of any attachment to the product of our labor. We are losing "the power of free initiative, of originality, and the interest in, or desire for, the things (we are) making."[207]

---

[205] http://prospect.org/article/progressive-agenda-now-jobs-and-medicare-all

[206] http://www.sfchronicle.com/aboutsfgate/article/Why-universal-basic-income-is-gaining-support-11290211.php

[207] *Red Emma Speaks*, Emma Goldman, 1972. Pp. 66-7
https://libcom.org/files/Red%20Emma%20Speaks.pdf

The Bottom Line on UBI?

Where do I stand on UBI? My initial reaction: it is absurd. And depending on how it is implemented it could be tragic. Implemented properly, however, I now believe it can be a huge breakthrough for society. For one thing I was thinking about how more ethnicities need to be at the top (both politically and financially). Then I was like 'ok, well what ethnicities should be at the bottom and how do we improve the bottom.' And I was like 'well, in a perfect world, no one should be at the bottom.'

My mind works toward ideals. Public policy itself shouldn't settle. We need to think big and talk big on the way to realistic implementations. That will lead to the best breakthroughs.

The goal is not to try to placate the bottom. We don't try to make the bottom subsist. And we don't try to make it a little better. Welfare, basic UBI and such are like that. Some are fine with the belief of thinking they are helping people. Yes, giving people money does, technically, help. It is a means that does achieve the end. But, what is the *best* way? What is the *best* means to the end?

UBI? Giving them money? I just said giving people money doesn't solve the problems. Well, it can't be lazy, and it has to have purpose to it.

UBI could have value if we frame it properly and then build implementation around a corrected mentality. What if we all have the security of knowing we are not going to fail? This frees every individual to live as they are designed to live; and to pursue their dreams and follow their heart.

A lot more people might choose to give back with their time. A lot more people might be helping other people if they can simply follow their heart. In this way UBI, could completely re-make a better society. Same thing in pursuing knowledge and careers. People can follow their heart and choose what they really want to do.

Many problems arise with UBI. Basing UBI on money may itself be one of the big problems. Say what? This is the type of outside-the-box brainstorming that will put us into another plane. Like the horizontal vertical planes. But then an airplane of taking off to a whole new place. A UBI that is not money based?

People will be continually priced out. A UBI will distort prices. Prices around us go up—housing for one thing—and the UBI just may not fit all the scenarios that can arise. So, a conversation about UBI needs to run really deep. Just giving people money cannot be lazy like a welfare program. It needs to be strategic. It is about the means. How do we achieve it?

32
BOLD STEPS

WORK:
THE FUTURE OF JOBS
AND EMPLOYMENT

Most fundamental to each of us is our ability to make a living—i.e. work.

What is work?

Why do we do it?

These are rather simple questions. And yet conversations revolving around these simple questions can help revolutionize how we work in the future.

Most of us work to make money. We need to make money to pay our bills and to afford necessities. And beyond that to fulfill wants and desires.

There is not necessarily a purpose, or point, to our work beyond this.

People that have a time in their life when they stay home, usually after a period of time end up with an overwhelming desire to get out of the house and *do something*. It is common to hear of people that 'want to get out of the house.'

Even in retirement, we are wired not to just sit and lay around.

Health-wise, we *need* to move around. Our body depends on moving. Our blood needs to circulate. Our bones need the Vitamin D from sunlight. Our muscles and fascia tissue will tighten up if we are not moving.

Work also provides meaning and purpose. Work can provide fulfillment.

**What work does not necessarily mean is
just making money. That is pointless. And yet,
the two have become synonymous (work to make money).**

Some jobs aren't much better than collecting a UBI. A lot of the jobs that get created are more-or-less keeping a chair warm. Some jobs you earn a paycheck without hardly doing much. It might not be a big paycheck but there are a lot of sedentary jobs. Please don't confuse where I am going with this.

The point is simply, let's start dialoguing.

Sitting and staring at a clock and wishing you were on a cruise ship in the Bahamas. Many of us have had that feeling over and over again. There needs to be more freedom to our jobs. Can more of us be in control of our schedules? If the work is done the boss might go out and get their nails done or play a round of golf. Can regular employees have a little of that freedom? These are the types of questions that can make future work rewarding and purposeful.

Anyway, there are several key themes to touch on here regarding conversations we need to have about the future of work.

- Moral aspect of just giving money
- Technology taking jobs
- Employment statistics such as labor force participation
- Shortage of good workers
- Disparity of jobs and benefits gap
- Introducing new incentives and rewards for work

And then two larger discussions:

- Value of an hour of work
- Thinking big. Lack of big picture to create more jobs

MORAL ASPECT OF JUST GIVING PEOPLE MONEY

The latest big banker, establishment idea is to just give everyone a base of income. Universal Basic Income (UBI) is a concept that may have serious value. Regardless, because of strong support from the banking class and the Federal Reserve it is likely to be implemented one way or another.

Roughly half of Americans receive government assistance according to several different reviews.[208] So, just stream line it all and give everyone the same base of income.[209]

---

[208] https://www.forbes.com/sites/merrillmatthews/2014/07/02/weve-crossed-the-tipping-point-most-americans-now-receive-government-benefits/#181baaa13e6c and https://www.washingtonpost.com/news/wonk/wp/2012/09/18/who-receives-benefits-from-the-federal-government-in-six-charts/?utm_term=.aa5cd78a4daa

[209] Giving every person a base of income can simplify government by eliminating a multitude of overlapping programs that more or less touch on so many people already across society (such as welfare, social security, unemployment and such).

However, the idea of giving people instinctively rubs a lot of people the wrong way too.[210] And for good reason. The point of UBI must and needs to move beyond only giving people money. As welfare, and supporting pointless leisure it will become a problem that only feeds on itself.

And there are moral aspects to this as well:

Can people in the U.S. be given money just to buy goods that are made by people working in another country, such as Malaysia?

Thus, first, there is the human dignity of doing something and accomplishing something. Second, there is the morality of who is working for whom? Is it right for people in Malaysia to work while people in America are just given paper money by the Federal Reserve?

Working with our hands and our own action, activity and ingenuity provides us with true personal achievement and the sense of accomplishment.

JOBS DISAPPEARING BY TECHNOLOGY

A lot of our economic problems are—or can, and will be—worked out via technology. For example, routine, repetitive tasks can be handled by a computer and/or robot. This is good for our economy and it is good for quality of life. It is a definite positive if we are removing mundane, repetitive jobs.

However, we need to create the better jobs—and fast—that are necessary to replace the jobs that are taken away by technology. Estimates are between 800 million to 2 billion jobs could be displaced by robots by 2030.[211]

Some projections are that as many as half of all jobs will be gone in 30 years.[212]

We only need to put our heads together to brainstorm a little bit to create all the jobs we need for people. There is plenty of work out there that can be done. We are limited by our imagination.

We are also limited by a stagnant financial system and a stagnant political

---

[210] A prolific example of trying to tap into this sentiment that backfired was Mitt Romney's infamous "47%" comment. He thought it would go over well. It *is* rather absurd that so many people in America receive some form of assistance.

[211] https://www.bloomberg.com/news/articles/2017-11-29/robots-are-coming-for-jobs-of-as-many-as-800-million-worldwide to http://www.futuristspeaker.com/business-trends/2-billion-jobs-to-disappear-by-2030/

[212] https://www.cnbc.com/2017/04/27/kai-fu-lee-robots-will-replace-half-of-all-jobs.html

framework. The status quo is protected by corporations and Wall Street. They only want to placate the masses while keeping their gravy train going and playing with all their expensive toys.

So, we need a) the big, new, innovative ideas and b) to get the old, status-quo protectors out of the way in Washington, DC and our financial system.

We simply do not think broad enough about people can do and how improved society can become.

EMPLOYMENT STATISTICS:
such as LABOR FORCE PARTICIPATION

Labor force participation is a government statistic tracking how many Americans are trying to find a job. Only 55% of American adults 18-64 have full-time jobs.[213]

It is the U.S. Department of Labor (the Labor Department) that monitors our economy and compiles the employment statistics.

Within the many statistics they track are some of the answers to improving our economic situation. And from these statistics we can also find the questions to improve on them and really get to the bottom of the problems in order to identify solutions to get all Americans the jobs they want and deserve.

How many Americans are making the money they need?

How many hours are they having to work to do it?

How many jobs do they have to work?

What if people are working a commission-only sales job? They are considered employed, but they may not be making the money they need to. And/or their pay may be fluctuating. Same goes for an Uber driver. In both of these cases the person is not collecting unemployment and may not be looking for work; however, they would definitely take a better job if they could.

So how many Americans would work a better job if they could only find one?

We need to track a lot more statistics in a more, personalized style: income, hours worked for that income, quality of jobs, number of jobs a person is working, self-employment. All of this needs to be tracked more deeply and intelligently.

SHORTAGE OF GOOD WORKERS

Really? A shortage of good workers?

Before getting into the serious aspect of this problem, what this does not at all mean is that everyone has a good job. Or that the economy is working properly. The Federal Reserve bankers want to look at a low unemployment

---

[213] http://lucyannlance.com/really-a-shortage-of-workers-729/

159

number as their proof that everything is fine and that is why we have a shortage of good workers and pat themselves on the back and go have more champagne and caviar. I digress.

Yes, it is truly a problem that there are a lot of small business owners and corporations that would be hiring if only they could find the properly skilled employees.

Many companies need a specific type of employee (that knows how to work a certain machine, or can write computer code in the language the company uses, etc.). And it can be a challenge to find these people. And the company does not have enough money, time or additional personnel to train these people to do the job. Plus, does not want to take the risk the person leaves quickly.

One possible solution is brainstorming ways to offset the types of risks these employers are concerned about. That way these companies can bring on workers that are close enough and/or could do the job if trained.

DISPARITY OF JOBS

We have a disjointed economy with respect to jobs. Several levels to the job market, so to speak. A disparity between many that are doing fabulous with great jobs and another segment that is just not making it.

First, it is impossible to look at America and say it is bad right now. So many people have great jobs, awesome houses, new cars, growing savings accounts.

So, a pause here. It is not all bad. There is so much good in America.

The point in this section is for those of us doing well (of which I definitely am not one of those lately) don't get lost in a bubble.

The job market is terribly for too many people.

Plus, a lot of people that are working are just working way too hard for not enough money, and not any benefits.

So, on the good side:

Corporate jobs with high pay and incredible benefits. The benefits are not just the traditional ones like pensions, savings, healthcare, etc. Corporate benefits include dry cleaners and gyms at your office. Foos ball tables and game rooms. Plus, extended paid vacation time and even "sabbaticals."[214]

**In the corporate world what is not to love,
L-O-V-E, about these jobs and this economy!**

---

[214] Read more about corporate sabbaticals here
https://www.forbes.com/sites/davidburkus/2016/06/29/the-surprising-benefit-of-work-sabbaticals/#1f19c9074d3c and https://fairygodboss.com/career-topics/sabbaticals-77-companies-that-offer-them-and-why-they-re-good-for-employees-and-employers

Government jobs too. Solid and predictable pay along with total job security. Plus, ridiculously awesome traditional benefits including bottom-bargain prices for top-quality healthcare. Flexible schedules. Want to come in to your government office at 4:30am and leave at lunch time? Go for it.

Tech jobs? Stock options. The best work environment. Tons of benefits. High pay.

Union jobs? Pensions, benefits, job security, rules that limit how much work you need to do during your shift. There would be a flood of people waiting outside to take any of these jobs. It is exclusive. Union employees have it really good compared to similar workers that are not part of a union. Union employees complain about their employers and bargain. They come off as a bit spoiled to other workers that are out in the rest of the economy.

Unions. Corporates. Government. Technology. And several more industries. Life is good in these lines of work.

Many of them simply don't know what it is like in the rest of the economy.

There are only so many of these jobs. It is like a lottery that you win and get a great job like that. A lot of government and union employees believe they are so entitled to their pensions and ever-increasing pay and benefits. On the one hand-- relative to CEO pay and just economic growth in general I do wholeheartedly agree to side on worker pay and benefits increasing. At the same time such employees should be mindful of how good they have it relative to a lot of others.

The flip side: the disparity from these great jobs is massive down to the other class of workers in this economy.

Many of them work a lot harder. Longer hours. Tougher conditions. Might have more than one job. And they have little, if any, benefits. Very low pay.

Retail jobs. Low pay. No benefits. Self-employed: no benefits, no paid vacation time. Well, that is the choices they make, right? People can work themselves into a better situation if they would only try? A non-zero amount, absolutely that is the case. However, I have come to believe there are deeper problems, structural problems, to the disparity of jobs. This must be addressed.

A final note though to those in the bottom half of this job disparity that complain about their jobs in America there are still lower categories. The situation for many of the worst in America is leaps above a worker in China.

Is it our own brilliance that we get to buy all this stuff from China? No. Not really. Philosophically... morally... we rarely (or never) stop to think about it.

BENEFITS GAP

Within the preceding section on the disparity between all the awesome jobs in America compared to the slog that many other Americans are experiencing.

The benefits gap.

This is an issue that could require some really, really alternative solutions.

What are the statistics? I won't go tracking it all down right now, but I will point out what needs to be looked into.

How many Americans have paid time off?

How many Americans have *employer* paid/subsidized healthcare?

How many Americans have a pension?

How many Americans have an employer chipping in to their 401(k) savings?

Tuition Reimbursement? Dental and vision benefits? Stock options?

Why is this an issue?

Is it right that hard-working Americans with no benefits pay taxes that pay government employees that have incredible benefits? I do not think that makes any sense. We don't even talk about it.

I am not sure what the solution is. But this is one of the reasons I stated at the outset of this section that something big may be needed. Government employees feel an entitlement to those benefits and feel that they have earned it as well. It is perhaps impossible (and certainly not popular) to propose to take those benefits away.

However, a solution is needed. It is hard to justify that a taxpayer that works as hard or harder out in the private sector with no such benefits is subsidizing benefits for another worker?

Just because one can land a government job should not entitle them to such amazing benefits—at the expense of their neighbors!

If someone in the civilian/private employment market is paying taxes and working as hard or harder than there is little reason why they shouldn't have the same benefits. That is one possible solution.

Perhaps a better, or rather easier solution to implement would be tax credits back to the private sector worker. So, if government employees are calculated to receive, say, $240 per month in taxpayer-subsidized benefits than private sector employees would receive tax credits in that amount toward their own similar benefits.

Paying taxes so others can qualify for amazing, free benefits is not right. Many are working hard and earning just enough to get by and have no immediate or long-term benefits whatsoever. that I am doing just well enough to not qualify for myself.

Another problem, I believe, is what I call "double dipping." Many government employees can retire with partial or full benefits after a certain number of years—such as 20 or 25 years. They might barely be 50 years old. And so, they go out and get a job. They are taking a quality job and at the same time getting taxpayer-provided benefits. The issue to me is when you are earning that pension and then also get another job. You are then taking a job someone else could need, and simultaneously draining the system. It is a complex issue. If a government employee has worked the number of years to qualify for a pension, yes, they should earn that pension. However, first maybe the benefits are *too good*. And second, if they go out and get another job maybe their other benefits need to be placed on hold.

Finally, not to mention subsidizing the rich and corporations.

How many Americans are working and paying taxes while General Electric and billionaires are avoiding all their taxes by deploying every accounting trick that was tucked deep into legislation in Washington, DC? I don't even want to get started on that one.

CAN WE INVENT NEW INCENTIVES AND REWARD?

Can we create alternative incentives to work?

We work to make money. But could we create another purpose? Perhaps, or likely, via different rewards?

Currently, our society revolves around the need and desire for money.

The more money you accumulate the more you can exchange for.

The basis for money is to act as a means for exchange. Ayn Rand, despite a reputation of spurring ruthless capitalism, was deeply curious in her pursuit of understanding the very essence and truth of what money is.

Money does enable one of us to work on one thing and then exchange our work for other things. The common denominator? Work.

Today, a lot of money has been detached from work. Money—the amount any of us have of it—does not bear significant relation to our work.

Can we find another way? Where to look?

Creating new incentives to work? New rewards.

There are a lot of incentives and rewards we haven't quite thought about. We haven't even pursued brainstorming and discussing this. Corporations flush with cash and technology firms are talking about this. But only in their 'flush with so much money we don't know what to do with it' type of thinking.

We need outside the box—and outside the champagne and caviar dining room—thinking.

How about a Hall of Fame for something besides the work of millionaires? We have Hall of Fames for sports stars and musicians.

What about a Hall of Fame for hard working manufacturers? What about a Hall of Fame for waiters and waitresses?

Flushing this type of idea through a little further: what makes a basketball player work harder? The chance to win a championship? The desire to do the best in front of a large audience? The potential to improve your statistics? Can we bring these types of incentives to more of society? Tracking statistics of everyday workers. Giving more people in a lot of different industries a 'championship' to pursue. From this type of thinking, brainstorming could move to ways to incentive and reward work that don't involve money at all.

163

How do we account for time worked to solve social problems? A solution to this question could enable a lot more charity and volunteer work.

Value of an Hour Worked

Why does the corporate worker get excellent pay and awesome benefits while a worker down the street working for a less successful private sector company receives a fraction of the pay and very limited benefits?

Would it be better that an hour worked is rewarded more equitably?

**How about if
You work 1 hour, and I work 1 hour, and
we receive roughly the same pay
and roughly the same benefits?**

Labor is in and of itself quite complex.

Consider two workers. Both sent to the field for an hour to pick blueberries. Each given a bushel basket, one comes back after an hour in the field and his basket is full (we will call him Jim). The other comes back after the same hour in the field, but his basket is filled about half way (we will call him Andy). If we count each of them as having worked 1 hour and pay them as such, is that fair?

Just this one simple question becomes a microcosm for our entire society.

How do we analyze this? What if Andy is paid less even though he also worked an hour? *Shouldn't he* be paid less? Pay them based on their effort and results! But there are tons of scenarios in which maybe Andy *was* working as hard. Or, maybe Andy was working as hard as *he* could, but it wasn't as good as the other. These scenarios only scratch the surface of what can be a very interesting discussion.

And there are layers of complexity to it. Building on the example, who is the manager of the operations? Who is the executive in charge of pay? Who owns the field? How would any of *them* <u>choose</u> to solve the problem? That might be considered a free market capitalist approach. The executive in charge might consider paying both the same wage while adding a bonus incentive to those that pick more blueberries.

The essence of this example is labor. Or succinctly, *the measurement and definition of labor.*

Is labor simply time?[215] Each of us has exactly the same amount of time available to us. If we define labor strictly as the amount of time you work that

---

[215] For more reading also see https://extranewsfeed.com/if-work-hours-the-value-of-automation-were-distributed-fairly-in-the-us-today-86d293ce0b6f

is at least a baseline that is comparable and equivocal for all people.

If Bill Gates works 8 hours on Tuesday and you work 8 hours on Tuesday is there any difference in what you should get paid?

The concept of _value_ comes to mind. Bill Gates is providing _so much more_ value in the work he is doing than the rest of us. He employs tons of people that are working on products used all around the planet. Microsoft is continually innovating and improving their products to such a level that he is earning based on the _value_ of his work. Is this correct? Is this fair? Is this the best way to organize society? The last question there is so interesting.

What if Bill Gates and you are paid the same exact amount of money for working 8 hours on Tuesday? Will he work as hard? Will he continue to innovate as much? Will we lose dynamism in our society by redefining labor? I don't think we would. So long as there is freedom. Some people have drive.

A slogan in the progressive movement says, "equal means equal." What do they mean by "equal means equal?" Is it just so that a woman or minority gets paid the same for the same type of job? Why stop there? If you work and Tom Brady works, what is the difference? You are both working! You should both be paid the same. Either your pay rate should increase to his pay rate, or his pay rate should come down to yours. Pay everyone the exact same amount. Is that what's best for society? Would that be fair? Would that be "equal means equal?"

If professional athletes were paid the same as McDonald's employees would the quality of the sports games decline? I don't think they would. It is beyond the scope of this debate but perhaps quality might even increase.

Thinking Bigger

We can create a lot more work that means something.

This gets back to placing entirely different people in charge of distributing money. If the people distributing money have different goals and objectives than entirely different projects can be funded.

Cleaning parkland. Improving parks. Keeping streets clean. Rebuilding blight. Cleaning up our waterways. The stream of ideas could go on and on with work that would yield real, tangible results that have a truly valuable impact on making the world a better place.

There is, frankly—and simply—a lack of big, good ideas today.

There is so much work that we—as a society—_could_ be doing.

Today, there are too many paper pushing jobs. We build a skyscraper and fill it up with paper pushing. The capitalist mentality right now—and through Congress—is to create more paper-pushing mouse traps. Accounting loopholes to keep accountants busy, and the like. Perhaps an overgeneralization, but in the aggregate the point is valuable. The point is not to take on the accounting profession. However, we can change what accountants count.

We can have more powerful outcomes if we orient society differently.

To work of value. The question is "what's the point of economic activity?"[216]

According to Lester Thurow we need more 'human capital:' "skills, education and knowledge."

"Replacing physical capital with human capital (may seem) a minor change at most-- but it isn't." Thurow goes on to state that essentially it comes down to the profit incentive. There is that word again: incentive. A 'human capital'-oriented world lacks the get rich quick ability of capitalism. Tracking 'human capital' gets back to the idea of accountants counting different things.[217]

E.F. Schumacher wrote that economic activity should be oriented around a foundational view that "people matter." Schumacher looked to India and Buddhism and some of the simple notions orienting economic activity around a goal of "maximum well-being," prudent employment with work that "nourishes and enlivens" people. The goal of the economy is not "maximization of production," more consumption, or even "maximization of employment." Rather, we need more fundamental objectives in our economy. We need to dig deeper—understand our 'why.' Schumacher asks, "what is the right path of development?"[218]

The rise of capital (money without work) has contributed to a general apathy toward real work in our society. Our economic goals are consumption-oriented and, given capital (money), we need to do things with that money: consume. And, as we go further and further along that path, we get disconnected from understanding what work could be done and whether we even want to work.

The Bible says God rested on the seventh day. We are supposed to be working. Nearly every day. Instead, we are trying to reduce the work week and reduce work. When you have so much capital (money stored up and access to more money) you want to spend it. And then we mistake our accumulation of capital with a need for more rest and relaxation—fancy dinners, laying on the beach. We are trying to lower the number of hours we work. And our work is detached from any real output. We are not producing anything with physical effort. Trappist Monks follow a very quiet lifestyle centered around prayer. However, one Trappist principle is work. Trappist Monks engage in daily manual labor.[219]

Is manufacturing really 'dead'? We revolutionized agriculture and stripped out much of the manual labor on farms? Now, are we stripping out all manual

---

[216] http://www.agjohnson.us/glad/if-not-capitalism-what/
[217] *The Future of Capitalism* Lester C. Thurow 1996 pp 280-281
[218] *Small is Beautiful*, E.F. Schumacher. 1973. Pp 59-66
[219] http://www.trappists.org/monastic-life/day-life

labor in production of goods? What next? Have we moved on to a knowledge and information economy? There is much evidence that indeed we have new job creation in the way of knowledge and information work. However, is *building things* over? We may not farm, or manufacture cars and goods in the ways we did in the past. And, perhaps the factories that were at one time so popular will continue to change and be phased out.

But are we done building?

No, we have only momentarily lost our imagination.

There are so many things we can imagine and yet build and achieve.

We haven't even scratched the surface of thinking big.

We need purpose to our work. As Denzel Washington says of your work, "don't just aspire to make a living. Aspire to make a difference."[220]

---

[220] https://youtu.be/BxY_eJLBflk?t=8m13s

33
BOLD STEPS

WORKERS ORGANIZING: UNIONS, AND EMPLOYER-EMPLOYEE BALANCE

Two basic themes to cover here: employer unions and employer-employee balance. Unions serve a very valuable service. The creation of unions has provided enormous positive breakthroughs for employees. For decades, however, unions have declined in their membership, relevance and most sadly, their impact. It is not as easy to simply say employees should be given all of this and that. There must be employee responsibility and understanding of the value of the business over-and-above what employees bring to it. However, overall, union strength needs to be restored at a minimum. And workers need to gain more fruits from their labor. First, unions.

Unions

Union membership dropped to 10.7% in 2016 down from over 20% in 1983.[221] In the 1950's the level of union membership was over 30%. Why the continued decline? One theory is unions are unique to manufacturing and thus membership in unions has declined as manufacturing jobs have also declined. Others contend that "skilled" jobs are harder to organize into

---

[221] http://thehill.com/homenews/state-watch/316310-union-membership-hits-new-low

unions because each person has different capabilities that are not easily grouped together. "Unskilled" jobs, such as working on an assembly line were naturally conducive to workers banding together.[222] And what about the conception: "labor unions" when we don't really have "labor" as much in the traditional sense. Many people go to work at desk and retail jobs and don't consider themselves "laborers" that would even consider a union.

Whatever the reasons for *the past* rise and fall of labor unions, there is plenty of brainstorming that could be done with respect to what *the future* should be.

The so-called 'Gig economy' could be one area where unions could regain a foothold. Thinking of, say, Uber drivers. They have routinely complained of their treatment and have on occasion tried to organize. Government (public sector) jobs have been seeing a rise in union membership in the last 20 years. Certain states still have lots of union jobs (such as Illinois, Michigan, California, New York and New Jersey) while other states, such as South Carolina, virtually ban unionization via "right to work" legislation.[223]

The 1880's were a turning point in the employee relationship with the boss. And, union membership really took off in the 1940's following the National Labor Relations Act of 1945 (the so-called Wagner Act).

Many workers are without healthcare benefits and without retirement plans and pensions. Union workers get many of those things and simply argue against their companies' management for more money out of the corporation. However, so many workers are outside this corporate structure and don't work for companies that are flush with cash and provide such benefits. For most workers, there is not an orange to squeeze. Unions have traditionally been organized at companies that are ripe with bearing fruit.

Galbraith noticed this and speculated about "direct action by the state on behalf of those in need outside the unions;" which is interesting. It is a very important distinction that those with a union protected job are themselves doing quite well compared to many in society.

The concept of unions will, in part, have to be completely reinvented. Perhaps around new ownership models and/or cooperative arrangements. Efforts in collective bargaining will have to be better developed.

New, different approach are found in small-scale movements such as the "Lucas Plan," which posits that discussion is needed about developing more "Socially Useful Production."[224] "What so inspires me about the Lucas Plan is the democratic egalitarianism which runs through its every

---

[222] https://www.theatlantic.com/business/archive/2012/06/who-killed-american-unions/258239/

[223] https://www.bls.gov/spotlight/2016/union-membership-in-the-united-states/home.htm

[224] https://www.theguardian.com/science/political-science/2014/jan/22/remembering-the-lucas-plan-what-can-it-tell-us-about-democratising-technology-today

part – the work processes, the products and even the very technology they propose."[225]

Employer-Employee Balance

What is the proper financial relationship between an employer and employee? Not sure if there is a one-size-fits-all answer. However, let's look at sports professionals. Many of them believe the fans are only there because of their great ability—so the players deserve all the pay.

Another view is that the stadium all the finds are watching that player in was built and there before that player joined the team. The fans have been there for years. The TV contracts, too; already in place. It is not all about the current player. For this moment in time, yes, the fans are coming to see that player. But they are coming to the stadium that is nice and fun. They are coming for the experience that has been wrapped around you.

A relevant analogy to companies and their employees and unions. The company was already there. The ideas were already there. The machinery the employee works on. Already there.

Thus, it is a balance. Yes, all the work is done by the employees. The game is played by the athletes. However, it is a bigger issue to discuss.

In one respect, employees should be thankful they have a job and thankful for the customers that keep money flowing in the door.

That is where this discussion could go beyond the corporations and owners and then beyond even the employees and the players.

Who really owns the team? Who really owns the company?

There is no revenue for the sports team without the fans.

The company is successful for reasons beyond the owners and employees. The company has customers. *That*, is where the revenue comes from. Without anyone buying the products there would be no company and no employees.

Much more discussion is needed in this area of 'stakeholders' and profit sharing. And, still, overall, an orchestrated shift in the balance toward workers is needed.

---

[225] https://www.opendemocracy.net/neweconomics/when-the-workers-nearly-took-control-five-lessons-from-the-lucas-plan/

34
BOLD STEPS

CORPORATE RESTRUCTURING

Corporations have been around since prior to 1400.

The modern corporate structure evolved out of the Gilded Age (1870's and 1880's), with tycoons like John D. Rockefeller, Andrew Carnegie, J.P. Morgan and the so-called "titans of finance" looking to protect their wealth, *and control*, from outside influence. Firms such as Goldman Sachs were formed amid this same era[226] and sought to spread this concept of tightly controlled corporations.

The mega corporations of Rockefeller and Carnegie ruthlessly took over industries, building monopoly businesses so large that public backlash ensued.

The America that emerged out of that era has ended up dominating the globe. The achievements of men banding together around an idea through the establishment of a corporation[227] is actually quite impressive.

Corporations are an amazing invention.

The first commercial corporation dates back to 1347 in Sweden.[228]

---

[226] Marcus Goldman founded Goldman Sachs in 1882. By 1906, they were leading major IPO's and made a big splash with the public offering of Sears, Roebuck and Company. Goldman's son Henry then influenced the creation of the Federal Reserve with a position inside the Woodrow Wilson Administration.

[227] Articles of Incorporation of Standard Oil, 1870. https://en.wikipedia.org/wiki/Stephen_V._Harkness#/media/File:Standard_Oil_Articles_of_In corporation_-_1870.png

[228] The Stora Kopparberg established in 1347 by a charter from King Magnus Eriksson for the Falun Mine per https://en.wikipedia.org/wiki/Falun_Mine and

So many corporations have made incredible accomplishments: Microsoft, IBM, General Electric and Coca-Cola.

An organization with a collection of people all working in the same direction. Most of these businesses, and the work of their employees, you could also say do truly serve the people.

Still, corporations have been around for a long... long time.

It is time to update the framework. It is time for radical improvement.

We are smart enough. And we are capable enough.

We must improve on the corporate structure to accomplish more for society at large.

For several reasons, the modern corporation needs a substantial overhaul.

- Corporate focus must change beyond merely its own profit seeking.
- Accounting gimmicks and earnings manipulation must be addressed.
- CEO pay must be brought back in line for a number of reasons (addressed in another chapter)
- Corporate influence in government (and specifically corporate power in Washington, DC) must be reigned-in and dramatically reduced.
- Reigning-in CEO/Board power and ending stock buybacks.
- Ownership of corporations needs to be vastly diversified and broadened throughout the economy (addressed in the next chapter).
- Entirely new corporate structure needed (subsequent chapter).

As with the overall theme of this book it is not so much about the past as there isn't anything that can be done about it.

We are well into the 21st Century now and we need to modernize—radically, and fast.

Innovation and continual improvement is essential. And corporate America—ironically—is in dire need of an overhaul... for its own good[229].. for our economic good, financial well-being... and to the benefit of world security.

That is the benefit-of-the-doubt perspective.

Galbraith puts a sinister view on the rise of corporate power. Galbraith has a view of history in which "imperial power came so suddenly to an end" but he asks "whether, it still continues in more disguised but not necessarily less

---

https://en.wikipedia.org/wiki/Corporation

[229] https://www.reuters.com/investigates/special-report/usa-buybacks-cannibalized/

effective forms."[230] Continuing, Galbraith asks "did one kind of colonial rule give way to another?" And then he alludes to how a "more sophisticated form of imperialism" now rules, not "government-sponsored imperialism" but rather today it is "privately sponsored imperialism" carried out by the "transnational corporation."[231] So much worse?

Many corporations are as big and problematic as the biggest banks. They aren't "too big to fail" in the sense that they could bring down the entire economy, but many have become TBTF in their own minds. TBTF in the minds of politicians and Washington, DC. Corporations, like banks, are filled with people that worship their own brilliance.

Who leads our corporations in the future and how they are led is a very important issue to work out. We must not get complacent or belief for one second that how things are today is how they have to be in the future. Change is the name of the game. Corporations thrive in the economy because they continually refine and improve their products and operations. In the same manner, we must take a deep look at how our corporations are structured. And we must refine it. Fast.

Governance of corporations must change to reflect more worker involvement and stakeholder participation. Corporations are not for just a handful of graduate school buddies to divide up all the value amongst themselves. What are the problems and potential new directions? Starting simply and moving to more radical:

Beyond Short-Term Profits

Short-term profits. Short-term focus.

Corporate management tries try to beat Wall Street earnings expectations. They want their stock price going up so the value of their stock options increase. As a result, companies have incentives to manage income to meet earnings targets or to make earnings look less risky.

Corporate management is not focused as much as it should be on creating long-term value in a wholistic way. It is a problem for economic balance. It is also a problem for these same corporations in their own self-interest.

Our society would be a lot better with less emphasis on corporate profit. It starts with asking different questions. Such as, how is the profit used? Are profits reinvested in the business, community and employees? Are profits used to increase CEO pay and give more stock options to board members? From new questions it continues from there to new metrics, new targets.

---

[230] *The Good Society*, John Kenneth Galbraith, 1996, pp 123
[231] *The Good Society*, John Kenneth Galbraith, 1996, pp 126

There are completely different metrics
that could be tracked
to monitor corporate success.

We can manage a company to achieve goals outside of simply "the bottom line" and short-term profits.

Already there is a lot of work in this area. Much of it is liberal leaning or liberal sounding: sustainability, social responsibility, fossil fuel use. The point is to get creative about achieving more out of our corporate action.

The "triple bottom line," is another of the new metrics. Also, liberal leaning that tracks the economic bottom line as well as the environmental bottom line and the social (social justice) bottom line.

And short-term management of earnings is being kind. As indicated in 1998 by one SEC chairperson, "managing may be giving way to manipulation; integrity may be losing out to illusion."[232]

Accounting Gimmicks:
No More Earnings Manipulation

Corporate earnings are increasingly manipulated. And they have been manipulated extensively for just about two decades. The pressures started in the internet age when investors began paying so much attention to earnings reports. Analysts make projections of their expectations for earnings. And if you 'beat' the analyst forecast your stock price usually goes up. If a corporation 'misses' the analyst forecast their stock price would sometimes get hammered.

The untrue financial condition along with added borrowing due to low interest rates has led some to warn about another problem, that of "zombie companies."[233] Companies that are dinosaurs that don't have the growth and new products to thrive, instead have been able to raise money in our current low-interest environment to perpetuate their existence. Companies like General Electric and Cisco have convoluted financials that mask possible bankruptcy.

Worse is the rise in "pro-forma," "EBITDA" and "non-GAAP" earnings reports. Companies have started to report "earnings before all the bad stuff."[234]

---

[232] A. Levitt, "The Numbers Game," Remarks to NYU Center for Law and Business, September 28, 1998 (Securities and Exchange Commission, 1998)

[233] https://www.bloomberg.com/news/articles/2017-07-24/zombie-companies-littering-europe-may-tie-ecb-s-hands-for-years

[234] https://www.wsj.com/articles/one-more-reason-for-investors-to-worry-about-earnings-

It is 'well, this is what our earnings would have been if we didn't have to do 5 or 6 things.' It's like going to your bank and saying 'well, my income would have been $80,000 if I sold these 5 deals that I didn't sell. And my bank account would have $15,000 in it but I had to pay the rent.' And the bank says, 'oh, no problem. Got it. Well, here is your big loan then.'

Investors don't really care. Investors don't know what they own. Investors hardly look at any financial ratios.

Investors do not care what they are buying.

The mutual fund owners don't care. They don't ask questions. They don't raise an eyebrow about "pro forma" just so long as the stock goes up.

As long as the market is going up.

When things go south *then* accounting will matter. A lot of this stuff will be written about in hindsight. Massive accounting fraud and gimmicks for stock prices and managed earnings. Misleading, but widely accepted, norm of behavior across many companies.

"Pro-forma," "adjusted net income," "adjusted operating income," just about anything a corporation wants to report the media kind of just runs with it. Most investors don't know and don't care. Mutual fund managers just plug that number into their spreadsheets. Whatever the company says their earnings are, that is what they are.

No one digs into the numbers. There is no apples-to-apples comparison. So, you have some companies that still report a true earnings number. But we value them just the same as a company that is making up their numbers. Even big-name tech stocks like Amazon engage in this process.[235] It also makes it difficult to compare a company from one quarter to the next. One quarter they are "adjusting" because of x, y and z. The next quarter they adjust because of x, a and b. There is no meaning even from quarter to quarter in some companies' earnings reports. The media and accountants are complicit. It is an accepted norm for everyone. Company management, accountants, investors. As such it becomes another reason the stock market is simply a casino. There is very little bearing between what people buy and any reality of

---

before-bad-stuff-1470261290

[235] In some earnings reports, Amazon has released a separate list of "adjustments to net income" for items such as "share-based compensation, amortization of goodwill and intangibles, impairment charges, and equity in losses of its subsidiaries." These adjustments make the reported income higher than actual income. Per: https://www.slideshare.net/HarunRashid87/income-statement-and-related-information-chapter-4-intermediate-accounting-15th-edition

what they actually own.

Another way to look at modern accounting is to call it "fake accounting." John Perkins used this term in describing how so much is left out in the narrow way that we define accounting.[236] A solution to "fake accounting" is movements for approaches such as "Full Cost Accounting (FCA)" and "True Cost Accounting (TCA)" that account for visible as well as hidden costs, past and future costs, life cycle costs and indirect costs.[237]

Ending Corporate Dominance in Government and Washington, DC

Too much corporate power in Washington, DC. All the corporate-funded lobbying results in welfare to corporations. There is far too much collusion in writing laws. Corporation lawyers write the laws and the Congressmembers jam through massive pieces of legislation to fool the public.

We currently have a corporate driven economy. This isn't really a surprise for anyone to hear. And it is not necessarily that corporations are bad. I wish all of them great success. The point certainly is not to bring anyone down.

Matters just need to be taken into our own hands—or someone else's hands—when it comes to fixing everyone else's economy.

There are far too many corporate loopholes, tax shelters and dodges.[238]

Corporate leaders are up-and-down the streets and buildings of Washington, DC. They have their lobbyists, but worse is corporate executives taking high-level government posts. On that same morning in early March 2017 that I heard the words of Treasury Secretary Steve Mnuchin, CNBC was also reporting on a meeting of CEO's at the White House.[239] It was the second time in a matter of weeks that President Trump met with CEO's. They referred to the Trump Administration as the most pro-growth President in a long time, if maybe ever. And all that is great. Appointing people like Steve Mnuchin to Treasury Secretary is a demonstration of the same old, same old.

Yes, CEO's deserve their input and they deserve to do better just as anyone else. However, they are not the voice for all of America. Nothing they work on is going to solve broader economic problems. Period. As great as

---

[236] For one thing Perkins believes we should account for externalities.

[237] *Hoodwinked*, John Perkins, 2009, Pp 102-105

[238] http://www.sanders.senate.gov/imo/media/doc/Tax-Dodge-Report-3.pdf and http://www.politicususa.com/2013/02/07/sanders-report-corporations-tax-dodge.html

[239] The whole moment of watching CEOs as the key (and really only) economic leaders discussing how to shape a better economy was also a contributing factor to getting this book project really swinging into motion.

these CEO's are. And some of them are amazingly talented people. And they work very hard. They are not going to solve any problems for the rest of America.

Regular hardworking Americans need to have a say in how this economy grows. Totally new people at the table. Or—at the very least— *expanding* who has a say. It is an echo chamber right now. They have like a 28-hour game of Monopoly going. No one gets to play until they are done. Worse, the people are the pieces on the board they are playing with.

Big banks and CEO want the status quo. They want commissions to be set-up by Congress to look into things and make a report. Preferably, a "bipartisan commission." They want to do reviews. And audits. None of that changes anything. It buys them time. We need action. Starting today.

Reigning in the Power of the CEO and Boards; And, the Problem of Stock Buybacks

One of the biggest problems in our current economy is big corporations buying their own stock back.

Why do board members and CEO's implement stock buyback plans?

First, this helps boost the stock price. The stock price is the prime metric for judging their performance. If the stock price goes up, they must be doing a good job. Hence, order up a stock buyback.

Second, the CEO—as well as the board members-- own tons of shares. And if they can make their own shares worth more money why not? So, management is taking profits from the workers and using it to enrich their own holdings.

These moral hazards are creating enormous problems in the larger economy.[240]

First, they are exacerbating the gap between rich and power.

Second, stock buy backs are distorting our economic performance.

Third, we are wasting colossal amounts of money. Instead of investing in their own business they are buying shares of their own stock. They are not using the profits to invest the money back in better equipment, and to grow the company. Instead of paying more profits out to their workers corporations are taking the profit money they have and buying their own stock certificates. This money could be used for more productive outcomes.

Fourth, it is used by Wall Street banks for manipulative purposes. The big banks help the CEO and board buy back the shares in the stock market.[241]

---

[240] https://blogs.cfainstitute.org/investor/2014/09/24/maximization-of-shareholder-value-flawed-thinking-that-threatens-our-economic-future/

For one thing, they know when a stock buyback plan is going to be announced. Then, the big banks are the ones buying the shares. They can buy when it is convenient to them. Influencing prices to their advantage.

Stock buybacks are a huge abuse of CEO and board power.

Money used to repurchase shares could have been reinvested to grow the companies. The money could have been reinvested in the employees. Anything really, except buying back paper.

We will look back on these years where large corporations are relentlessly focused on buying back their own shares of stock as a totally wasted opportunity.[242] Companies are using their profits to buy shares of stock while simultaneously cutting employees. They are buying stock shares instead of using that money to acquire businesses and expand. It does nothing for the long-term benefit of the business, or the economy. It helps the board, CEO, banks and largest shareholders become ever richer.

Stock buybacks have been out of control.[243] Even Apple, which just continually reports having so much cash on hand takes out bonds to buy back shares.[244] Thus, low interest rates enable corporations that are already flush with tons and tons of cash to get even more cash. And they use that cash to buy their own shares! The money is essentially free because interest rates are so low.

This charade is spurred by Federal Reserve easy money, their buying of bonds and keeping interest rates low. All of this gives a false sense that the economy is coming along better. We are masking major, significant problems. And Federal Reserve policy is doing nothing for Main Street America.

There is so much wealth in this country that can be tapped into. We need different accounting principles, different (and more) people in charge, reorganized corporate structures.

---

[241] http://www.zerohedge.com/news/2015-08-12/mysterious-dip-buyer-found-goldman-buyback-desk-has-busiest-day-2011

[242] https://www.forbes.com/sites/investor/2017/07/24/stock-buybacks-the-greatest-deception/#41d9819f6968

[243] Cisco spent $37 billion in cash on buybacks from 2007-2011 while spending $6 billion on capex during that same time! From late 2004 to early 2011 S&P 500 companies spent $2.3 trillion on stock buybacks! ExxonMobil has been the leader repurchasing $160 billion of its own shares from 2004-2011. IBM had a massive program that kept a near perfect rise in the stock going. Bought 550 million shares or 36% of the outstanding while floating a lot of that right back to management stock options. CEO Sam Palmisano made $110 million off stock options right after his retirement. Read more: https://www.reuters.com/investigates/special-report/usa-buybacks-cannibalized/ and https://www.theatlantic.com/politics/archive/2015/02/kill-stock-buyback-to-save-the-american-economy/385259/ and https://www.cnbc.com/2015/11/09/more-buybacks-less-capex-in-2016-goldman.html.

[244] http://www.bloomberg.com/news/articles/2015-02-03/apple-raises-6-5-billion-from-bond-sale-funding-share-buybacks

How about a solution such as companies that are buying back their own stock must first pay a "share repurchase tax" of 20% of the purchase amount. And then, provide that money directly to the population at-large? And/or radically different ownership structures could unleash huge amounts of wealth that just otherwise is left to sit around.

35
BOLD STEPS

BROADEN OWNERSHIP
IN STOCKS AND COMPANIES

Too much of the stock market is owned by too little people.

Great idea Bill Gates. Great idea Mark Zuckerberg.

At a certain point, however, the company and its success and ideas eventually become about more than just the founder.

The top 1% of households owns 38% of all stock shares. And, 10% of Americans owned over 80% of the wealth in the stock market.[245]

Far too much concentrated wealth!

**A rising stock market simply
does not impact enough of the population.**

Government policy should not be focused—at all—on helping the stock market rise. It is targeted help and assistance for the wrong people.

There are ways to grow the economy that can impact all people. Running the economy to grow a stock market that has such narrow impact is ridiculous.

---

[245] *Household Wealth Trends in the United States, 1962-2013*, Working Paper No. 20733, Edward N. Wolff, National Bureau of Economic Research, December 2014
http://www.nber.org/papers/w20733 and
http://www.marineconomicconsulting.com/w20733.pdf via

A first solution is to simply diversify stock ownership. Put shares of stock into the hands of more people.

Give all people some shares of stock?

Radical, but somehow necessary.

The purest step to solve this would simply to get more of the broader public participating in investing. Step one, however, is having enough money to save and invest. Another path is providing more ownership to employees and workers of companies. What about those that work at companies that are not publicly traded? Is enough ownership provided to employees? Who else should be an owner? Who else should share in the profits and success of a business?

Along the more radical path, on way to do put shares in the hands of more people—the first way that comes to most people's minds—is that you have to take shares away from current holders and give them to others.

That would be the drastic path. Hard for me to justify something like that.

An easier way, that heads in this direction, is through secondary offerings.

This is common in the stock market to conduct secondary offerings.

More shares are made available for the public to purchase.

A company that had 1,000,000 shares outstanding yesterday could issue another 1,000,000 shares today. And at the end of the day the company now has 2 million shares outstanding. The existing owners of the stock would be affected by their ownership share being reduced. In this example, by 50%. Fifty percent is easy for a quick illustration purpose, but the actual implementation could be a far lower percentage implementation.

If stock prices are the be-all and end-all for Washington, DC policy makers and New York City banks that we have to have more diversity in ownership. It is not alright to focus so much attention of economic growth on driving stock prices up when only half of the population even own stocks.

Disperse ownership more broadly.

Spread ownership in corporations.

Who are the *real owners* anyway? Many like to say a business is nothing without its employees. I like to point out that a business is nothing without its customers. The people are ultimately the reason why Coca-Cola, for example, rolls in the money.

There is too much concentrated wealth.

This is not an indictment of capitalism or free markets at all. The market is not what it once was. More to the points, there are improvements to be had. The way stocks and stock ownership are structured needs to be improved; perhaps revolutionized. Change in this area could take a long time. This may not be a political movement. However, change in the current era is happening fast. Ideas can spread quickly, and technology can speed implementation. Consider Facebook was founded in February 2004 and had an IPO valuing the company at around $100 billion just 8 years later.

Diversifying ownership in the stock market is an essential point.

The fact is that not that many Americans own stock.

Moreover, the vast majority of stock is owned by very few people.

So, it is a double whammy. Most people don't own stocks anyways. Plus, those that do in reality hold very little relative to the vast amount of stock wealth that is tied up in very few hands.

Even those that think they own a lot of stock, do not really own much in the grand scheme of things. If you own $10,000 of Microsoft. And let's not kid ourselves, most people do not own $10,000 of any company. But if you did, that is a stake of just 0.0000016% of the company. With that percentage of ownership if you were to get your share of Microsoft's annual income, your share would add up to 1 penny after 50,000 years.[246] The math is far worse than any Ponzi scheme.

It is similar with sports. Professional players complain more and more about getting a bigger share of the owner's profits. And players make a ton of money already! Multi-million-dollar contracts. As their annual salary! So, for me, they are already doing quite, quite well. And they should be thankful. They may be the game today. But the team was there long before they came along. There wouldn't be a stadium and fans for them but for the many years of growth prior to their arrival on the scene. But where I am going with this is that the players believe it is only *they* who make the owners wealthy? The players go after the owners.

What about the fans? Fans are the ones that are paying for all of it. Couldn't the fans benefit from the owners having less profit? If there is less profit for the owners, shouldn't the fans have first dibs on that? What about tickets for people that can't afford to go to the games? This sports analogy could really be pulled out and could have lots of play (so-to-speak) in determining some real-world alternatives for our economy.

Corporate profits and corporate ownership can be related to this sports analogy.

Is it all because of the CEO and the current corporate board members that the company is so successful? Is it even only the employees? What about the customers? Is it right to want to give ownership to employees? In what circumstances? And how? Can we slowly roll to a new manner of corporate ownership? Stock ownership? Or what about something more direct? Ownership of a rights to a proportion of future profits? The benefit to this type of arrangement is that it can be more universal. No matter whether a

---

[246] Microsoft annual income was $55.19 billion in 2017 per https://www.marketwatch.com/investing/stock/msft/financials

company is publicly traded with stock to own, the employees have a stake regardless. Owning a portion of the company they work for.

Activist Investing and Impact Investing

Changes in ownership are likely to come about one way or the other.

The activism of Colin Kaepernick is portrayed innocently by the media as #takeaknee for police brutality but the objectives and goals behind the movement run much deeper. Far broader in scope and ultimately economically disruptive: stemming from, branching off from and/or paralleling movements such as Occupy Wall Street.[247]

The protest of the Dakota Access Pipeline is a microcosm of a movement that is far more mainstream then some people believe. The richest universities such as Harvard and Yale have huge pension funds and endowments (money accumulated from donations) that invest just like mutual funds. They are making decisions to stop adding to investments and even "divesting" out of the fossil fuel industry. Banks themselves are making changes about what they will finance. U.S. Bank will no longer provide "financing for construction of oil or natural gas pipelines" and the bank is also implementing strict standards for oil and gas industry companies, requiring "enhanced due diligence processes."[248]

These changes in investing trends started as "socially responsible investing" and are now called "impact investing" or "activist investing." Activist funds have been created—primarily in Europe. Groups such as FairPensions, BankTrack and Platform London are becoming shareholder activists.[249] Greenpeace is also buying shares of stock, so they are able to go into shareholder meetings and make speeches. They even disrupt corporate shareholder meetings if they can.[250]

Change is coming one way or the other. People are so upset about what they believe is egregious about corporations (from extreme wealth to energy use) and they are tracing to the sources of the problem, so they can do something about it. They want to take over companies. Robert Reich called something like this "diffusion of ownership."[251] All of this is why I believe we

---

[247] http://www.occupy.com/article/black-lives-matters-shift-economic-issues-echoes-black-panthers#sthash.k5p43V9V.dpbs

[248] https://www.commondreams.org/news/2017/05/15/us-bank-stop-funding-pipelines-divestment-movement-expands-worldwide

[249] *The Heretic's Guide to Global Finance*, Brett Scott, 2013. Pp 128.

[250] https://www.reuters.com/article/us-credit-suisse-gp-agm-greenpeace/greenpeace-gatecrashes-credit-suisse-shareholder-meeting-idUSKBN17U1BW

need to broaden stock ownership fast. Sound extreme but financial experts can easily implement.

---

251 *The Work of Nations*, Robert B. Reich, 1991

36
BOLD STEPS

BEYOND CORPORATIONS: NEW ORGANIZATIONAL STRUCTURES

The way corporations are set up and managed—all of it can change. There is no reason why it needs to be the same in the future.

CEO's and management do not need to have so much control over the entire company.

Decision-making can become more democratic—especially with respect to how to divide the pie.

Corporate boards can be filled with a lot of different people.

And the goals for a corporation can change too. It does not need to be all about the bottom line.

It is past time to reform corporate structure.

There is too much power and false incentives for CEOs, upper management and board members. Furthermore, all of the above have abused their roles. Finally, the interests of the CEO, upper management and board members are not in the true interest of all shareholders. And there is no reason why employees should not have a better stake in their own production.

Even as far back as 1913 there have been calls to create a new form of corporation—with different objectives, beyond only profit-seeking. Pope Pius XI called for a "tripartist corporation" in which government, labor and industry would collaborate for the greater good.[252]

Believe it or not, another way does already exist.

---

[252] https://en.wikipedia.org/wiki/Quadragesimo_anno#Tripartist_corporatism

B Corporations. Benefit Corporations.

The outdoor fitness company, Patagonia is set up as a B Corp.[253]

Well, it is not totally a legal structure in and of itself (it is more like a certification such as LEED buildings or Fair Trade coffee); however, it makes this discussion a lot more real.

We are already well on our way to starting to make corporations different, and better.

The conversation can get quite deep and even philosophical if you ask me. I might say that just because you are one of the lucky people in the town to have a good job at a corporation does not necessarily make you any more entitled to great pay and benefits than the CEO. Depending on how great the benefits and pay are for employees, they are "CEOs" relative to the population around them. The spoils of a corporation might belong not just to workers but all stakeholders. Stakeholders. What is a stakeholder? People affected by the company in any way. And what about the customers? The purchasers of the products and services are the ultimate reason why the corporation stays in business. Robust discussion could be had.

Dialing it back a little. At a minimum, we need to make the CEO and top management accountable not only to a board but to the employees. And the community.

What if employees got to vote on CEO compensation?

If employees voted on CEO compensation my guess it would be fair. There are a lot of CEO's that deserve, and earn, their pay. A lot of CEO's have the respect of their employees; based on how they manage, and based on the skin they have put into the organization. The point is who is afraid of who? A good CEO shouldn't be afraid of letting employees determine their salary. Let them make their case. Let the board makes its case of what *they* think the pay should be. And then let the employees decide. It's an idea.

And beyond pay, what are the best ways to improve corporate management and the boards? Is there a way to have oversight of the Board of Directors? Independent directors was a movement fueled by Sarbanes-Oxley. Diversity.

Legendary management guru and author Peter Drucker wrote in 1994, "we have to rethink *the governance of corporations.*"[254] It is long past time to dig deep in conversation and start embracing some new ideas.

---

[253] http://www.patagonia.com/b-lab.html
[254] *Post-Capitalist Society*, 1994, Peter Drucker. Pp 67.

37
BOLD STEPS

DIVIDENDS FOR AMERICANS

How about corporations pay citizens every year, or quarterly, a dividend—a portion of their profits?

This might be more simplistic, and easier to implement, sooner; rather than the more drastic step of shifting ownership.

It has been common over the years for companies to pay "dividends" to their shareholders. That is, paying a portion of the company profits divided up among the shareholders. Usually this is done on a quarterly basis.

Why not instead require all companies to pay a base percentage of their profits directly to the people? Divide the profits up among all Americans.

Utility companies (electricity providers) have traditionally paid dividends. Dominion Energy pays $0.77 (77 cents) each quarter for every share owned. So, if you own 1,000 shares (about $80,000 worth of stock) in Dominion you receive $770.[255] Four times per year. Multiplied by four quarterly payments that is $3,080 every year. Shareholders earn that dividend. Simply for buying and holding the stock the shareholder earns $3,080 per year for their 1,000 shares. That is a return of about 3.9% simply for already having that $80,000 to invest and hold 1,000 shares of Dominion Energy.

With 642 million shares outstanding, Dominion pays out about $50,000,000 every quarter to its shareholders. Multiplied by four quarters, Dominion Energy pays about $200 million every year in dividends.

So... how about paying this money to the people instead of the

---

[255] As of October 2017, the stock was trading around $80 per share. Thus, you need to have about $80,000 of stock to earn that $770.

shareholders?

Radical. Absolutely!

There are numerous ways to look at this.

It could be seen as a "tax" on profits. And instead of the tax going to the government the tax goes to the people.

It could be seen as a return for the people. All of the collective productivity of the country is paid back to the people.

It could be seen as leveling the playing field. Do we need to give so much money to people that already have tons of money?

Call it "Dividends for Americans" or "Citizens Dividends."

The Citizens Dividend is 10% of "reported profits" per share. This is because companies routinely make up their own 'adjusted earnings' and such to meet and beat earnings estimates. So, whatever that crazy number is they publish, the Citizens Dividend will apply based on that. Call it a double solution. Helping people while at the same time take away incentivizes for accounting tricks and accounting manipulations.

How will the citizens dividend be distributed? How about citizens with incomes in the top 10% will not receive dividends. How about making it an "earned credit" for people working, or in need of work and/or in school. Basically, a "qualifying event," single mother, what have you.

Let the brainstorming begin.

38
BOLD STEPS

CLOSE THE
STOCK MARKET

Close the stock market? Say what?

There is entirely too much focus on the stock market. At a minimum we must find ways to grow GDP—or even more specifically, personal income—faster. We should spend more time trying to improve GDP and personal income than we do on the stock market. The economy should drive stock prices. Instead, policy makers keep trying to make stock prices lead the economy.

There does not seem likely any kind of change to big bank, mafia-like manipulation and definite Federal Reserve interference in continuing massive gamesmanship of the stock market.

It will not end until the keys are taken away.

Should the U.S. stock markets be closed down?

For the benefit of all U.S. citizens, I contend that the current stock market exchanges in the United States need to be shut down.

This may be the only way to truly turn around national incomes and provide meaningful employment for more Americans.

Nothing has worked to get the Federal Reserve champagne sippers to try a better approach to fix more problems in our economy.

So, close down the New York Stock Exchange.

Quite radical.

I claim to be a steadfast believer in markets and free economies. I *am* a big-time believer in market-based economies and capitalism.

What I am *not* a believer in is crony capitalism or false markets. I believe in *free* markets. We do not have free markets in America.

Shutting down a *free*, *market* would be the wrong path.

However, closing manipulated casinos that are not regulated like a casino would be a positive step for freedom.

**Closing down the stock markets as they are today
has the potential to unleash true free markets
and spur a more helpful and beneficial form of capitalism
(or post-capitalist world). A financial system that is truly
new and improved and better for a modern age.**

The pieces are already in place.

Closing down the stock market is not as outlandish as it might at first seem. There are so many great ideas out there already. And there is a lot of market-based finance already in motion that can serve to fuel economic innovation that is extraordinary while at the same time bringing more and more people up.

There are better ways to raise money for the best ideas.

There are better structures for businesses that can benefit more people.

We are ready now.

**At a minimum serious discussion must start
immediately to include such radical prospects of
if and how to close the U.S. stock markets.**

The basis behind this is that we do not have free trading stock markets.

More importantly, we have a Federal Reserve and government policy makers that are entirely too narrowly focused on only rising stock prices.

We do not have open access to capital in the markets for a broad, competition among all new ideas.

It is entirely possible that a whole new technology and platform can spring up and take over the entire stock market industry.

This is akin to how, say, Facebook came in and dominated MySpace.

Or, better yet how Netflix totally eclipsed Blockbuster. Google's better algorithms taking over search engines; Uber reinventing the taxi industry.

The New York Stock Exchange (NYSE)[256] and even the more technology-based NASDAQ could be eclipsed by a better technology. Are the ideas already there, and in practice, such as forms of crowdfunding.

---

[256] The New York Stock Exchange (NYSE) is now, interestingly, owned by an Atlanta, Georgia based company, the Intercontinental Exchange (ICE).

In this sense, starting discussion about a future without the NYSE and NASDAQ would be healthy. It is a distinct possibility to occur even without a populist revolt such as I imply.

NYSE is a self-regulating organization (SRO). At a minimum need to be regulated. The realization has hit many people, perhaps most convincingly based on the corruption market observers witnessed in the 2008 crisis: "the model-- the ideal of markets as self-regulating and safe-- was deeply flawed: 2008 proved it."[257]

Majority of Americans Not Invested

Just about half of Americans own no stocks.

Those that do own stocks, most of them, in aggregate amount to little with respect to all the wealth in the markets. Many of these people too own stocks in a 401k as part of a distant savings plan to access on retirement. In other words, for most Americans the day-to-day increase in the stock market does... *absolutely nothing*.

Policy makers-- mainly the Federal Reserve and politicians-- are too focused on the level of the S&P 500 and the Dow Jones Industrial Average.

**A rising stock market has little to do
with the day-to-day economic well-being
of most Americans.**

According to Gallup polling, only 54% of Americans own any stocks.[258] Of course, that means the rising stock market leaves nearly half of Americans out and behind. The 46% of America that does not own *any* stocks receives no direct benefit at all from all the Federal Reserve, politicians and media attention to the rising Dow Jones Industrial Average.

There is much more to economic growth than the U.S. stock market. Indeed, we can have a thriving and growing economy even with a massive drop in the stock market or no stock market at all. It is all about the orientation of leadership and the framework of finance. And with a significant new direction a lot more people can and will stand to benefit. A decentralized financial system can work from the bottom up to feed what may be called growth. Or maybe a new term altogether.

---

[257] *The End of Wall Street*, Roger Lowenstein, 2010, Pp 305

[258] https://finance.yahoo.com/news/trump-keeps-reminding-america-much-hes-helping-rich-155620003.html?.tsrc=applewf

Valuation Now Meaningless and Pointless

Many may wonder, will the stock market move up or down? If the stock market does go up it should be driven higher by fundamentals.

Fair value on the stock market is, looking at the Dow Jones Industrial Average, anywhere from about 38,000 to 2,000. If you aren't prepared for either you shouldn't be in the market. A positive scenario says consider the growth potential in a world of over 6 billion people for the likes of Coca-Cola and other international companies? A negative scenario might be like this: what happens when baby boomers start withdrawing their money from the stock market? And, at the end of the day, owners of a stock, all they are holding is a paper stock certificate.

Corporate accounting is all rigged and gamed. Many companies can use various 'adjustments' to their earnings report to make the end result whatever they want it to be. And in the Federal Reserve money printing era, they could make the Dow 50,000 tomorrow if they wanted to.

The stock market has lost attachment to the reality of what it is supposed to do: raise capital.

When it hits home to some regular investors about how much of a casino investing in the stock market is, the bottom could fall out. Especially as they learn more about the corruption and insider rigging. **If prices do go south some investors are going to demand their money back.**

Insider Manipulation

The U.S. stock market has not always been a casino. But where there is money crime elements come. And within an environment with so much money at stake the incumbents so to speak that may have never realized or ever thought of intending to become a crime element, become such.

With new options and futures contracts popping up all the time, you can now basically simply bet on the market going up or down. It is red or white.

And the crime element oversees all trades. Electronic. They know all the trades going into the system. So, they front run. They skim off the top. Every buy and sell order from the public is skimmed. Even E-Trade and TD Ameritrade look to make money off of orders placed by their own customers.

At this point it ceases being a "market"

It is not random. It is not a random walk. All of that is nonsense as well.

The VIX (volatility index: a gauge of investor concern about big price movements) is now artificially low on the market. The cost of protecting a stock market portfolio is so low because no one has to protect anything. They know the Greenspan-Bernanke put will float the markets onward and upward.

The owners of stock have such a grip on government and political power and the levers of the markets that they could literally do anything to protect against a market move against them. They could even close the markets themselves. So, no one feels they need to buy any insurance. And that becomes a *big* risk!

Bye Bye Casino

Basically, the keys to the Porsche need to be taken away from the reckless teenager. Reasoning is not going to work.

If you were looking to get in control of the biggest money-making venture on the planet what might it be? Well, it would be two things. One is actually printing the money. That is the Federal Reserve. The other is the stock market. The U.S. stock markets are infinitely bigger than the alcohol industry of Al Capone, or the Las Vegas casinos of Bugsy Siegel.

The biggest casino on the planet earth in 2017 is Wall Street. And the casinos need to be shut down. And right away they need to be regulated. Like a casino. They either need to be regulated like a casino and treated as a casino; or, closed down for not being properly licensed as such.

And no more fox watching the hen house.

This is not to say shutting down free markets or capitalism. Rather it is a move to unleash true free markets and capitalism. Or a post-capitalist world that is new and improved and better for a modern age.

There really is no other way. Total outsiders need to be placed in charge of the stock markets. The markets need to be left to float as markets will float.

Close these casinos—the futures markets, stock markets—shut em all down.

Then open fresh, new, true markets.

With much less, significantly less top-down control. This would be a big step to decentralized markets.

Closing the New York Stock Exchange will not matter as much as people think it would. If we set up a new bar across the street the fact we have to close down the old bar will just mean people take their after-work drinking business to the new watering hole. The difference will be the management, and the drink selection. The difference will be in how the new exchange is established. Who runs it? How it is regulated and overseen. That is why a new market would be so much better. We need to completely abandon the existing market so that the old actors can no longer pull the strings. And so that it isn't grandfathered in to a faulty regulatory system with shanty oversight.

How to Close the New York Stock Exchange

What would be the process for closing down the New York Stock Exchange (NYSE)? They have become crooked casinos. Via consolidation, most of the U.S. exchanges are all a part of the same breed.

The ultimate goal is new and better jobs. New and better infrastructure. Higher incomes across the board for the population. A structure of economy that has a lot less control by a few. A lot less ability for insider manipulation. A lot less ability—or no ability—to rig systems.

The goal is not fairness or anything like that. The goal is to unleash the freedom of entrepreneurs. Artists. Alternative talents. They must have a way in the world. Starting now.

The timeframe could go something like this. Pick dates following a major Congressional election (to provide time to debate and roll over Congress):

1) Close down the New York Stock Exchange by January 31, 2020
2) Close down the NASDAQ Stock Exchange by January 31, 2020
3) Close down the Chicago Mercantile Exchange by January 31, 2020

Once the dates are set… the conversation can begin. So many details to work out. It doesn't all need to be hashed out here and now.

But without a target date nothing gets done.

We all like a deadline. So, there it is.

The conversation about what to do beginning 2/1/2020 can start now.

And that—conversation—is exactly the point. If we accept working around that fixed date of when the stock markets will be closing, then discussions about what that means and what the implications are, and ramifications might be. All of that can start to happen in earnest.

I am 100% confident that:
The world will get on much better
with whatever solutions are developed.

What is entirely clear is that the economy has verged toward stagnation. Yes, we have the internet now. Yes, we have social media. Yes, we have a lot of innovations. We also have dinosaur institutions and archaic industries. We have an aging infrastructure. We have a lot of big ideas that aren't going anywhere as fast as they should and need to.

We must be bold in brushing away this stagnant present so that we might boldly harness the new potentials before us. For example, with a focus on the railroad, aviation and transit industries we cannot embrace much bigger new transportation potentials.

Whether it is much faster trains, bigger tunnels, new spaceships, education institutes and/or solving poverty. We got bigger problems to solve. IBM is probably not the venue for the 21st century. Truly beneficial disruption is possible. Radical modernization needs to be better enabled and facilitated. Our current financial system is not going to get us there. We need to take innovation to the next level in America. We need to continue boldly leading the world. And new financial entities can be the catalyst to unleash American ingenuity and enable the potential revolutionary breakthroughs that are right in front of us.

We cannot wait for a stagnating, easily manipulated stock market to provide the economic framework to harness innovation. The stock market is making our economy too stagnant. Are there major ramifications? Yes, absolutely. That is why this is bold in its vision. Don't need to be afraid.

A Better Future, A Better Exchange?

Closing the NYSE does not mean closing all stock markets.

In fact, a better exchange might be the best solution.

It also doesn't mean everyone's investments are wiped out overnight.

We are only talking about money and 000's in a bank account. The Fed can buy anything right? One quick fix is to take a look at your 401(k) holdings of stock and magically turn it into that same amount of money in your bank account. Point is I am not saying close it and stiff everyone.

What needs to happen is take the mafia-like, crony capitalism out of our exchanges and turn back power to the people.

Many of the insider corruption issues in this book bother a lot of traders. Therefore, already competitor ideas are getting going. Their path is not legislation but rather simply making an end-around the existing markets within the existing regulatory environment. IEX is one such stock exchange that promises to take a lot of manipulation out of trading.[259]

It's also possible to take important, game-changing steps today that would not close the NYSE or stock exchanges but rather a) change how they are overseen, and b) spur new competition such as IEX and even better ideas that are out there. Finally, new competition will emerge in any regard.

Ban Self-Regulation of Exchanges

In this way, a first step can be a simple rule passed by Congress to ban "self-regulation" of markets. Currently the New York Stock Exchange—as many exchanges in the United States—have styled themselves as "self-regulatory organizations." No longer can $20 trillion be monitored by "self-

---

[259] IEX, the Investors Exchange https://iextrading.com/about/

regulation". A new regulatory entity could be established to oversee exchanges. This does not mean more regulation. It is only common-sense.

"Free" Exchanges

The "markets" we have today; the exchanges that we have—regulations have been designed and implemented around the notion that the current markets and exchanges are the *only* ones. This is quite like all industries in the U.S. right now. Competition is regulated out.

Therefore, at a minimum, broad changes in regulations are necessary to even have the possibility of competition in stock markets and exchanges such that alternatives can truly breakthrough.

We can keep the current exchanges and their existing regulatory framework.

However, other exchanges could be opened under a different regulatory landscape (beyond IEX, as mentioned IEX is trying to go within the existing legal framework). It can be as simple as a piece of legislation that sets up a new entity to oversee exchanges that want to be "free," i.e. different from the current, crony capitalist system. This process would leave "self-regulatory exchanges" to continue operating in their own crony world.

Meanwhile, a parallel group of exchanges wouldn't be subject to any of their mouse traps. Remember, the NYSE, NASDAQ, CME and such get all the banks and power brokers set-up within the government agencies: Treasury Department, SEC, Federal Reserve.

"Free exchanges" would be overseen by a new entity; placing them outside the Wall Street umbrella. The work for this can begin now.

Other Competition

Some new ideas will breakthrough of their own accord and with or without the help of whatever the process is. Whether they are simply revisions on the same-old mousetrap will remain to be seen. Consider though, the Social Stock Exchange[260] (SSE) in London. Over 50 companies are listed on the SSE now.[261] They vet the companies that can be listed based on how much good they can do for society, such as clean energy. And, SSE is actually a class of exchanges because Canada now has the Social Venture Connexion, SASIX in South Africa and in Singapore it is the Impact Exchange.[262] One issue is that these competitor, new-idea exchanges are themselves branded as 'the only regulated exchange'[263] in their country. They might be all that will be

---

[260] http://socialstockexchange.com/

[261] http://money.cnn.com/2017/11/28/investing/social-stock-exchange-positive-impact/index.html

[262] https://ssir.org/articles/entry/the_rise_of_social_stock_exchanges

[263] http://socialstockexchange.com/about-ssx/what-we-do/ via http://www.nex.com/about-

allowed. They are controlled competition. I want to see "free" exchanges. Real competition.

39
BOLD STEPS

ENDING THE
NEW YORK FED PRESIDENT

We do not need a New York Federal Reserve President.
This is one of the little-known most powerful positions in the world.
Set up outside of government interference.
Set up definitely well outside any accountability to the public.
Officially, the title is President of the Federal Reserve Bank of New York.
The New York Fed President is the center of control over manipulating the markets. The NY Fed President oversees the "open market operations:"[264] buying and selling in the markets.
A primary step to change society will start there.

**The position of New York Fed President,
originally formed in 1914 at the start of the Federal Reserve
has had
only 10 leaders in over 100 years of existence.**[265]

New York Fed President is commonly known as "the second-most important job at the Fed."[266] With a statement you wonder if even the Chair

---

[264] https://www.newyorkfed.org/aboutthefed/whatwedo.html

[265] https://en.wikipedia.org/wiki/List_of_presidents_of_the_Federal_Reserve_Bank_of_New_York

[266] https://www.cnbc.com/2017/11/10/ny-fed-president-dudleys-replacement-likely-to-be-controversial.html

of the Federal Reserve Board is themselves a placeholder. So much is run out of New York. And when it comes to manipulating the markets, the operations are run out of New York.

Breaking this monopoly of control over the financial markets is a key to changing the financial system and improving economic results.

Specifically, it is the head of open market operations that can powerfully influence so much. Broadly speaking, the entire Federal Reserve Bank of New York needs to be audited, re-regulated and the nexuses of power it maintains over the entire country needs to be broken up.

40
BOLD STEPS

CLOSE THE FEDERAL RESERVE, END THE FED

The Federal Reserve came into existence in 1913 through legislation. Written in secret and rammed through Congress.[267] Not much different than the mega-bills of today. It was written on a retreat to Jekyll Island, Georgia, by a handful of the richest bankers of the time.[268]

There was widespread criticism of the bill, but with the insider support, they got the votes they needed. Among the 'no' votes, representative Joe Eagle of Texas said banks would now be "guaranteed against loss" by virtue of this establishment of a "paternalistic relationship or partnership with the government."[269] And another Texas congressman, Robert Henry said the legislation was "wholly in the interest of the creditor classes, the banking fraternity, and the commercial world, without proper provision for the debtor classes and those who toil, produce and sustain the country."[270]

What needs to be corrected now is the last part of Henry's critique. Giving "proper provision" to "debtor classes and those who toil, produce and sustain the country." The Federal Reserve was one of several steps that have detached

---

[267] Glenn Beck had an extensive expose of the founding of the Federal Reserve about a month before leaving Fox News. Available online and worth a watch https://www.youtube.com/watch?v=vB5LK-jihgk

[268] There are a number of good resources to study the founding of the Federal Reserve. One of the most detailed accounts *The Creature from Jekyll Island*, G. Edward Griffin, 1994.

[269] http://studyres.com/doc/10315546/the-inflation-book

[270] https://www.thenation.com/article/why-federal-reserve-needs-overhaul/

work and effort from reward. This must be corrected. Doesn't mean the people of the Federal Reserve are bad people. It just means we must do it a different way. It was rammed through improperly and it is time to correct the mistake and do our financial system the right way. This is America. We can do better.

Why a Monopoly in Charge?

Why do we have a monopoly in charge of our economy?

One national bank?

The last thing a free economy should have is a national bank.

The last thing a free, democratic country should have is an unaccountable central bank (the Federal Reserve) run in secret by a small number of people. A central bank is a concept in the middle of Karl Marx' book on communism.[271]

A board room of bankers deciding what they want to fix the national interest rate level at? That is not free. That is not a free market.

Do we stand for exclusive monopolies in America? No! We break them up. Consistently. The Federal Reserve is the biggest monopoly ever. In charge of making and distributing money.

The Fed is the ultimate monopoly. And that will have to change.

The Federal Reserve does not have a budget. It doesn't need one. There is no supervision. There is the Supreme Court. There is the Executive Branch. There is the Congressional Branch of government. Those are co-equal branches of government. Then there is the Federal Reserve. Outside all of it. Part of the government, but not accountable to the government, or the people?! The Federal Reserve is more secretive than the CIA, with no similar rationale.

It is as if Congress voted on legislation to start a private company. And that private entity gets to counterfeit money and give it to their nearest friends and allies.[272] Plus, make market-moving announcements that they come up with and do so on their own time frame. What is in that interest rate statement that is released on Wednesday? They know. They drafted the decision a week prior.

Government-created entities like the Federal Reserve must be accountable to the people and to the legislature.

Murray Rothbard refers to the Federal Reserve structure as "absolute self-

---

[271] Karl Marx advocated for "centralization of credit in the hands of the state, by means of a national bank with state capital and an exclusive monopoly."
https://www.marxists.org/archive/marx/works/download/pdf/Manifesto.pdf

[272] https://thedailycoin.org/2016/09/29/warning-we-are-going-to-be-living-in-an-incredibly-chaotic-world/

perpetuating oligarchy, accountable to no one and never subject to public (vote)." He continues that the Federal Reserve is essentially a dictatorship.[273]

According to the first secretary of the Federal Reserve Board, Parker Willis, the Federal Reserve had "gone off the rails almost as soon as it opened its doors for business."[274] He thought the Fed would help in the balance to offset cycles of demand. Instead, the Fed itself created credit (capital money), something Willis never felt was the point. Moreover, the Federal Reserve quickly became a manager of the growth of the macro-economy rather than letting the free market rule. Willis published his frustrations some 20 years after taking the helm at the Federal Reserve in a book entitled *The Theory and Practice of Central Banking.*

The Federal Reserve as constructed, and in operation, is completely outside any concepts of democracy. The Federal Reserve operates outside of the economy. Its members and leadership are not accountable to the people.

For most of us, it is all about
the President, Congress and Supreme Court.
Who cares about the Federal Reserve?
We are beginning to understand about our money.
With money driving so much of society, people are digging
around and finding another source of the problem:
The Federal Reserve. And it will change.

The Governors need to a) be accountable to the people, b) of the people. The Federal Reserve need not be only for bankers and finance heads and their university puppets. The composition of Federal Reserve governors could be to include working people.

Within the U.S. you have those close to the Federal Reserve with centralized control over the economy, money printing and money distribution. In the 21st century there is no reason why so much power must be so centralized.

The founders of the United States did not intend for there to be a Central Bank. That is why there was not a Central Bank when the Constitution was written. It was a movement by European bankers that took over 100 years to finally result in jamming through legislation in 1913.

Audit? Audit the Federal Reserve?

---

[273] Quotes from Murray Rothbard, *The Case Against the Fed*, as published https://mises.org/library/myth-fed-independence
[274] https://mises.org/library/over-you-h-parker-willis

An audit of the Federal Reserve is nothing more than a delay tactic. For several years, some in Congress have tried to pass legislation for an audit. Most notably, Ron Paul. However, the moves have gone nowhere. Usually, the bill is referred to as the Federal Reserve Transparency Act.[275]

Whatever it is in concept, if the idea ever did get through Congress (which it has never come close) I am sure it would be watered down to something along these lines: set up a "bipartisan" commission (which takes a year or so to get going) then they spend 3-5 years auditing the Fed. They finish and gather a bunch of media fanfare with a conclusion to make, say, eleven meaningless adjustments.

Audit? Better is an autopsy. We can perform an autopsy on the closed entity. The Fed can be closed down and then we can look inside to find out why we had to close it.

No Need for an Audit.
End the Fed. And then perform an autopsy.

Once the doors have been shut if people want to go in—then—and perform an audit and see what they were doing, go ahead. The U.S. has always been a country of action and innovation. We can close down the Federal Reserve and have an even better, more dynamic economy.

The very concept of a central bank to command the entire economy ought to be an absurdity to a supposedly capitalist country such as the United States. And yet we allegedly operate a free market financial system while a Federal Reserve of a handful of bankers fixes our interest rates and conducts "open market operations."

The original intent in the 1913 establishment of the Federal Reserve was to ensure a stable monetary system and sound dollar. The motivating drive was to contain wild economic cycles and end financial panics. Instead in just the first 20 years of the Federal Reserve we got World War I, a speculative boom and then the biggest stock market crash and recession (the Great Depression) in the history of the world. The truth is that all of that was coordinated by the Federal Reserve. And they were just getting started. World War II came shortly after that. Subsequently, we have seen incredibly drawn out, long cycles where interest rates slowly climbed up to the highest they have ever been and then slowly taking them down to absurdly low levels.

Auditing the Federal Reserve doesn't accomplish anything. An indictment of the past is not a solution. That is a glorified way of kicking the can down the road. That appeases the masses while accomplishing nothing. If people want to know about the Federal Reserve corruption we can find out in performing the autopsy after closing it down. This institution is not worthy of

---

[275] https://en.wikipedia.org/wiki/Federal_Reserve_Transparency_Act

an audit.

Why Close the Fed? Outdated and We Never Needed it in First Place

The Federal Reserve could be innovating every day. Coming up with new and better ways to help Americans. Why have incomes been stagnant for decades? And why have prices of goods gone up? Why are most Americans not able to save money? We know the problems. Do they ever talk about fixing any of that? Do they ever innovate? No. They eat caviar. They drink champagne. And then they fix prices in our supposedly "free" "market."

Why doesn't the Federal Reserve work on ways to:

1. Increase household income.
2. Monitor job quality and work on ways to get more people higher quality jobs (including reduce the number of people that have to work multiple jobs to make a living).
3. Improve their own transparency.
4. Get more regular people involved in decision making.
5. Disperse money in different ways. To more organizations besides big banks; and to more people.
6. No more fox watching the hen house. Former Goldman Sachs CEO becomes treasury secretary all the time. Forget it.

The ink was dry on the Constitution by 1780. And the Federal Reserve was founded in 1913. The United States economy managed, grew and thrived for over 130 years without a Federal Reserve.

The U.S. successfully operated without a Fed for longer than it has had one.

The United States had only $1 billion in Federal debt when the Federal Reserve was established.

The Federal Reserve is an organization that fixes problems it creates. We need to eliminate the booms and busts created by the Federal Reserve. Return to a natural, common-sense economy with free-flowing markets. No more Federal Reserve control and interference. No more legalized counterfeiting.

As Ron Paul said, "the Fed has one power that is unique to it alone: it enables the creation of money out of thin air."[276]

"Ending the Fed would be the single greatest step we could take to restoring American prosperity and freedom and guaranteeing they both have a future."[277]

---

[276] *End the Fed*, Ron Paul, 2009.

Ron Paul has been at the forefront of listing all the reasons we don't need a Federal Reserve.

1. Not authorized by the constitution
2. Too secretive, no transparency
3. Counterfeiting, prints money from thin air into the hands of big banks.
4. Fixes the interest rates
5. Manipulates markets through open market operations
6. Monopoly power
7. No accountability
8. Need more people and more democracy
9. Has a goal to create inflation in prices of everything but not a goal to increase incomes, thereby destroying purchasing power of Americans
10. Causes wild swings in our economy (bubbles in housing and tech stocks; interest rate swings, depression and more).
11. Enables financing of huge government deficits and thus funded our biggest wars.
12. Do not have any goals to actually help people with quality jobs and higher incomes.

Up until a bit past the Civil War the battle over finance was out in the open and ongoing. Back in the 1800's, the rest of the country didn't like the idea that powerful interests in the Northeast had all the banks and money. Since the Federal Reserve was established in 1913[278], the debate over a central bank and all power consolidated in New York City has been relegated to the sidelines. Time to bring that American debate back!

Can the Federal Reserve Be Improved?

There are a number of changes that could be implemented that could radically alter the Federal Reserve and make it a better institution in lieu of closing it. My concern would be that any process to improve it would end up watered down and not change much of anything. Hence, like an audit, need to just skip closing it. Before getting to that, however, lets at least lay some ideas on the table. They can be helpful principles for understanding both a) why we will benefit from revamping our economy and b) how to structure any future organization that might be developed.

---

[277] *End the Fed*, Ron Paul, 2009.
[278] https://www.federalreserve.gov/aboutthefed/fract.htm

What could be changed?

End open market operations.

Let the discount rate and federal funds rate float in the free market.

Open up the "discount window" to a lot more banks and other entities.

Add citizen advisors to the FOMC.[279] Said, David Stockman, "the twelve-member FOMC is about as close to an unelected politburo as is obtainable under American governance."[280]

Add citizen advisors to the Board of Governors. Expand the number of Governors and add real people to the meetings and decision-making. How about some waitresses and truck drivers sitting at the table?

Reorganize the regions of the Federal Reserve and empower smaller cities.

Increase reserve requirements for banks.

Ban creating money out of thin air. Only allow if it is to give money to all the people, or if the people vote and allow it.

Ban letting the Federal Reserve implement programs such as "Quantitative Easing" where they just buy things, like buying bonds from banks. What an absurd idea that was? And the Federal Reserve shouldn't have the power to do silly things like that.

Separate the Board of Governors from the FOMC. Currently 7 of the 12 on the FOMC are from the Board of Governors. That makes no sense.

Publish full transcripts of all meetings immediately.

Impose a penalty on any bank that uses the discount window.[281] The Federal Reserve is supposed to be a last resort lender. So, the discount window should be either a) closed, b) open to pretty much anyone, and c) be costly to use so that it is rarely, if ever, needed or utilized. Big banks borrowing money needs to be based on real collateral, just like it is for people in the real world. What we have now with the big banks getting free money whenever they want it from the Federal Reserve is a total sham!

Reduce the terms of people serving at the Federal Reserve: 14 years? Really?

Allow "wildcat banks" in the U.S. and/or any and all forms of more banking competition.

Allow competing money. Something like the Texas Bullion Depository which is a gold-backed bank initiative looking to repatriate gold currently held in New York and bring it back to Texas.[282]

---

[279] The Federal Open Market Committee (FOMC)
http://www.federalreserve.gov/monetarypolicy/fomc.htm
[280] *The Great Deformation*, David Stockman. 2013. Pp. 267.
[281] Some recommend a "mobilized discount rate policy/regime" based on going to the interbank market because there would be a Bagehot penalty at the fed window.
[282]

http://www.thenewamerican.com/economy/economics/item/21271-texas-launches-gold-

Close it Down; Just Like That
End the Federal Reserve

Pass the "Repeal the Federal Reserve Act."

It could be that simple. Legislation started it all and now legislation can change it and end it and put us all on a much better track, fit for the 21ˢᵗ Century.

We are smarter and more capable. And there is nothing to fear.[283]

"The only thing we have to fear is fear itself."[284]

Our economy would be just fine without a Federal Reserve

With the doors closed, the actors will fade away. The Federal Reserve will be out of sight; out of mind. And… life will go on.

There was never intended to be a Central Bank or a National Bank. The founders didn't include one and didn't want one. England opened their central bank in 1694 so the founders knew all about the idea. And there was, from the start, a concerted effort, by the British loyalists and European financiers, an intention to somehow, someway make a national bank. America resisted. It took a. long. time. for them to finally get there way.

America didn't need the Fed before 1913. It is not necessary now. There are other ways to manage economic policy. Like it was done before 1913. Or better a way for the 21st century. This is the beginning of a movement for the democracy of money and finance. Close the Federal Reserve.

I'm not one to cry over spilled milk. The Federal Reserve has gotten us here. For better or worse. But it is not the right way. And, it is the 21ˢᵗ Century and we can do a lot better in coming up with the institutions and manner in which to run our economy.

What would it mean to close the Federal Reserve?

Wouldn't have to worry about their balance sheet and what affect it might have and whether we have to liquidate bonds or anything. We pay them interest. That's crazy. Wouldn't have to do *that* anymore. The Federal Reserve does supposedly hold a lot of gold in reserve. We could divide that up among the people.

We are capable of a new and much better system. A more citizen-focused,

---

backed-bank-challenging-federal-reserve

[283] One fear might be a temper tantrum from the establishment because we take away the keys to the convertible (i.e. Goldman Sachs 'burning the oil fields, aka Saddam Hussein').

[284] Franklin Delano Roosevelt 1933 https://www.youtube.com/watch?v=6EuAZsz_z_U

democratic, accountable, decentralized system would be established. And the distribution of money would be more localized and as close to individual people as possible. We don't need 11 people in a room deciding money for everyone. Whatever path we go, we will be just fine without a Federal Reserve. Time to start the conversation and draft the legislation. It is time for a new era. The U.S. had an era before the Federal Reserve. It is time for an era after the Federal Reserve.

41
BOLD STEPS

BREAK UP THE BIG BANKS

If something sounds too good to be true, it probably is. That is how the saying goes. If our banks seem like they might be too big, if we talk about how they might be too big… they probably are. We probably ought to break them up sooner rather than later. For our own good.

We just need to do it.

Go with the gut.

Too Big to Fail (TBTF)?

If you even have to ask, they are too big.

We need more competition too.

What steps can we take now?

Regional and smaller banks need to be able to compete more evenly with the bigger banks. This can start, first, with legislation that reduces burdensome paperwork that the big banks can handle but which overwhelms their smaller competitors. Ending the Federal Reserve would also help with this; or, more banks need access to the Federal Reserve free money that the big banks get.

Second, allow more competition to the system itself. Other currencies, other types of banks, etc. The radical ideas.

Third, break up all aspects of the fox watching the hen house. No more Goldman Sachs running through every hallway of government. And no more writing burdensome regulations that are too costly for small banks to compete.

Finally, just break them up. Break up the major banks. Literally break up Goldman Sachs. Turn it into Goldman A, Goldman B and Goldman C.

And make a Sachs A, Sachs B and Sachs C.

There are several key problems with banking in the United States today.

Concentration of wealth among the top banks never trickles out and down to the population at large. So much of who is wealthy in America is unfortunately determined by proximity to banks and proximity to the Fed.

And the biggest banks themselves benefit from their proximity to Wall Street and the stock market.

The biggest New York City banks have turned Wall Street into a modern Las Vegas. It is the ultimate mafia casino. There is nothing better on the planet than being able to skim off the top of every single stock trade.

Five large Wall Street banks account for most of the trading profits every single quarter: Goldman Sachs (founded 1869) JPMorgan Chase (1799 as Bank of the Manhattan Company. It was Chase Manhattan Company in 2000 when it merged with J.P. Morgan & Co which was founded in 1871), Morgan Stanley (1935 as a Glass-Steagall branch off from J.P. Morgan & Co which was founded in 1871), Citigroup (founded 1812) and Bank of America (1904). Bank of America is here also in part by virtue of their 2008 crisis government-adopted takeover of Merrill Lynch which was founded in 1914).[285]

How Big
Should a Bank be Allowed to get?

How big should a bank be allowed to get? Now they call TBTF by a more clever politically-correct term, "Systemically Important Financial Institutions."

The size of banks and the control exerted through banking has been a prime discussion throughout U.S. history.

Glass-Steagall legislation in 1933 separated commercial banking from investment banking (so banks could not use deposits for speculative trading). In 1999, the Gramm-Leach-Bliley Act was passed by Congress and signed by President Bill Clinton, effectively repealing the important provisions.

In 1791, the Bank of the United States (sometimes referred to as "B.U.S.") was established—and later the Second Bank of the United States—as the original attempts by Alexander Hamilton Federalists to establish a Central Bank in the United States.

When Andrew Jackson ended the Second Bank of the United States in 1836 the nation went through a period of "free banking" or "wildcat banks" in which there was no centralized control until the Civil War when several major pieces of legislation pulled more control of currency and banking to the federal government. And, ultimately, the Federal Reserve was established in

---

[285] Bank histories gathered via internet research.

1913; placing the U.S. banking sector under the control of a central bank.

Fierce debates were had up until the time the Federal Reserve was established. However, since then there has been virtually no conversation of trying to have a free banking system. There was not really a single politician throughout the 20th Century that tried to rally the nation to end centralized control of banks. More recently, the most prolific attempt has been the Ron Paul movement.

Monopoly corporations is a similar type of debate that has engaged the American public. How big can the largest companies get? The American people get deeply engaged in these discussions. And the battle to ensure no monopolies control certain U.S. industries has been more sustained and perpetual. Consider AT&T in the early 1980's. And the 1880's Gilded Age with the rise of Carnegie's U.S. Steel and Rockefeller's Standard Oil. Dealing with Rockefeller was among the biggest challenge Americans faced in dealing with monopolies.

In 2017 we have newly developing problems of monopoly—especially in the tech sector. Amazon and Google. Before this the focus was on Microsoft.

Right off the radar from these discussions is the size of the nation's biggest banks. They seem to be quite crafty in keeping their own issues off the minds of the public. It is time to break up the big banks. Some of them maybe even just need to be shut down!

Wildcat Banks?
Back to the "Free Banking Era"?

Time to go wildcat. We have had "wildcat banks" before. Bring 'em back!

The use of the term "wildcat" has painted a rogue picture on an era of banking in 19th century America. Sounds like dangerous, unauthorized banks. This period of time—1816 to 1863—is also known by a less threatening term, the "Free Banking Era."

Prior to the Civil War state laws permitted banks without federal regulations. This created much greater competition. It is also created power outside of New York City and Washington, DC. Wildcat banking refers to the practices of banks chartered under state law during the periods of non-federally regulated state banking.

However, New York City has never liked competition. Anytime that banks in western states and agriculture states have started to gain any traction of power in America, new rules were devised to ensure the power center was New York and the Northeast. The Gold Rush too, tested New York City's dominance.

When too many banks were popping up, Federal control became the path to protect the establishment of that era. As Abraham Lincoln came into power at the start of the Civil War, the Legal Tender Act of 1862 and the National Banking Act of 1863 put the brakes on "free banking." The resulting new monetary framework drained the rural/country banks into the big NYC Wall Street banks. Several financial panics took hold including 1873, 1884, 1893 and 1907. J.P. Morgan, John D. Rockefeller, Andrew Carnegie, all rose to power following the end of "free banking."

Andrew Jackson said, "when the laws undertake to... make the rich richer and the potent more powerful, the humble members of society who have neither the time nor the means of securing like favors to themselves, have a right to complain."

Jackson, who fought Federal control of the banking system more than any other American in history added, "There are no necessary evils in government... the rains fall "alike on the high and the low, the rich and the poor." That is how it should be in banking and government.

Alan Greenspan in a 1966 essay said, "a free banking system stands as the protector of an economy's stability and balanced growth."[286]

Localize Banking and Unleash Innovation

There must be room for local and small-scale innovation in finance and banking. Significantly more regional bank autonomy is necessary now.

The U.S. is far too big for only Washington, DC/New York City control. Movements in England are also trying to break up banking power and spark local innovation. Brett Scott reviewed some of the alternative proposals being made in the U.K. for smaller banks. One proposal, by Tony Greenham of the New Economics Foundation, called for "breaking up state-owned bank RBS into chunks." The move could "revitalize local banking networks." These types of ideas will go nowhere with the current, firmly-entrenched establishment because they make "some people in suits twitch and grimace."[287] We need to unleash innovation in banking.

Heading in the Wrong Direction

More and more power and control continues to be consolidated and centralized. In August 2017, the Federal Reserve finalized its rules for

---

[286] From a 1966 Alan Greenspan essay, quote as published at
https://www.barrons.com/articles/SB120312013624372883
[287] *The Heretic's Guide to Global Finance*, Brett Scott. 2013. Pp 181.

protecting banks that are too big to fail. The Fed calls these banks global systematically important banks (GSIBs).[288] As the saying goes, 'if you trust the management of the medium of exchange to bankers, it will be manipulated to the benefit of the bankers.'

From 1998 to 2008 the combined balance sheet of Goldman Sachs, Morgan Stanley and their now swallowed up competition grew from $1 trillion to $5 trillion. A five-fold increase in just 5 banks in only 10 years! They all were even tinier in the early 80s. As interest rates have declined for over 30 straight years these Wall Street banks have ridden an unprecedented bond binge higher and higher. The trade of the century. They have profited the most from the financial scheme that has seen the U.S. stock markets torpedo higher.

These banks are too big to fail, too big to compete against. Laws they wrote, such as "Dodd-Frank" have helped to solidify their power.

---

[288] https://www.reuters.com/article/us-usa-banks-fed/federal-reserve-finalizes-rules-to-help-unwind-big-banks-idUSKCN1BC576

42
BOLD STEPS

LAND AND REAL ESTATE
(PRIVATE PROPERTY)

Will land be the final frontier of finance and economics?

Land is uncharted territory for economists. It is too complex for me to do it justice here. And that is how it is for the sharpest minds in finance. No one really ever wants to... 'go there.'

We have all kinds of textbooks about capital, money and interest rates. However, it is past time to take the conversation up a notch. Better accounting (for lack of a better word) of how land should be treated in our financial system is likely to both a) yield far better long-term economic results in and of itself, and b) by delving into its complexity open many other doors to economic innovation.

Why land?

Before capital... before fiat money, it was land. Land was the original form of wealth inequality. Think kings and feudalism. Kings owned all the land.

The same inequalities of Kings were perpetuated into the Victorian Age. As late as 1813, popular culture portrayed income inequality in land.[289]

Land *was* the source of wealth and value. So, in the late 1800s, when one economist went looking into the depths of economic problems like poverty and explored how to make progress another way, his research brought him to... land.

---

[289] In Jane Austen's novel, Pride and Prejudice, she portrays the Bingley's in a positive light for acquiring wealth via trade instead of through inheritance and landlord payments from tenants.

Time to dust off the works of Henry George; review and debate his economic concepts, such as land value taxation.

"Nothing short of making land common property can permanently relieve poverty."[290]

George couldn't reconcile that we create so much wealth but why "could not everyone benefit" from this "prodigious wealth producing ability."[291]

George's research had a primary goal to change the ownership and control of capital in such a way that wages would have to increase. He wanted wages to increase.

Ironically, more than 100 years later we struggle with… the. exact. same. problem.

For George, land became the focus. The supply of land is fixed and finite with is a key differentiator. Perhaps, better than gold in that sense. A true financial benchmark and reference point.[292]

A little ironic that given the history of land and kings, George was pinning the economic hopes of the poor on land. Plus, capital (money out of thin air) was in the process of lessening the importance of owning land anyway.

Rothschild succeeded in creating a new form of wealth and income. Out of paper. It was more liquid than land. It could have a higher yield. And it required no real work to possess. Of Rothschild, Heinrich Heine said, "the system of paper securities frees… men to choose whatever place of residence they like; they can live anywhere, without working, from the interest on their bonds, their portable property" thereby "raising up the system of government bonds to supreme power" and "endowing money with the former privileges of land."[293]

Thus, what George was arguing than was that a) wealth and income would be best determined if originating out of land, but that b) land needed to be commonly owned by all. We are born to the earth. And no one should own the earth. Or any part of it.

An extension of thinking about land ownership is to consider ownership of resources. Norway has abundant oil reserves in the North Sea. And those reserves are "owned by the country as a whole and not private corporations." Therefore, the income from these resources is "distributed across the entire population."[294]

---

[290] *Progress & Poverty*, Henry George, 1880. Pp XVIII (preface)

[291] *Man and Mission: E.B. Gaston and the Origins of the Fairhope Single Tax Colony*, Paul Gaston. 1993. Pp 28

[292] *Man and Mission: E.B. Gaston and the Origins of the Fairhope Single Tax Colony*, Paul Gaston. 1993. Pp 3

[293] *The Ascent of Money*, Niall Ferguson, 2008, Pp 89

Finite Aspect of Land Makes it Ideal to Build Economics Around

Land is finite. And it is fixed—more or less!

As such, land has made for interesting economic debate among the more astute theorists. Henry George was among these deep philosophers.

With only limited amounts of land it makes land among the more valuable true assets on the planet.[295] As I like to say, "You can't live in a 401k." Not only is land finite but it is where we live. It is also where we produce food, find our energy and on and on.

Should land therefore be the center of economics?
Time to dust off the Henry George books.[296]

Was Henry George on to something in the late 1800's? What if we had a land-based economic system? Instead of money-centric? Is that possible? In some ways it is so far from our minds as to be like day and night; earth and space. It is hard to come to terms with. We simply haven't considered it or talked about. So, it's a question of: where do we begin?

Henry George

Henry George has lapsed into a near-forgotten economist. Much of that is because he was not an educated economist in the first place. Today's intelligentsia—economics establishment—surely holds him at arm length, with a tad of contempt, since he was not a trained economist.

When *Progress & Poverty* was first published in 1879 it became one of the most popular books in the United States and worldwide. In Cleveland, a statue still stands downtown in which Cleveland's Mayor from 1901-1909, Tom Johnson, is depicted holding a copy of *Progress & Poverty*.

George upended economics with his treatment of land. To this day no one has been able to wrap their heads around the concepts he introduced. There is virtually no talk today about taxation of land as it could serve as a possible balancing factor in the ongoing disparity between labor and capital.

It remains to be seen if George was just so far ahead of his time or whether his concepts and ideas are simply not going to work.

---

[294] http://www.agjohnson.us/glad/if-not-capitalism-what/

[295] Thinking about land as finite can set this discussion in motion for other things as well, such as natural resources like crude oil.

[296] *Progress and Poverty*, Henry George. 1879. Dedicated to "those who, seeing the vice and misery that spring from the unequal distribution of wealth and privilege, feel the possibility of a higher social state and would strive for its attainment.

The ideas are, in a nutshell, too radical.

Implementing the economic plans of George would mean no less than the reordering of society. Removing all taxes except for a tax on land. No income taxes, sales taxes or taxes on capital. It is almost like a total do over. It is hard for anyone to wrap their head around who might be helped or hurt. And it is scary for anyone to consider implementation as it would surely be disruptive.

Where would we start if we wanted to implement Georgian economics?

Movements were underway quickly to discredit George. Wealthy owners of a lot of land stood to lose a lot. Businessmen such as John D. Rockefeller directed their own money toward economics departments at universities that would work to undermine the progressive idealist economics of George. Marxists were also not enthused by George. Their rationale was that his tax on land still fell within a capitalist framework and was thus not revolutionary enough.

What Henry George ultimately wanted was to increase the value of labor in the economy. And so that could be a more fundamental question to focus on.

How to increase the value of labor within our economy?

Capital has advantages over labor that land does not. Or in other words, land cannot be exploited such as capital can. You can't magically expand the supply of land. As we know, financial big cats can wave a magic wand and create more money. They cannot do that with land.

More paper money can be created at the wave of a hand
You can't do that with land.

This is where George may have been on to something.

By taxing land, it is said by Georgist economists to be more efficient, fair and equitable. Georgist theory contends wages would rise and the massive up and down cycles of capitalism would be reduced. Land would also have to be used efficiently. Use the land or lose it. Could probably help with blight too.

Some have tried connecting Georgist economics to a "citizen's dividend" or "basic income"—specifically to the extent the land tax resulted in surplus public revenue. George's "land value tax" could be paid as an annual dividend to every citizen.[297] Finland is pioneering a related plan of basic income.[298]

The natural world (all land) is the common property of all people. Thus,

---

[297] https://www.progress.org/articles/henry-george-in-favor-of-a-basic-income and https://www.theguardian.com/global-development-professionals-network/2017/mar/04/basic-income-birthright-eliminating-poverty
[298] https://www.progress.org/articles/finlands-basic-income

taxing land helps to ensure the people are getting a return from the land around them. The underlying principle is sound, though basic. To truly implement such ideas requires delving into the weeds of questions like: How do you adapt a land tax to account for that there is only certain land at the beach that is better than the rest around it? All land is not the same. You can't do the same things with all land. Some is on a hill facing south with sunlight for great vineyards. While just around that same hill, the land cannot be used that way. Is it 'fair' that some have land in better places then others?

Improvements on land

George didn't necessarily address some of the complexities of actual implementation of his ideas. He worked out the math of the matter sharp enough to note that his "land value tax" should apply only to "improvements on the land" and not just ownership of that land. However, it is unclear how much further he took the depth of the issue. For example, it is not just the land itself but the location. Improvements on land are usually related to the specific land that is owned.

You could improve on the land in one place the same as another place with totally different results. Consider the amount of rain or sunlight for a vineyard. Two sides of a hill. Geographically basically the same location. However, one side of the hill faces north and the other south. Completely different results if, for example, the owner of one side and the owner of the other side both plant grape vines.

Consider the location of land such as right on the beach or 10 miles inland. Each owner could invest the same amount of money building a nice restaurant. Which owner will do better? So, there is a delta involved. There is a derivative to the calculation that makes land value taxation a deeper question.

Affordable housing and Homeless Camps

Homeless camps have started popping up in urban areas. Cities have had to crack down. Part of it is a manifestation of poverty. Part of it is the lack of opportunity for jobs. Part of it is the insanely high cost of living in urban areas—a cost of living that fewer and fewer are able to afford.

Along with all that, what seems to be occurring is that a growing number of people are *choosing* to be (for lack of a better word) homeless. Rather than shell out monthly payments for rent, sleeping in a tent in a city park is a way to save money.[299] It is a way to be able to live in a big city on the meager

---

[299] Some of this new style of the homeless population is living in RVs. They find cities that have no ordinance against RV street parking: http://crosscut.com/2017/08/seattle-city-council-legislation-homeless-rv-vehicles/ and http://www.kiro7.com/news/local/looser-rv-camping-regulations-seattle-councilmans-draft-legislation-could-do-that/585801130

amounts of money that most jobs are now paying.

Big cities across America are having to come up with policies and ordinances to deal with the rise in "homeless camp" living. Seattle now has "City-Sanctioned Encampments."[300] Portland, Oregon maintains a map of the countless homeless camps they have.[301]

Cities, such as Los Angeles, are grappling with the legal changes that are necessary to, in effect, address what has become a pervasive problem of homelessness. Los Angeles invented "HOPE teams" to combat homeless encampments.[302] HOPE (Homeless Outreach and Proactive Engagement.[303]) is a perfect example of how keeping the old financial system and existing power structure in place will be attempted via fancy, positive sounding terminology.

They may solve the problem in the short-term. However, this is a movement at this point. This is like the swell that rose up and elected Donald Trump as President despite all the naysayers. The movement is not just going to go away. It will adapt and find ways to make this new lifestyle work.

It is a homeless lifestyle. It is a financial strategy. Just as the rich find loopholes to avoid paying taxes, these people are looking for ways to move off and out of the current financial system. In some ways it is sad that perhaps a lack of opportunity in America is the reason for this rapidly growing trend. In other ways it is quite interesting and almost entrepreneurial.

Government Controlling More Decisions Regarding Land-Use; Requisition?

New York City's controversial mayor, Bill DeBlasio wants to see an end to favoring private property and instead put the city government in charge of decisions of who owns which land, what they can do with that land and how much the rent will be.[304]

In London, the "requisition" of the mega-mansion homes of the ultra-rich has been proposed.[305] Requisition? Taking away the property from the rich and repurpose the homes and/or land for use as affordable housing for a lot of low-income citizens.

These concepts sound quite extreme. However, I believe it will become increasingly real. There will be problems that are likely to arise out of the

[300] https://www.seattle.gov/homelessness/sanctioned-encampments
[301] http://www.kxl.com/see-portlands-homeless-camps-new-interactive-map/
[302] http://www.dailynews.com/social-affairs/20170823/las-response-to-homeless-encampments-isnt-working-councilman-says
[303] http://www.dailynews.com/government-and-politics/20170404/lapds-hope-teams-sees-results-in-cleaning-up-homeless-camps
[304] http://nypost.com/2017/09/05/a-plea-to-democrats-to-back-anyone-but-de-blasio/
[305] http://www.telegraph.co.uk/news/2017/06/15/jeremy-corbyn-empty-homes-owned-rich-should-requisitioned-grenfell/

massive wealth that has been created.

Consider the mega-mansions of the Gilded Age. Today they are museums. No one could afford to maintain them in the long haul. Too much land property and then too many rooms and bathrooms. The cost of it all became too much a generation later. Could that problem be multiplied many times over today? Have we today created mountains of such homes? Homes so big that no one will be able to afford them over the long haul?

The economy of the future is going to be different. We don't really think hard about what *is not* free about our current financial system. In other words, the future will involve a scrutinized focus on some different things than we are used to. Whereas all we see now is the base unemployment rate, the stock market Dow Jones Industrial Average and capital and bonds… in the future we will be thinking more about quality jobs, improving the world right around us (the land… its parks, wasted spaces, blight, beauty, neglects) and more.

Freedom is a key prerequisite for society and our best future. Freedom should permeate as much of our financial system as possible. When it comes to collective decision-making about land, and especially the radical ideas of this section (such as reducing the freedom associated with private property as well as ideas such as requisition) it should not be left to the mayor. No way should one administration, such as DeBlasio or anyone else (no matter how benevolent and good they sound) be in charge of deciding how land is used by everyone else. That is what a King does.

We must have decentralized finance.

We must have democratized finance.

Community-based committees and associations must make the larger decisions, and include input from all.

43
BOLD STEPS

UNLOCKING WEALTH FOR THE VELOCITY OF MONEY

A lot of wealth is too concentrated. More than that it doesn't move. It doesn't flow through the economy. It just sits, as a number in a computer, in savings.

One of the most important aspects of a prosperous economy is: the velocity of money.

**Velocity of money:
How fast is money flowing
around and throughout the economy?**

Consider a small-scale example: 1 ten-dollar bill in a small town. One day in the life of that ten-dollar bill. First thing in the morning, Jill gives that $10 to her neighbor John for sweeping her walkway. John takes the $10 over to Bill's farm to buy 3 gallons of fresh milk. Bill takes the $10 to Sarah's bakery to buy a dozen cupcakes. Sarah takes the $10 over to Tony's wholesale shop to buy some more baking supplies. Tony takes the $10 and pays the cover charge to see the band at the local bar. $5 of that money ends up with the band at the end of the day and $5 ends up in one of the bartender's pockets. That is velocity of money. That ten-dollar bill moved all around and throughout the town in one day. Contrast that with a ten-dollar bill that sits in a wallet.

When money is moving it benefits everyone.

Now consider all the money printing by the Federal Reserve in recent years. It has, basically, just sat with big banks and high-net worth individuals. Not moving through the economy in a way that would benefit everyone. The Federal Reserve money printing has helped bond and stock prices to rise. However, that money has a very low velocity.

The Fed has been wasting efforts in creating wealth that has little velocity.

In addition, there are other problems of concentrated wealth. It begets new wealth. Rather easily. Too easily. The problem of unearned wealth[306] include earning interest on it. I am not talking about trying to take away earnings of retired savers who worked decades to squirrel up a nest egg. The issue is working on the larger issue of multi-billionaires. I don't have a problem with multi-billionaires. I do believe in freedom and capitalism. My goal is to improve our economy for the future, discuss all topics and explore ways to address structural issues that negatively affect the overall economy. The best solutions I believe are outside the existing monetary system all together. However, if we cannot move out of that then it is past time to start changing the insides of it.

Ok, so that said…

What kinds of options are there? Of course, there is replacing the Federal Reserve with a better idea that can manage an economy better than the scarecrow.[307] We need decentralization of finance. We need democratization of finance. And we need to change how money is distributed. That is how we can start to achieve different, better outcomes that affect more people.

Within the existing financial system, options to get money flowing and to unlock wealth include negative interest rates and a tax on all wealth.

Negative Interest Rates

Negative interest rates are an idea. If you have over $x million sitting in an account a negative interest rate could be assessed. It is, in theory and in practice, a "tax on wealth." For example, a 2% negative interest rate could pull out $20,000 per year from every $1,000,000 in savings.

Tax on All Wealth

It is one thing to tax money sitting in savings accounts. And another step would be to tax all wealth. Bernie Sanders recently officially proposed such a tax—a "wealth tax." Sanders' wealth tax would impact those ultra-rich with over $21 million in assets. They would be assessed a 1% tax every year on all

---

[306] *With Charity Toward None: An Analysis of Ayn Rand's Philosophy*, William F. O'Neill, 1972

[307] https://youtu.be/nauLgZISozs?t=1m2s

of their assets. In Sanders' words a tax on "everything they own every year. Every tractor, cow, and acre." Sanders calculates this type of wealth tax could raise $1.3 *trillion* in its first 10 years.[308]

Consider that $32 billion per year could be raised from a 2% tax on wealth. That number is based on data that the richest 62 people in the world own a combined $1.6 trillion in wealth according to one study (which is equal to the amount of wealth of the bottom half of the world's population; 62 people own as much as the combined wealth of 3,500,000,000 other people on the planet).[309]

This type of number is only scratching the surface.

The combined market value of the U.S. stock markets is over $27.5 billion. In total global wealth, stock markets are worth over $69 trillion.[310] Average Americans hold a very small bit of that. In 1989 the top 1% of households owned nearly 40% of wealth in America. The lowest 20% of households owned 6% of wealth.[311]

Sharing Wealth

Robert Reich is an economist that doesn't get as much respect as he should. Reich and I probably rarely if ever vote for the same politicians but in terms of economic analysis and passion and ideas about the financial system, Reich is someone I respect. A recent book of his is *Saving Capitalism*. In there is one of the most succinct and powerful lines that I wholeheartedly agree with. It is just a simple statement. Yet, it probably should be the center of extensive analysis and debate to break open the radical new path our economy desperately needs: "Instead of directly taxing the income or wealth of a few and transferring it to the many, a more sensible approach is to more widely share future wealth."[312]

"A more sensible approach is to more widely share future wealth."

It is a profound statement. Many of the concepts buried in the depths of this notion have been covered in previous chapters. The point is basically, don't give all the wealth to a few in the first place. For example, there can be better ways to structure corporations and to fund businesses.

---

[308] https://www.buzzfeed.com/rubycramer/with-popular-single-payer-plan-bernie-sanders-enters-new?utm_term=.kwd8ewdgnP#.jsQK0no7pm

[309] http://money.cnn.com/2016/01/17/news/economy/oxfam-wealth/index.html

[310] As of February 17, 2016, as captured August 21, 2017 via http://www.visualcapitalist.com/all-of-the-worlds-stock-exchanges-by-size/

[311] *The Good Society*, John Kenneth Galbraith, 1996, pp 60

[312] *Saving Capitalism*, Robert Reich.

Specialized Taxation Policies?

Can we implement tax policies that could affect big bank bonuses? And what about past bonuses? So-called "back capture" or "clawbacks."

In other words, how to make up for Goldman Sachs bonuses for years? All the easy money they gave away. Goldman Sachs (and big banks like them) get TARP bailout money from taxpayers and then are right back and off-to-the-races with million-dollar bonuses? Can we impose supra-, ultra- taxes on purchases of expensive items? I do believe we can get this specific and we should.

Progressive tax rates are the norm in America. And we can stretch this concept out. We had very high tax rates on high income back in the 1940's, 50's and 60's.[313] It didn't affect the American economy then.

The distribution of income can be leveled-out via progressive taxation. To Galbraith "a more equitable distribution of income must be a fundamental tenet of modern public policy in a good society" and a key solution is that "progressive taxation is central." To achieve greater income equality "the most effective instrument remains the progressive income tax."[314]

Amid the 2017 debate in Congress to pass "tax reform" legislation that included tax cuts for corporations and high-income Americans, some very wealthy individuals went public asking that they receive *no* tax cuts. A group called "United for a Fair Economy" sent a letter to the U.S. Congress imploring "Do not cut our taxes."[315]

Means Testing Taxes and Fees

Fees to enter National Parks have been increasing and there is a move to significantly hike the cost.[316] Who likes this? Environmentalists and the liberal, rich suburban elites. Because it keeps people out of the National Parks and preserves the earth. However, it is exclusionary. Is it fair that only the rich could afford to enter National Parks? No way! A problem like this is a perfect illustration of a public good. Land owned by the government and it should be open to all. A possible solution is "means testing."

As a tax policy solution, Means Testing is a form of calculating the tax by linking the amount the government would collect from an individual to the amount of money each person earns. In other words, what means do they

---

[313] http://2.bp.blogspot.com/-NbAzw1SjuCk/TpO1gyZIJ9I/AAAAAAAAACU/q9Qhy04L1H8/s1600/Federal+Tax+Rates.jpg
[314] *The Good Society*, John Kenneth Galbraith, 1996, pp 63-65
[315] https://www.salon.com/2017/11/13/400-millionaires-tell-congress-not-to-cut-their-taxes/ reporting on letter sent by United for a Fair Economy (http://www.faireconomy.org/)
[316] https://www.usnews.com/news/best-states/articles/2017-10-25/national-park-service-proposes-70-entrance-fee-into-some-parks

have available for paying the tax? If they have a lot of means, then more money is collected. If they have very little means, then less money is collected. Depending on the issue that comes up means testing is either very common sense or quite controversial. It can be seen as unfair treatment on something like a National Park fee. Everyone should be subject to the same entrance fee. However, means testing is already quite prevalent. And we probably need to use it more.

Means testing is utilized when providing welfare benefits. And, to judge whether one can file bankruptcy. Means testing has being considered as a solution for Social Security. The rich that have enough other income do not really need to receive a Social Security check also. Progressive taxation is itself means testing. We tax a higher percentage to the rich then we do for the poor. So, is "means testing" another of a string of "cute," obscure words the elite come up with for things they don't want the public to catch on to using?

44
THINKING DIFFERENTLY
BEYOND BITCOIN, BEYOND MONEY: TRULY ALTERNATIVE FINANCE

Money is going to change. How we value things is going to change. The internet has revolutionized many things and money and value will come. Thus, regardless of views of whether the Federal Reserve is this or that, the Federal Reserve could quickly become behind the times. The current financial system is not creative enough now. It is incapable of the creativity that will emerge.

The end of money as we know it could (like any industry) end just about overnight if the technology and other factors all align. Or it will happen anyway, either via legislation or some other manner.

Regardless of whether it does not come for 3 more years or 5 more years or 10 more years. Doesn't necessarily matter. It *is* coming. When it does come, it is likely to happen so very quickly. I suspect something truly different comes along. If it happens the 'right way' I a) don't believe it will be something you can foresee and b) don't believe it will be anything you can profit on by getting in earlier than others. That is a short answer of why bitcoin is not truly unique. Bitcoin is just a part of the current financial system. Bitcoin is a 'currency' or 'commodity' so you can 'get in on it' early. And there is nothing unique about bitcoin with respect to changing, for example, the nature and value of work. What I envision is 'truly different.'

Store of Value (SOV)
Yes, But Not the Essence

What is the purpose of money? What is the point? If we know why we have it; if we know if we need it; and why—then we can begin to conceptualize and establish what money can become in the future.

As Ron Paul said in *End the Fed*, "everybody thinks about money and almost everybody wants more". However, "we use money without thinking much about its nature and function."[317]

The biggest key is it must be accepted by people. To be used for exchange the form of currency must, in the simplest explanation, be **trusted**. You accept a dollar from me because you know you can use it elsewhere. We have faith in our currency. It has value because everyone collectively recognizes it as having value.

The other critical feature is that it must hold its value. If you are going to hold onto it for any period of time you need to know it will still be worth what it was when you earned/received it. Hence the phrase "store of value."

A good medium of exchange must be generally desirable, easily portable, easily divisible. Durable over time. Consistent in production. Available (though not too easily in order to control supply). Gold and silver emerged for most of humanity. Today, gold is losing its... luster.

A store of value of the future could be a "bundle of commodities." Jim Rickards outlined such an SOV as "a portfolio of 20 percent gold, 20 percent land, 10 percent fine art, 20 percent alternative funds (hedge funds with specified strategies) and 30 percent cash should offer an optimal combination of wealth preservation... while offering reasonable liquidity."[318]

Money is a store of value. Accumulations of the store of value (accumulations of wealth) fostered much of the problems we have today. As elements of power discovered what a "store of value" could be, they devised "capital" that is just created out of air and people have their "store of value" without even working (as we discussed in Chapters 31 and 32). Thus, money is more basic than that.

Breaking Down Money:
a Medium of Exchange

Is a "post-money" society possible?

---

[317] *End the Fed*, Ron Paul, 2009.
[318] *The Death of Money*, James Rickards, 2014 pp 300

Will the definition of money itself change?

I believe that it can and will. And I definitely believe that is where the energy should be focused.

What *is* money? What is the point of having money? Money is a store of value. It is to take and use some time else, somewhere else.

In the short-term that means money is a medium of exchange. We need a way for transactions that exchange our work for the work of someone else. Instead of literally bringing a large number of coins or heavy metals (such as gold) to make a transaction, paper is lighter and easier.

In another simplistic definition if you make a blanket and want the cheese I made we don't want to try and barter how much cheese to give you for the blanket. We have prices in the economy and a medium of exchange (money) and it makes the transaction a lot easier. That is the Adam Smith definition. What will people accept that they are reasonably confident others will accept?

Money is:
a store of value, and
a method for exchange

Is it both?

Is one aspect more important than the other?

Well, we need a method/medium of exchange. We don't necessarily need to store money. The storage, or accumulation, of money is what becomes a problem in society. In this, a devout Catholic or Christian can agree with a progressive liberal.

The leftist sees money as the ultimate source of corruption and problems in the world.

The religious find in Biblical scripture that you either love God or love money; it is impossible to love both. The bible, in the Gospel of Matthew chapter 6, says "Look at the birds of the air, that they do not sow, nor reap nor gather into barns, and yet your heavenly Father feeds them. Are you not worth much more than they? ... So, do not worry about tomorrow; for tomorrow will care for itself."

Surprisingly, it is similar principles and values by both the religious and the leftist progressive. Just coming at the problem in different ways.

Where we are today with money goes beyond these core aspects. As discussed earlier in the book, because we now create money out of thin air there is no attachment to work. Money now is capital. And capital takes money outside the individual and, frankly, trivializes humanity. Money printed out of thin air money loses its relation to work, time, quality and effort.

We need money as a medium of exchange. Each of us has unique talents and abilities. And we can each master different skills, based on those abilities, as well as our interests. And then trade on that ability for something else that we need. We work producing all the corn while another produces the milk. We exchange milk for corn. One builds the houses while another paves the roads. One cleans the streets and the parks while two others are the preacher and the teacher. We don't need one man in the town that owns the housebuilder, the roadbuilder and the farm.

Overly simplistic? Perhaps. However, this concept becomes the foundation for understanding how easy it might be to create a completely different future.

Truly Different Finance Beyond Money

What will happen is that money will get back to its roots.

I can offer some thoughts about how this might come about. I do think though that it is going to be something unforeseen. I also believe it will not have any advantages anywhere in it. You won't have to get in on it early.

That is, if what comes through, is as pure as I think it can be.

That doesn't mean it will be the first thing to break through. There could be any number of innovations that seem to be the way it is going to be.

Probably, there could be several different things that catch on. There may not be one way.

I don't believe the media will be excited about it. And I definitely don't think Washington, DC or New York City bankers are going to like it.

Many of the best efforts will likely get (quietly) stomped out by the regulators. They let Bitcoin go because it is part of the globalist plan. If someone tried to start something outside of bitcoin but similar to bitcoin it would get shutdown in a hurry. Bitcoin has competitor coins, but it is all under the Coinbase and Blockchain umbrella. It is all tightly controlled. Not yet regulated, but controlled. What I am envisioning is completely outside the system.

Post-Money, Beyond Money. Not money at all. The sad thing is that as hard as some may try to create something different that is not money and does not fit within our existing financial system and economy, is that Washington DC and the corporate-banking establishment will do everything to make sure it is branded as an illegal form of money, a Ponzi scheme, or whatever negative connotations they can come up with in order to regulate it out of existence.

So, what might it be?

Points

I believe "points," could be the type of innovation that could start to grow outside our current financial framework. Think, perhaps, like loyalty points of an airline program. Different, but conceptually helpful. Earning points based on the time you put in on something. Earning points based on the quality of your efforts and the value of your work. Earning points for connecting others. And then your points become your "medium of exchange." Such an idea could take years to grow. It could start small but take years before anyone is making their car payment and mortgage payment with their points. But envision a local café accepting points, and then a local store. And it could bubble up.

I am thinking beyond money to a post-money society.

"Move Your Money"

"Move Your Money" is a movement to take money out of the biggest banks and place it in alternatives—most popularly community banks and credit unions. There is 'branching-off' within the move your money movement to other goals. For example, African-Americans moving their money to "banking black," #BankBlack. OneUnited[319] is the largest black-owned bank in the country and Citizens Trust is another growing black bank; both have benefited from this new thinking.[320] This movement is not revolutionary. It does not break society into a completely different realm. However, it is evidence of growing awareness to moving outside the traditional Wall Street banking establishment.

Borrowing

There is so much potential for simple 'why didn't I think of that' ideas. Borrowing items is one such area with unlimited potential. Consider cans and bottles and even bags at stores and fast food restaurants. There is a lot of waste. Sometimes you are given a bag, you pull the sandwich out of it and throw the bag away as you walk out of a restaurant. One bag, wasted in under 10 seconds.

So, you could instead pay to borrow the bottle or can. And you return it and get that money back. You don't *have to* return it, but there is at least some incentive to do so. If the price is set low, you might not return it but someone else might. If the price is set too high the people might not support the idea in the first place. Obviously the higher the price the better the results can be.

When I went to college—back in the 1990's—in Iowa—there were bottle (and can) deposits. Five cents a can. It was common for some enterprising students to gather cans and bottles off the pavement after a party. You could

[319] https://www.oneunited.com/
[320] https://www.washingtonpost.com/business/economy/move-your-money-move-society/2017/03/31/68cb95c8-036d-11e7-b9fa-ed727b644a0b_story.html?utm_term=.d06be57247bc

make a little bit of spending cash collecting the used cans at 5 cents a can!

In Iceland, it seems this is a new idea which is just now seeing some adoption of the so-called "bottle deposit."[321]

Simple and small ideas could really start to revolutionize society.

Giving and Sharing: From FreeCycling to Couchsurfing

From giving to sharing, there are operations being developed in society that do operate outside traditional money. You can share items of your neighbors instead of buying them. Saving resources and money. You can give old items away that others need. It doesn't take much more than a Facebook post to give and share with your friends, family and neighbors.

Lots of positive innovation out there. On the giving side, The Freecycle Network[322] is kind of like Wikipedia meets Craigslist meets waste. It is a simple website organized for local and community gifting of goods that might otherwise end up in the garbage and a landfill. Instead of throwing something away, or even recycling it, you can "freecycle" it. A similar organization broke away and formed in the United Kingdom, Freegle.[323]

Freecycling is a giving network. Finding items that others are trying to give away. It is just one idea of "giving" of which there could be countless more that could be developed.

Couchsurfing is of the "sharing" economy. You share your house (your place) with someone needing a place to stay for a night or so. It is like Airbnb, but free. Instead of paying for a hotel room you stay at someone's house for free. You stay on their couch; or really, whatever the space is they make available (i.e. couchsurfing is just the catchy name they came up with). The mutual benefits? Well, if you share your house it makes you feel better when you stay at someone else's. So, you give back in order to receive. Another benefit of sharing your place is meeting new people. A lot of times it is unique people that are traveling and don't have the money to stay at a hotel.

Timebanking

What is an hour of your time worth? With "timebanking", my one hour of work is basically exactly the same as anyone else's hour of work. The concept of "timebanking" is also a currency movement—for a "time-based currency."

As with a lot of "new ideas" this one has roots that go back a while as well. It is like old ideas that get dusted off and made new again. Like a cover song of an old hit. As far back as 1832, Robert own introduced "Labour Notes" in Birmingham, England. Hours were the denomination of the currency—for

---

[321] https://www.theguardian.com/environment/2017/nov/30/co-op-iceland-bottle-deposit-scheme-uk-reduce-plastic-pollution

[322] https://en.wikipedia.org/wiki/The_Freecycle_Network

[323] https://www.ilovefreegle.org/

example, 2-hour notes, 10-hour notes, 40-hour notes, etc.[324]

The biggest potential now for this concept might be in providing some form of value for people who volunteer their time. Traditionally, volunteers only get the reward of "feeling good" about giving back. That is definitely reward enough. However, so many more people might volunteer if they could. And in a money-centric society most people have bills to pay. They cannot afford to use their time volunteering with no return.

Timebanking would mean that the 1 hour of volunteer work could qualify you for a 1-hour "time dollar." You could then trade that 1-hour time dollar for the benefit of work from someone else. So, you might, say, get that leak under your kitchen sink fixed by a plumber. It can get more complex—even enabling to get big projects done based on the accumulation of your "time dollars."[325]

The idea is being researched by the federal government: hOurworld involved funding from the National Science Foundation.[326]

With timebanking an hour is an hour, but it can get more complex. People could be allowed to put a value on their own hour beyond an exact exchange of time. This can get philosophical based on life choices but suffice to say that it takes more skill to do certain types of jobs than others. I can offer to rake the leaves in someone's yard for an hour and earn 1-time dollar. Then I am able to trade that 1 hour for dental work, or computer programming? The dental office, or the computer programmer, might be willing to offer their services into the timebanking community but only if they can accept more "time dollars" to perform the work. And it makes sense. And that is how more and more people could start to timebank. There become other barriers. How much of the economy could potentially timebank? Most of our bills require real money: like your mortgage, car payment and on-and-on. So, you might be willing to timebank your skills at the margins—exchanging a few hours of gardening for someone to paint your living room. But how big could timebanking *really* get. That is why it would need to be tweaked and include some variations. But it could be quite fun to get it going.

Positive Money

"Quantitative Easing" got a lot of people's minds turning. As I have discussed, the Federal Reserve (and central banks around the world) let the cat out of the bag so to speak. When the Fed started buying bonds from big banks a lot of people started wondering, well, why not buy something else.

---

[324] https://www.britannica.com/biography/Robert-Owen#ref221950 and https://www.worldsocialism.org/spgb/socialist-standard/1970s/1971/no-801-may-1971/labour-time-vouchers and http://www.coinbooks.org/v20/esylum_v20n01a31.html
[325] https://www.aarp.org/money/budgeting-saving/info-02-2012/time-banking.html
[326] https://hourworld.org

In England, the Positive Money movement popped up in 2010 for "quantitative easing for people."[327] The Positive Money movement continues to gain momentum as part of an attempt to change money creation.

---

[327] http://positivemoney.org/what-we-do/qe-for-people/

45
THINKING DIFFERENTLY

PRITCHARD, ALABAMA: REPARATIONS AND BLIGHT

What to call this chapter? At the end of the day, just "Pritchard, Alabama." Enough said.

Couldn't talk about the utopia of a quaint, charming bayside village like Fairhope without going into the town of Pritchard.

Few would dare. At night for sure.

Call it the opposite of Fairhope.

Less than an hour away, also in Alabama, Pritchard is immediately to the north of Mobile.

I have driven into Pritchard a few times. Driving through when I worked in sales. Several more times as an Uber driver. I have driven through Pritchard in the late nighttime hours for Uber. I am afraid of a lot of things—such as heights. And I am timid in a lot of respects—such as in making something of myself career-wise. When it comes to sharing—such as sharing my house with complete strangers via Airbnb and sharing my car with complete strangers via Uber and driving wherever it is the GPS takes me—I have a naivety. I guess that's why I do it. I don't think anything will go wrong. Other people have that confidence when speaking in public, or asking for a raise or moving up in their career. We all have our areas where we are more-or-less prone to do something.

So anyway, it was a very recent trip into Pritchard that I decided it needed to be a part of my book.

Can't just make it all about a quaint, Maybury-like town such as Fairhope. For the big changes I envision a lot of it needs to start in places like Pritchard.

Pritchard is not safe.

It is the part of the area people tell you to avoid.

It is high crime. Drug deals. Murders. Gang violence.

When I last drove through Pritchard I didn't see the type of 'cool' and 'innovative' renovation that is going on in Fairhope and downtown Mobile, all over Washington, DC, Nashville and on and on. Plenty of investment goes on in the good parts of town and the well-to-do areas.

Not in Pritchard. And not in a lot of places like Pritchard.

Who would *want* to invest there?
Why should they?

Why would we? Should we invest somewhere filled with so much crime?

Is it just the free market at work investing in the right areas?

The market does make informed decisions and invests where it makes the most sense right?

So, it is kind of a chicken-and-egg scenario.

Do we, 1) wait to see improvement in Pritchard such as dramatic reductions in the amount of crime? *Then* we can invest.

Or... 2) do we need to invest a lot to change the cycle, give a lot more people hope and then see the crime rate drop because of the improvements?

I am not sure either question necessarily needs to be answered.

What I can say that struck me when I had that moment that Pritchard needs to be in this book.

People from Pritchard are not at the decision-making table.

They can't answer either question.
Because they aren't even in the room.

They aren't part of the discussion.

That is where it must start.

The elected officials and smartest business minds from Pritchard—the best of what they have for those that are like, say what—those people need to be invited into the biggest banks. They need to be part of bigger discussions.

And that is just a start. Because corruption can be even bigger in the biggest problem areas.

What about *the people* of Pritchard.

Real, ordinary citizens should be at the table with the richest bankers and decision-makers in order to bring about true progress. And that is the type of improvement that ripples through the entire economy. It is what a 21st century thriving economy will take.

Pritchard, and the people of Pritchard, need as much opportunity as any other area. Do it their way. Is it new, nicer, larger homes? Clean, new grocery stores? Freshly paved streets. Inviting parks. New business centers. Whatever the vision is, the vision is needed, and action is essential. Fast.

Bringing new faces to the table will enable a flow of answers to the question. It is not so much for outsiders to sort out. It is time to bring the benefits of what is around Pritchard and let Pritchard grow Pritchard.

A metaphor for so much of the rest of the country.

Reparations

Reparations. Payments made for past wrongs. Some have called it accounting for "moral debts."[328] In this book I am trying to 'go there.' Walking the walk. Putting it all on the table. Some African-Americans talk a lot about 'reparations.' The Black Lives Matter (BLM) movement supports a list of a number of fixes, primarily revolving around access to education.[329] Blacks point to the long, systematic oppression under slavery, segregation, lack of voting rights and more. All of which, 'set them back' so-to-speak. Blacks, for so long, did not have the same opportunities as other Americans. I am not saying invest in Pritchard as a reparation. Invest in Pritchard because it is just common sense. I am not saying to invest in Pritchard because it is a black community. Invest in Pritchard because all areas that are economically left behind need to be part of the rest of the economy. The fruits of American success need to be felt *throughout* America. Should we discuss reparations too? I think it should be on the table. I think it wouldn't hurt. Long-term, however, it doesn't solve problems. It is a one-time 'feel good' fix. Overhaul of money, who distributes it, how, why and where. That is the fundamental fix that can change everything.

The concept of reparations is also discussed for American Indians. Andrew Jackson and the "Trail of Tears" and the fact "native Americans" were forced out of some territories and subsequently confined to "Indian reservations."[330] In 2012, the U.S. government finalized a $3.4 billion payment to American Indians across the nation. Not specifically a "reparation" payment, but out of that movement.[331] Short-term. $3.4 billion today looks like a drop in the bucket. We need a lot more than reparations. Not to right the past. To make a better future.

---

[328] https://www.theatlantic.com/magazine/archive/2014/06/the-case-for-reparations/361631/

[329] https://policy.m4bl.org/reparations/

[330] https://en.wikipedia.org/wiki/Indian_reservation

[331] http://www.cnn.com/2012/11/26/politics/american-indian-settlment/index.html

Blight: Rural and Urban

Blight is not unique to Pritchard, or its equivalents.

Blight is all around us. Empty storefronts along rural small-town Main Streets, abandoned manufacturing factories down country roads outside town.

Blight is a couple blocks away from fancy new buildings in our biggest cities.

Too much blight. We have so many run-down buildings and vacated properties and no answers or ideas on how to utilize those spaces and beautify the world around us.

We can put a lot of people to work repurposing buildings. To some, this is a delicate issue. Even very controversial. This delves toward the right of private property ownership.

Well if it is an elephant in the room it is time to start building a bigger door and getting that big boy out and moving.

There are initiatives already going that can provide the ideas. Project for Public Spaces. Urban Commons Projects.[332] And we can dialogue the details. It is time to get to work!

---

[332] https://www.shareable.net/blog/9-awesome-urban-commons-projects-in-ghent

46
THINKING DIFFERENTLY

RELIGION IN
OUR FINANCIAL SYSTEM

Is the answer in the Bible?

Can that question even be legitimately posed?

For so much in our daily lives many of us turn to our religion. We say prayers, Christians read the Bible, we go to church. Yet, when it comes to society at large-- our jobs, our government… and our financial system-- we are expected to leave religion at the door. Keep it out of mind. It is like the separation of church and state is also the separation of church and business and the separation of church and the economy.

Could religious principles at least have an important say in building a better financial system and economy?

It is a question almost out of left field for this era.

Religion as part of a healthy economy and financial system is just about a complete and total non-starter to so many in the U.S. today—most notably, the intellectual crowd, liberal urban areas and journalists. We have a very secular society and the principle of a separation of church and state leaves religion in its corner. It is simply not appropriate to even discuss.

It is simply hard to believe it could even be possible. Religion—as part of how we operate our economy and financial system?

I believe it is vital that the deepest and most core values and principles of religion-- of Christianity-- need to be on the table and openly discussed as we design and build a 21st century financial system. How would it happen? How would it be integrated?

The reason religion is not involved now is because we don't study it and we don't consider it.

We rarely, if ever, talk about religion's role in a healthy economy.

Why not? That can change.

We go to our churches. And we go to our houses of worship. And for the hour we are there, we seem to "get it."

About how we are supposed to live.

Yet, why don't we really, and actually, go out there and make our world that way?

Why don't we live in the image of Christ, or God?

Is it ok to be so blunt? Can we talk much about Christianity? So directly? In a book about finance and our economy?

I would contend religion may be a large part of the ultimate economic and financial system frameworks of the future.

This does not have to be direct. It does not have to be overt.

However, we totally and definitely can structure our financial system differently and utilize the principles, values, concepts and ideas of religion, of Christianity, to build an economy that functions more optimally.

In this sense, I am envisioning religion at the very center of the financial system. The core foundation that is behind making it all work.

Thus, a whole stand-alone chapter that at least plants the seed.

The best economy for all may be possible by integrating religious values as guiding principles

Some may have already thrown this book up against a wall.

This is an 'out there' idea when you first hear it.

How might this occur?

It doesn't have to mean we have "Christianism" as the post-capitalist financial system.

It simply means having new people at the table discussing different things. And allowing some individuality. Several Christian "health shares" have popped up recently in which Christians without health insurance, or unable to pay the rising costs of monthly healthcare premiums can join together to share costs as they come up.[333]

When a liberal or progressive reads this list, there is a lot of commonality.

It is about finding ways to get on the same page and moving in a better

---

[333] For example, Samaritan Ministries https://samaritanministries.org/

direction. It is about a totally new way that is much, much... much better.

- How do we solve poverty?
- How can we help more people?
- Does everyone have adequate food, clothing and shelter?
- Does our financial system truly care about the individual?

The bible says things like "you can't love both God and money." And, so bringing that concept to the table. The Federal Reserve isn't talking about any of these issues. They are monitoring GDP. They are monitoring the stock market and the Dow Jones Industrial Average.

How about completely different people talking in a radically different way about the humanity of it all? What is our purpose?

Christianity in particular, and all religions in general, discuss help for the poor and living a meager life. And so why wouldn't we work this into our economy and financial system?

The answer to that question is I strongly believe: we will. Religious principles, such as Matthew 6:34, *will* become a part of our economy and financial system.

> Do not worry about tomorrow; tomorrow will take
> care of itself. Sufficient for a day is its own evil.[334]

The Bible says: "give to Caesar what belongs to Caesar."

These bible verses lend themselves to saying we should not focus on accumulating wealth or storing wealth at all. And that money is a product of the government and therefore of no concern to a good Christian citizen. These are deep and profound statements. We need to take time to consider whether and how to integrate these values and principles into our financial system. Is it possible? We haven't even considered! Maybe it is. Surely it is. It is simply a matter of starting the dialogue and getting our minds focused on the issue.

Related heady material from Matthew 6:24.

> "No one can be a slave of two masters,
> since either he will hate one and love the other."

Money is not supposed to be our primary motivator and the underpinning organizer for society.

The truly religious, we know... we *know*... how we should act and how it should be. And yet, year-after-year we go about the same ways. The focus

---

[334] New American Bible, 1970.

needs to be entirely on God. God should be guiding and leading us.

This is not to say the fixes need to be 100% religious or 100% Christian. The point is to bring humanity into the discussion to truly differentiate the economy of the future and ensure it is achieves better outcomes.

The point is to introduce new ideas and concepts to the discussion.

Religion must be at, and on, the table.

Religion should be a large part of our economic and financial future. Hard to digest. Hard to fathom. Certainly, not talked about.

How can we truly talk about a better economy and financial system for all without looking at religion

This idea, of religious values at the center of our economic framework has been studied and developed by some. For example, Brent Waters, author of *Just Capitalism*. In the book, Waters discusses the principle of "koinonia:" joint participation, sharing-in-common and fellowship. A non-religious progressive activist might shut down at the thought of religion as part of the discussion; and yet the actual principles that are brought up are thought-provoking across the spectrum.

Is there "financial fair hope" to be found in religion? I think religion and morality are factors in part of a future financial order. I don't necessarily believe God wants everything to be "fair." Why is it that God does not want "fair?" Consider the parable of an eye for an eye.

Religious principles have more than potential to eliminate the "me first," "me only," ruthless nature of our current society. We must have a moral foundation to ensure better behavior. Unfortunately, there is a mentality prevalent that thinks if 'they play ruthless and get ahead then we need to also.' This must change.

Ron Paul has talked morals when he wrote there is a "moral argument against the Fed." In his words, "very simply there can't be a more immoral system of money than one based on a banking monopoly that can counterfeit money in secret with no oversight and protection of the people."[335]

The Federal Reserve and Central Banks place all their energy toward maintaining the financial system. They promote the possibility of another crisis. And then it is the "fragility of the financial system, its vulnerability" to crisis that becomes "the very source of its spectral power."

Even deeper than this, Philip Goodchild writes[336] that all of us focus our

---

[335] *End the Fed*, Ron Paul, 2009. pp 156

[336] *Theology of Money*, 2009. Philip Goodchild

energy first on making sure we have enough money and in that pursuit, we are unable to properly focus on higher values:

"All other ends must be suspended until sufficient money is obtained... Money thus posits itself as the focus of attention and desire... Striving for wealth and freedom has had the effect of subordinating humanity to the impersonal and abstract force of money."

In effect, we need to completely flip our perspective. Money needs to—somehow—be moved to the background. That way, our truest and purest motivations can be the drivers. That is one major reason some people ardently support a UBI. They believe that once people are free from the concern of not having money that they will be able to pursue better paths.

The terminology used in our financial system and economy can be much more positive and honed-in, so to speak, to help make a difference to more people. In Galatians 5:22-23, there is a string of words we could consider: "love, joy, peace, forbearance, kindness, goodness, faithfulness, gentleness and self-control."[337]

What other aspects of religion might we take into consideration? Islam does not permit usury-- money making money (interest). However, the Bible doesn't speak negatively about interest. And in fact, the Bible seems to validate interest by discussing accumulating debts. What *is* in the Bible is mention of relaxing debts every 7 years. That is something we don't do in society. Forgiveness of debts every seven years is a very distinct point made in the Bible, such as Deuteronomy 15 and even the Lord's Prayer, the popular Our Father, mentions forgiving debtors.[338]

What if, say, Mother Teresa was at the table to discuss how our economy and society should be organized? We must inquire and get ideas from people such as Mother Teresa.

Jesus said you cannot serve two masters. The Bible says that sufficient for a day is its own evil. How could we live that world? Does that mean giving up the house that you have? Maybe. What if we built houses for everyone? Really nice amazing houses. For everyone.

---

[337] https://www.biblegateway.com/passage/?search=Galatians+5&version=NIV
[338] https://bible.knowing-jesus.com/topics/Cancelling-Debts

47
THINKING DIFFERENTLY
NEW TRACKING STATISTICS

New statistics. Alternative ways of monitoring and tracking our economy and financial system. New metrics to target.

We can only improve by
Targeting new goals
Measuring alternative statistics

Do we measure the right statistics? Do we track the economy in the right way? No. And no. This is not to say that what we are doing is wrong. It is to say we can do a lot better.

There *are* completely different and better ways to monitor our economy. Currently we track things like GDP, inflation, unemployment and the stock market. We need to sink deeper into these numbers while simultaneously reflecting on 'what exactly is it that we want to do?'

What you measure is what you care about?

We need to analyze to the core what the actual desired outcome is. More money? More happiness. Both?!

We need other metrics growing like the stock market grows. Home prices? Incomes? How about GDP growth relative to the stock market? The stock market does not run deep enough in terms of impacting the broader population.

The establishment literally hides behind their limited statistics. The Federal Reserve would prefer the very abstract national unemployment rate. One meaningless number to target. Our numbers show people have a job.

Do you have a job? That is not the type of economic management that is going to keep the U.S. dynamic and a leader of innovation in the 21st century.

We need to up the game in America!

Forget the dinosaur Federal Reserve, we need a modern way of managing our economy to:

Increase Incomes

Target Higher Job *Quality*

Measure number of people working multiple jobs

Measure number of people receiving employer benefits

Do people want to be working multiple jobs? Some people do. Some of it is seasonal. Some of it is a matter of time and day of the week. Working a bar or restaurant on the weekends and something else on some other days of the week. Overall, though, we need to start getting at the root of problems. And we can only do that by delving deeper into the numbers.

Obviously, we are capable of deeper analysis.

It isn't going to happen with Princeton educated, Wall Street banking insiders leading obtuse, outdated government operations.[339]

The Federal Reserve tries to target economic growth with their power to print and control money. These two powers should be separated. Some other entity (perhaps the people at large) should have "control" (for lack of a better word) over growing the economy. And from there it could also be dictated to the Federal Reserve what should be done to achieve those goals.

Facebook founder Mark Zuckerberg has talked about an economy that measures progress beyond the traditional "economic metrics like GDP" to something more "meaningful."[340]

What is a successful economy?

How much are we investing in employees and our workforce?

Can we get broader decision-making about how to grow the economy and what actions to take in that direction?

How do we grow the economy? Is *grow* even the right term?

We are capable of a much better economy. Whatever that means. In other words: what is our economy? What is the point? The point certainly extends beyond 'growth.'

We can ask the right questions and get better answers and outcomes. It will take totally new people in charge.

---

[339] https://en.wikipedia.org/wiki/Jerome_Powell

[340] https://www.forbes.com/sites/johnzogby/2017/05/29/zuckerbergs-most-powerful-idea-yet/

48
THINKING DIFFERENTLY

BEYOND RETAIL—BUILDING BIG

Too much retail. It is a consumption-focused economy. Locked in with the very statistics we use to monitor progress.

We are spilling chemicals into our waterways. So-called environmentalists talk abstractly about "climate change" and trading carbon permits, meanwhile the simplest, truly ecologically-friendly fixes could be made much closer to our own backyards. Focusing on specific factories and making them cleaner and more efficient.

We need radical changes to society.

We should not be afraid to even discuss so much as a complete reorganization of the economy.

Not only to fix problems but in order to remain dynamic.

So much more could be accomplished if we set out to do more.

We have a society run by a few for the benefit of those same few.

For our collective best interest, it is time to reach higher.

We must break through our stagnant ways of business and government. A 10% approval rating for Congress is just one very telling example of why immediate changes are needed. We all know and recognize there are _major_ problems we just don't know how to fix them. In part, a lack of leadership. We need fearless, bold leaders to step up.

1. New tracking statistics
2. Too much retail
3. Too much urban blight
4. What to build. Think big

5. Less time complaining and protesting. More time coming up with solutions and actions. Reusable cups. Common sense things that make a real difference. Clean water instead of a corporate carbon trading scheme

Too Much Retail

We are creating entirely too many retail outlets and retail jobs. The reason we have so many calling for minimum wage increases is because that is the bulk of the job creation out there. And **retail jobs** pay at, or near, minimum wage. It is not a long-term career option. And yet we have so many of us that are relegated to working these minimum wage jobs.

In the words of a book review of *Nickel and Dimed*, our country has abandoned "manufacturing and the high-paid union jobs in favor of a low-wage service economy."[341]

Retail has been good to the construction industry.

There have been so many jobs created in recent years *building* new strip malls and retail outlets. Everything from 'dollar stores', new Wal-Mart's, and opening and/or remodeling fast food outlets. Our politicians and our government representatives don't want to put people out of work and want to keep people in their jobs. So, we perpetuate what we have going. We need to think about a different step B, C and D so that once we build retail there is something else to build. Instead, all we do is build retail, and more retail and retail over and over.

It is narrow thinking. Politicians believe they are helping the economy with job creation and new construction and new store opening. Short-term thinking.

We need to think bigger. Much bigger. Bolder.

A simple twist can work too.

There are a lot of other things we can build.

Vision: Radically Different, Big Ideas

We can begin massive new infrastructure projects. Ideas completely beyond our imaginations even just 10 years ago. Currently we have an Interstate Highway System that facilitates transportation across the United

---

[341] http://www.businessinsider.com/best-ever-classic-non-fiction-business-books-2017-5/#nickel-and-dimed-2001-a-rare-detailed-look-at-the-real-lives-of-the-modern-poor-7

States of America by personal vehicles. The Interstate Highways were begun in the 1950's. First, we can radically improve the existing interstates. We could add a lane across the entire system. We could replace dozens of old bridges with new bridges.

We are in the era of "money for nothing." The stock market rains money to existing millionaires and billionaires. Technology entrepreneurs from Jeff Bezos to the founders of Google to Elon Musk are using their millions and billions of dollars to pursue radically new ways of living and operating.

Space ships. Musk transportation visions. Google automated cars.

At the same time, change and development take time. The computer wasn't just invented with a snap of the fingers. When it was, think of all the steps and time it has taken to get to the world we have today.

Thinking Differently

What is the best solution? What is the best path forward?

It is not always the first idea. There is no substitute for your own action. The solution cannot be rested into the hands of government. Most often the government solution is going to be co-opted. It is going to benefit a few with the power to right the law. It will sound all good. It will seem everything will be solved because the name of the program will be something like "Program to End all Poverty." The mistake is too many of us believe that is enough. It is particularly a fault of progressives to believe Wall Street funded politicians are going to use government to solve your biggest problems. They will not. Government is not going to live up to high ideals. The solutions will be co-opted by bad elements. Moreover, frankly it is a lazy approach. The path forward belongs to you. The hard work rests on your shoulders. It is not enough to say tax me and let government do it. It is not enough to outsource your own responsibility. It is the easy way out to say government needs to be the one to force people to do something. Or to force others to be the solution that you are not yourself willing to be. Reality check is to take Al Gore and Leonardo DiCaprio. When it comes to "global warming" and "climate change" they are not going to 'walk the walk.' They simply talk a big game. Others must make changes but not themselves. Washington, DC cannot be the scapegoat. Washington, DC is not the one fixing the problems. You must be the one.

Clean water is an example. Do not believe for a minute that a government program is going to help the environment. Big corporations will be looking out for themselves and will see that a government program is instituted with a tough, positive sounding name while in reality not changing much. So, do not be fooled.

Go out into your community and make the changes. Yourself! There is no substitute for what you can do. This is a call to believe in yourself.

We do need to protect our environment. We can take a win-win approach to this issue. We can have "economic prosperity" alongside "environmental protection."[342]

Nine out of ten people are going to want clean air and clean water. Ironically, though, a gun-toting NRA member may actually do more to protect the environment than a progressive liberal activist in San Francisco. The NRA member might be an avid hunter. They want their grounds (air, water and land) protected and preserved so their children, and grandchildren, can hunt and fish just as they do. They are simply less likely to believe Washington, DC government programs are going to help the situation; whereas the San Francisco liberal activist will likely be dedicating tons of effort toward government-led solutions. The hunter will believe in individual freedom and common-sense action and preservation; while the San Francisco liberal wants to control the situation by placing rules and restrictions on others. The truth, I believe, is always a little of this and a little of that. Neither perspective should be written off. And the San Francisco liberal should be more willing to engage in conversation and understanding with others that they hold in disregard when in reality they might be their biggest advocates. Their biggest advocates for the bottom line that is.

What is the **bottom line**?

What is it that you really want?

Do you want a carbon standard?

Or… do you want land, air and water protected, clean and preserved?

What do you really want? In the words of Justin Bieber, "What do you mean?"

---

[342] http://business.edf.org/blog/2017/03/21/a-path-to-prosperity-that-we-can-all-embrace/

49
THINKING DIFFERENTLY

POST CONSUMPTION?

Might consumption itself be a fad in humanity? We haven't always had so much easy money and so many things to easily buy.

Plus, we manage our society by trying to achieve more consumption? It is rather absurd if you step out of the whole process and look down on it. The economic statistics we track and aspire toward are for more consumption. Really?

Overall, I am a believer that we are here on this planet to live life. Live to the fullest. Explore. Taste. Experience. Build. Create. Dream. Inspire. All of this is good, in my personal and humble opinion. Even if there is waste and too many trinkets it is not—in and of itself—bad. Making the most of our planet and enjoying life are indeed purposeful, and have their own value.

Naturally, we might change. And perhaps society totally should.

Many things in life and the world are seasonal and/or cyclical.

Just as we cycled into an era of mass consumption will the pendulum swing bank the other way? Call it an "action economy," or "activity economy." Instead of going places to shop; we go places to actually for activities and to see people.

There are small and large indications of the desire, or need, to reduce our emphasis on consumption. There have been small efforts to alter the consumption mindset have not gained too much traction in society. For example, "Buy Nothing Day," started in 1992, coincides with the heavily promoted shopping day of Black Friday, the day after Thanksgiving.

More actively, environmentalists are concerned about protecting the earth, air and water. Some religions, such as Catholic, challenge our "materialistic" ways. The Bible too is filled with references, including Matthew 6:19-21: "do not store up for yourselves treasures on earth, where moths and vermin destroy, and thieves break in and steal."[343]

Minimalism is becoming a bit of new fad. Joshua Fields Millburn and Ryan Nicodemus have worked to define it and frame it as more than a fad. Ironically, the root purpose they express in their brand of minimalism is to "assist you in finding freedom."[344] That word again. Freedom.

Beyond Consumption

Too much consumption in modern society. We are also too consumption driven. And this is similar to the cycle we have been thrown into due to the overbuilding of retail. All we really think about is consumption.

Our economy is too consumption driven and motivated.

Now I am not an environmentalist or a "sustainability" advocate by any stretch of the imagination. However, I do believe in common sense. I like to breathe fresh air. I like to swim in clean water. I like to hike and otherwise enjoy the scenery of the great nature around us. We do not always need to think about consumption. The Union of Concerned Scientists raised its first alarm over too much consumption in a 1992 "warning to humanity'" that the environment was at long-term risk. Recent updates to that opinion state developed nations "must greatly reduce their overconsumption, if we are to reduce pressures on resources and the global environment."[345]

Joseph Schumpeter likened it to "Buddhist Economics" in saying that we should be looking to 'maximize well-being' while "minimizing consumption.' We currently try to consume ourselves to happiness. Rather the end is happiness and it is not consumption that needs to get us there. Look at our economic statistics (the subject of our next chapter). Wall Street and economists track "retail sales" numbers and "production."

One biblical story that is part of every 1 of the 4 gospels is the "Cleansing of the Temple," in which Jesus throws out all the "money changers" and overturns their tables. There are more important parts of life and living than consumption. At a minimum we need to track our economy in ways that place emphasis in other places. It is not that consumption is bad. It is that we definitely do not need to be organizing society almost entirely for it.

---

[343] https://www.stewardship.com/articles/what-does-the-bible-say-about-minimalism

[344] https://www.theminimalists.com/minimalism/

[345] http://scientistswarning.forestry.oregonstate.edu/sites/sw/files/Ripple_et_al.%20_7-18-17_scientists_warning.pdf

50
THINKING DIFFERENTLY

PARADOXES

Paradoxes are a great reminder to help us be open to what is possible and what may come. The best solutions may actually be nearly the opposite of what you originally would think. And by that—the best solutions to achieve exactly what *you* want may come from sources you would least expect.

There are paradoxes in life and there will be paradoxes to our future.

Murphy's Law. Ironies. Contradictions. Paradoxes. Call it whatever you want.

Plants need carbon dioxide (CO_2) to thrive and survive.

Food for plants *is* carbon dioxide?![346]

Climate change and global warming proponents spread dire concern about increases of CO_2 in the atmosphere. But is that exactly what nature needs?

We are cutting down so many trees and clearing vegetation (which needs CO_2 to grow back) and now we have data showing more CO_2. Almost, a natural, and necessary, feedback loop of earth?

These are the paradoxes around us.

Photosynthesis—the process that spurs growth in plants—is a combination of CO_2 and H_2O (carbon dioxide and water).

So, we have more plant food now? Precisely when we need it.

Not saying this is right to be cutting down trees and increasing CO_2. Just showing there are deep paradoxes all around us.

---

[346] https://en.wikipedia.org/wiki/Photosynthesis

The best financial and economic solutions may come from unexpected sources in unforeseen ways.

The person who dislikes computers will never be a computer hacker. In other words, you do have to like the subject to be able to change it. But you don't have to have cancer to be a doctor that cures it. Balance. My view of the world is a lot of grey. My view isn't helpful when it comes to just getting things done. I want to find grey. But, just because I am not good at this or that doesn't mean seeing a lot of grey in the world is a bad thing. It is *my* contribution.

The start of agriculture in ancient Egypt?

"Agriculture began in the Nile River Valley," despite not having plowing or fertilization.

Why?

Since they had "annual floods and inundations of mud, plowing and fertilization were unnecessary. One had only to seed."

Therefore, they got an earlier start than the rest of us. They didn't need to plow. They didn't need to fertilize. They dropped seeds and their crops grew. "Missing two key technologies (plowing and fertilization)" didn't matter![347]

In a similar way, major changes in society have occurred without social media and technology. Big changes in political parties and elections happened over the years (such as back in the 1800's) with sweeping shifts in voter's minds occurring despite not having Facebook or the internet.

Related, the right *mindset* alone can be more important than the technology. Athletes can beat better players then themselves simply by believing they can, and putting together a good game. David vs. Goliath. As Lester Thurow says, "success came to the Romans not because of technology but because of their ideology."[348] The unexpected is possible. Jimmy Valvano: "ordinary people do extraordinary things… the lord must have loved ordinary people, because he made so many of us."[349]

Ordinary people do extraordinary things.

Another paradox is with respect to just how we will move forward.

Who has the best ideas?

Who has the right ideas?

We will all be right. To varying degrees.

---

[347] *The Future of Capitalism* Lester C. Thurow 1996 pp 12
[348] *The Future of Capitalism* Lester C. Thurow 1996 pp 13
[349] https://www.youtube.com/watch?v=2KESjF-W79Y

And we will all be wrong. In varying degrees.

Some of what we hope for will happen. Some of what we hope for won't. It doesn't make the ultimate outcome any better or worse. We really have no control over the ultimate path. What we can do is work as hard as we can as proponents of our beliefs.

We all see the world a little bit differently.[350]

There is no permanently right answer. Society and an entire global economy are far too complex. As soon as we figure out a right answer, there will need to be changes. Must keep innovating.

---

[350] *When Breath Becomes Air*, Paul Kalanithi, pp 172.

51
THINKING DIFFERENTLY
LOCAL VS. GLOBAL

Globalization is all the rage. It is being pushed through popular culture. A familiar saying comes to mind:

Think globally, act locally.

We don't do much of this at all. In fact, we are doing the exact opposite. It is not just a corporate global agenda. Individually, we don't act on anything. We certainly aren't doing much individually in our own back yards. We are drawn into discussions of larger issues. The environment is a perfect case in point. Well-meaning environmentalists don't really do much to clean up the water in their community. Rather, they protest about global, abstract issues. Parts per million in the atmosphere.[351] And, worse, they protest for a corporate agenda.[352]

Big corporations, banks... and the politicians they fund... are implementing all kinds of globally focused laws, regulations and organizations.

There is a definitive push to globalize much of the economy and government decision-making. The entities are already in place. World Bank, the International Monetary Fund, United Nations and related global entities. The consolidation of more and more power and control is ongoing.

---

[351] https://350.org/science/

[352] For example, "carbon credits" given to corporations becomes a major rallying call to environmental groups in Washington, DC.

Around this theme of globalization is "convergence" and harmonization of different rules and systems from one country to another. Step-by-step this is taking place. Just about every country on the planet has a central bank. Creating a central bank for the world is part of a globalist solution. Currencies are being consolidated. The Euro was a major step in this direction; consolidating several of the world's biggest currencies into one. Now, the exchange rates of remaining major currencies have been converging to near parity.

Counter to this trend is the idea of local decision making.

We need to preserve our differences. Our unique cultures and our unique traditions. Instead we are doing the opposite. Whatever the globalists like they allow and whatever they disagree with is being shamed out of existence.

A lot of issues that the United States tries to solve at the national level should be left to states and localities.

There must be local balance.

We need to retain our unique differences and advantages.

We do live in a global economy and we do need to have solid ways of staying in good relations with all nations of the world. However, we can do that with new organizations that respect our differences; and allow differences.

As E.F. Schumacher pointed out we can keep trying to regulate and tax the bigger and bigger corporations; believing we are keeping them in check and making the system run more efficiently. However, if we do not start breaking things down into smaller pieces with localized control we are not serving the true public welfare.[353]

It will take real effort. The global agenda is way out front.

U.S. Senator Mike Lee recently discussed how "federalism and localized decision-making processes are crucial to restoring civic connectedness, unity, and faith in the American government."[354] Lee believes we need more "social capital."[355] I don't trust any movement originating in Washington, DC especially with a goal to restore "faith in the American government." However, the point is, getting discussions going at the local level… connecting with people… to make a difference in communities.

There is truth in a lot of perspectives. There is at least *some* truth, or *some* benefit to take away. Hillary Clinton made famous the phrase "It takes a village." To some extent it is dumb to try and argue with lines such as this. First, let's say this much. It does not take *only* a village. Sure, it takes a lot of people around you to aide in making the best of any situation. However, it

---

[353] *Small is Beautiful.* E.F. Schumacher. 1973.

[354] http://www.aei.org/events/localism-and-social-capital-sen-mike-lee-r-ut-on-why-federalism-is-key-to-restoring-civic-connectedness-and-faith-in-the-american-government/

[355] https://www.lee.senate.gov/public/index.cfm/socialcapitalproject

also takes personal initiative and individual responsibility. At the end of the day it is you that needs to take action and to act reasonably and morally.

It is the same in constructing an economy for the future and a better, new and improved financial system. It needs to have elements of a village mentality. And it also needs to ensure personal responsibility by incentivizing (encouraging) individual initiative.

It comes down to matters of degree. That one aspect of a solution requires, say, 80% of a "it takes a village" mentality and structure does not make the entire solution "it takes a village." And, vice versa.

In 2008, the U.S. Federal Reserve not only worked to consolidate more power within the U.S. for Goldman Sachs and major banks but gave money away to banks around the world to increase global power. For a time, Alan Grayson was one of the few congressmembers that challenged the status quo in Washington, DC; not surprisingly, he is no longer one of our representatives. Grayson routinely called out the big banks and Federal Reserve.[356]

Business looks out for its own self-interest in Washington, DC. According to our selfish and un-responsible capitalist mentality that is how it should be. And to some extent, absolutely, you make your own case. There are two points here. First, fine take that. Then, the opposition must organize and work in similar manner. New entities must pop up to press the message on behalf of 'everyone else.' Second, we can do a lot better than selfish. Take some responsibility. The corporate-global agenda needs to be challenged—externally and internally. Balance must be restored to emphasize local differences and local action.

---

[356] https://youtu.be/uGs_Qn5yEgs

52
THINKING DIFFERENTLY

MORE CAPITALISM
OR MORE SOCIALISM

More capitalism or more socialism? I see that as a false question. To me they are two principles to build around. Both capitalist and socialist approaches could work in tandem, or to varying degrees, in facilitating a future economic framework around:

1)   Free people and free markets
2)   More people obtaining income and sharing wealth

To me, our future goes far beyond capitalism or socialism. I am envisioning and helping to promote adoption of a financial system and economy that is radically better by being something completely different. I am not concerned in whether it is capitalist or socialist. I expect it is a combination of both. If, say, 80% socialist or 90% capitalist I still believe it is something wholly new.

Capitalism or Socialism?
Can we answer "neither; but both."

The solution-- so to speak-- lies, perhaps, not so much in whether we are capitalist or socialist but in utilizing the best and various elements of both.

Beyond this, understanding why, for example, capitalism has succeeded so successfully in places like the United States. Hernando de Soto contends it is not because of the culture of support for capitalism and the amounts of money itself. Rather, de Soto in analyzing the success of Bill Gates finds that much of it is due to the laws underpinning society. Because the U.S. has patent laws for example. What business could thrive if not for being able to patent its product from competition? And businesses need enforceable contracts protected by a steady legal system. The business owners need property rights. And, all this rule of law—so to speak—are what differentiates, for example, the United States[357].

Where the U.S. could lose its edge is in the triumph of too much capital in too few hands. Armies of lawyers that can literally redefine words and pick apart a tiny aspect of a patent in ways that allow big corporations to thrive and new innovations to be snuffed out and/or gobbled up into the vortex of the mega companies.

Should the future be 50% socialist and 50% capitalist? NPR once suggested that "a spoonful of socialism" could make capitalism work. They called capitalism "the 'least bad' economic system" echoing Winston Churchill on democracy that "democracy is the worst form of government — except all the others that have been tried."[358] Several spoonfuls of socialism, or anything/something, can be thrown into our capitalist society. Tripartist economy is one concept that has been proposed along these lines.[359] They can improve upon our society most likely without noticing much difference.

There are competing feedback loops that pull toward both the best and the worst of capitalism. A balanced, objective analysis that hopes to move us toward the future can acknowledge that both government and free markets are to blame for problems in our present economy. It is not necessary to move us in one of those directions, or the other. Rather, we need to move forward. Incorporating lessons learned from the failures of too much government as well as too much free markets. And at the same time taking the best from both government run properly as well as free markets run properly.

Are free markets the problem? Are capitalists to blame? Is government to blame? Is too much regulation to blame? Ultimately, we need to accept a little truth in all of those questions.

There is not enough discussion in society about the idea of more capitalism. Not "bad capitalism," more "good capitalism."[360] "The people in power and the people making money, they aren't practicing capitalism.

---

[357] *The Mystery of Capital*, Hernando de Soto, 2000. Pp 224

[358] http://www.npr.org/templates/story/story.php?storyId=114163098

[359] https://en.wikipedia.org/wiki/Quadragesimo_anno#Tripartist_corporatism

[360] https://www.economist.com/news/business/21669911-anti-capitalism-being-fuelled-not-just-capitalisms-vices-also-its

Capitalism is what happens to everyone else. We call it capitalism." Is that a quote from Scarface? I can't remember. Anyway, what do we have in America? Some could argue that the U.S. is kind of heading quite a bit in the direction of socialism without talking about it. Think about Wal-Mart. We are getting closer and closer to having one big store that sells us everything. Wal-Mart, and mega corporations like them, have so many lobbyists in Washington, DC, and they provide so much money to our politicians that it would not be too far-fetched to call them an extension of the government already.

So "competing feedback loops" is to say that proponents of both sides of this debate get caught further and further entrenching their own perspective. If you are so fed up by capitalism, free markets and the ultra-rich and mega-corporations dominating the economy and society, guess what? I think you are right! If you believe government is out of control, with too much regulation, too much interference and sky-high taxes—guess what? **I think you are right too!** The free market is *not* *all* bad. And government is *not* entirely the only problem. We need to have frank, politically incorrect conversation. Intelligent, deep conversation to move forward.

To quote President Obama, "you don't have to worry about whether it neatly fits into socialist theory or capitalist theory -- you should just decide what works."[361] Or Mike Huckabee discussing "vertical" politics instead of the usual left-right horizontal politics; calling it "an obligation" to focus on "making America a better place." In other words, not whether an idea moves us left or right, but does it make us better, or worse.[362]

One thing is sure, there *is* a lot of momentum to make capitalism better. There *are* people that have made their way successfully in capitalism and want to make it better for more people.[363] There are all kinds of ideas. It's time to embrace new directions.

---

[361]

https://www.realclearpolitics.com/video/2016/03/25/obama_forget_the_difference_betwe en_capitalism_and_communism_just_decide_what_works.html

[362] https://www.youtube.com/watch?v=YaAqnrpev44

[363] https://www.ted.com/talks/paul_tudor_jones_ii_why_we_need_to_rethink_capitalism/discussion

53
THINKING DIFFERENTLY

BEYOND GOVERNMENT AS THE SOLUTION

Do we need something akin to the New Deal? An even better New Deal? A New Deal for modern times. We do need to think big! During the Obama Administration there was a bit of a push to get something going along those lines. We had the "stimulus." These ideas were not allowed to go far enough, would be the contention of Obama supporters. If only we had passed even bigger stimulus bills, then we could have really pushed the economy ahead.

This is the Keynesian path: more government spending to stimulate economic growth. Cutting government spending is now termed "austerity" in Europe. So-called "anti-austerity" political parties popped up (first in Greece) to fight proposed cuts in government spending during their economic crisis.

The big *ideas* that come from the thinking behind proposals like a New Deal are definitely part of what is needed. The New Deal included massive infrastructure projects. The New Deal built dams so big they are still marveled at over 80 years later. Today we need to think even bigger than that.

So, we need the *vision* of a New Deal.

We need vision *far greater* than the New Deal.

Economically, however, we need something far more innovative.

This time, instead of looking to government, how can we fix the freedom and market-based system we have? Can we make it more innovative? Can we invent new ways to get big projects done?

Funding Projects by the People

Banks have the money. The government has the money.
Banks and the government determine which projects get done.
Could there be another way?
Yes. Absolutely, there can and should be another way to fund projects.
Let's give money to new projects that are great ideas. Give it a try!

If some people have a great idea.
If there is a movement for an idea.
Let's get that idea funded and moving.

A lot of innovation is held up by the status quo. Today's airline, railroad and auto industries have no interest in more competition. So, any new ideas for better forms of transportation are not getting helped along.

Stagnation due to the current power brokers and current economic interests blocking progress is a *major* problem!

Great, new ideas are blocked by the existing establishment.
We need new ways of funding
to move simple, good ideas along!

How could this work?
How about 100,000 people behind a movement = $70 million.
If you get 100,000 to sign your petition in person, then the money is granted to start working on the project.

The Federal Reserve can print money out of thin air—easily—for this type of project. $70 million? That is nothing. Nothing. When it comes to the big banks of Wall Street and the Federal Reserve this level of money could be provided with a snap of the fingers. The Federal Reserve simply has to print the money (err, punch the keyboard for the numbers of zeroes and hit send) and give it to the group. Start the project and go from there.

Another way? How about a governing board, appointed with real people, selected by a lottery (kind of like jury selection). The people decide which ideas will get funded. Which projects and loans are most deserving? Instead of the traditional way of a handful of bank executives deciding; everyday citizens can be making those decisions.

The money can come in other ways too.

Create a pool of funds by collecting taxes. For example, billionaires making philanthropy contributions would have to pay the first 25% as a "social tax" with that money going to a separate pot for projects of the people. Or special corporate taxes.

Another idea? Create a competitor to the Federal Reserve.

The People's Reserve.

Compassionate Capitalism?

Regarding capitalism—as Steve Forbes points out—trust and mutual benefit are the unlikely cornerstones of a truly successful free market.

Per Adam Smith, the neighborhood butcher does not have your dinner prepared for you as a free gift. The butcher has your dinner ready because you are going to pay for it.

The relationship—from both perspectives—is largely and purely, if not entirely, based on self-interest. And it is a win-win.

You want to eat.

And the butcher wants to earn money and has the food ready.

A win-win based on mutual, self-interest
The work of one, in exchange for the work of another.

Put another way by **Murray Rothbard** "both parties undertake the exchange because each expects to gain from it."[364] What do you buy at the grocery store? You buy the food that looks like the best value.

Adam Smith goes on to discuss "the invisible hand." For the doubtful in free markets, the base element, outside of markets, is to think of it as individual freedom.

Freedom for individuals is important. It can and should be a piece of a solution. It may sound like caving in to a free market mentality, but freedom for all is simply the basis for any of us to pursue whatever the best ways are as they continuously change and unfold. What wins the day now may not be the best path in the future. Only freedom allows change. It is essential to all our unique and independent interests.

None of this is to say: freedom to exploit. None of this is to say: freedom to make millions while others all around you suffer.

We are called to be better.
Can we be free? *And*, compassionate.

From Raj Patel to Rich Devos, there is discussion of more *compassion* in our economic structure. In 2009, Patel called for a "fairer and more compassionate society"[365] while ultra-capitalist Rich Devos wrote *Compassionate Capitalism* in 1994. There are wide differences in the details of

---

[364] *How Capitalism Will Save Us*, Steve Forbes and Elizabeth Ames, pp 11.
[365] *The Value of Nothing*, Raj Patel, pp 189

"compassionate."

Patel sees a "compassionate" economy that is a "collective enterprise" with "people getting together and working, sharing and giving things away for the common good" (referencing free software as a modern example) in which "property and government can be much more plastic," "more equitable and sustainable" and all facilitated by "more imagination, creativity and courage."[366]

Devos defines compassionate capitalism in the subtitle of his book as "People helping people help themselves." In 336 packed pages, Devos really delves into the issue of making capitalism work for all. Devos looks at the belief in our own "self-reliance" and challenges us to think back and recognize we can all "trace our self-reliance to someone in our past."[367] Similarly, he challenges deeper thought on charity itself: "I know there are people in this world who cannot help themselves... but... remember that handouts may send people down a road of diminished self-worth.... Government has confused the creation of social-service bureaucracies with compassion."[368] Devos goes on that "we *must* reward people who work."

In a truly compassionate system, all effort is directed toward making people independent and capable of standing on their own two feet.[369]

The visions of Patel and Davos are quite different when discussing the same idea, compassion in capitalism. However, the fact each of them mentions the concept must be taken as a huge positive sign for future collaboration toward a path-breaking, ultimately-pleasing, better and beneficial financial framework.

Government Crowds Out Giving

The Bible mentions being able to tithe 10% toward God. Part of a problem with the ever-expending size of government (as well as the impacts of monetary inflation) is the crowding out of people being able to donate time and money to volunteer efforts and giving. Most people do not have money available to save and don't have 'rainy day' cushions of money; meaning they aren't able to give. And that is a problem that needs to be addressed.

Should it be a 'right' to be able to give back and make a difference? It would seem that *somehow* everyone *does* deserve a little room to give back.

---

[366] *The Value of Nothing*, Raj Patel, pp 189-194
[367] *Compassionate Capitalism*, 1993. Rick Devos, Pp 266.
[368] *Compassionate Capitalism*, 1993. Rick Devos, Pp 267.
[369] *Compassionate Capitalism*, 1993. Rick Devos, Pp 268-269.

Can we all benefit by having the
freedom and ability to give back?

Maybe there could be legislation to enable 3 or 5 days a year that a person is off-work but must do some sort of charity work. Financially, people also should have 10% off the top of their income that is totally protected in which they can give back.

Making room for private giving is so important.

Government can't do everything and nor should it. A lot of what people want the government to do, could be better achieved by the private and non-profit sector. Today we are starting to see more "private funders tackling problems that government can't or won't."[370]

---

[370] https://mobile-nytimes-com.cdn.ampproject.org/c/s/mobile.nytimes.com/2017/06/20/opinion/jeff-bezos-bill-gates-philanthropy.amp.html

54
THINKING DIFFERENTLY

PHILANTHROPY, VOLUNTEERING
AND NON-PROFIT GIVING

Interestingly, how we got to this current, cutthroat, selfish form of winner-take-all capitalism might never have gained a foothold in the first place. Alternatives were stamped out just as they might have started marching forward as the defining organizational elements of our economy.

Perhaps our society today would already be more philanthropic—rich with broad-based volunteering and giving. Today, there is a lot of philanthropic giving; however, it comes from the rich that have accumulated so much via our capitalist system. They give it away because they have more than they can spend. Many of us would do the same but we don't have that level of income and wealth. What is the history? What is the path forward? What is the solution?

Mount of Piety

Before we went down the path of credit, loans, bonds, lending and interest rates there was an idea that came and went that perhaps could still yet lead us into a better future. Mount of Piety. You can go all the way back to the beginnings of modern finance to find the solutions to our modern problems? Organized in the late 1400's these charity entities were formed as an alternative to the new money lending—with an explicit goal to get funds to those in need at terms favorable to the poor.

Mount of Piety was swept under the rug. Kind of like how the first automobiles were planned as electricity/battery based. What happened to the idea of electric cars? Swept under the rug. Until now.

The objective of Mount of Piety was to benefit the borrower and not be concerned with profits of the lender. Thus, Mount of Piety was a benevolent alternative to the rising capitalist methods.

Basically, a non-profit bank.

**A non-profit bank?
Not looking to profit, and all the while
Working to the benefit of the poor**

Can we get something like this started today?

New organizations with lending that involves giving to more people, including the poor; charging the poor the same or better rates?

Instead, right now, we do the opposite! The poor are subject to loan sharks and cash advance retail outlets that charge exorbitant interest rates and late fees; meanwhile the for-profit banks beg to loan money to the rich and provide them with the best rates.

We exacerbate the worst economic problems!

**Non-profit banking can help enable
the poor to get treated the same as, or better than,
the rich at the bank**

Three hundred years after Mount of Piety didn't make it a revolution took up in France. The economics of Jeremy Bentham motivated the masses. The movement did overthrow the government in the French Revolution (due to executing King Louis XVI) of 1793.

However, they did not achieve the objective behind the movement: income redistribution. Powerful interests emerged in scoping and writing the referendums and new constitution. Income redistribution was basically included but was not defined. Thus, Bentham's work went the way of Mount of Piety. Bentham believed income redistribution would achieve the "fundamental axiom" of his work which was to achieve "the greatest happiness of the greatest number" of people.[371]

Giving Back: Volunteer Time

---

[371] https://www.utilitarianism.com/jeremy-bentham/greatest-happiness.pdf

In order to truly re-prioritize what we are doing as a society, we need to reward people for giving back. Not talking about the retiree or rich spouse that has the money and time. This is about freeing hard-working people to have balance in their lives. Rich Hollywood stars, professional athletes and corporate managers—they have the time and the money to volunteer. We see them out working with disadvantaged people and genuinely trying to make a difference in the community.

It should not be only the rich that are able to give back.

People who work hard—hours and hours in tough jobs—and then have just enough money to pay their bills and maybe make it to church. These are the people that can't take an easy-breezy trip to the homeless shelter to feed meals on a Tuesday afternoon.

How can we accomplish this?

Giving people the time to volunteer and make a difference.

Giving Back: Philanthropy

And what other ideas are possible?

The rich and the well-to-do, *they* get to go to Disney World with their family. They have the time to go to prayer groups at their church.

The rich get to go to the fancy restaurants; and stay in the highest-rated hotels and resorts.

Can we enable the homeless to have similar opportunities?

For one thing, mobile showers have been invented. The unit can pull into an area with homeless people; and they can take advantage of a free shower.

This type of initiative can be an enabler of many things. Now that homeless person can clean themselves up… can we get them into a 5-star restaurant?

Maybe it is via a voucher program. Maybe it is a non-profit that raises money for the poor to go to dinner. Maybe the restaurants collect additional money from willing diners and use those funds to allow a certain number of homeless to come in from time to time.

We are seeing movement in this direction: 'pay-what-you-can' restaurants such as "A Place at the Table" in Raleigh, North Carolina.[372] And there is the Kansas City Community Kitchen that adds a restaurant-like feel and operation to feeding the homeless.[373]

Compassion. Kindness. How can we get kindness and compassion into our world and our economy? Compassion is "the obligation of the fortunate

---

[372] http://www.newsobserver.com/entertainment/restaurants/article161008499.html

[373] https://www.huffingtonpost.com/entry/kansas-city-community-kitchen-restaurant-style-soup-homeless_us_56d87303e4b0000de4039a01

to the deprived"[374] per Galbraith who also adds "let there be a coalition of the concerned and the compassionate and those now outside the political system."[375] Right! How do we get a "coalition of the concerned and the compassionate" going? There is too much selfishness in our current way.

Philanthropy and Impact Investing

Much of modern philanthropy is amazingly cool. Ideas in people's heads—for a bigger and better city park, cures for cancer and Alzheimer's, better schools—large benefactors come forward to fund these projects. In the next 50 years over $20 trillion will go into philanthropy so says *The New York Times*.[376]

Non-profit organizations do not need to answer to taxpayers, citizens or voters. And they don't need to worry about shareholders either. Therefore, their missions can be bold. In a word, a philanthropy can fail.

So much private wealth has been created by the stock market itself (through IPO's) and the rising prices (for investors and corporate stock option holders) and that money needs places to go. Much of it goes to big mansions, fancy cars, high-priced restaurants and travel. When the dust settles, giving money away to causes people care about also fills a void.

Non-profit funding generates big, bold and revolutionary ideas.

When it is money being given and a legacy on the line many of these wealthy benefactors are dreaming very big. They don't just want a name on a building on a college campus. They want, for example, to fund a complete overhaul of how we do education in the first place. That is from one industry to the next—a desire to bring about radical, revolutionary change.

The rich get to make a difference with the vast amounts of wealth they have.

Water.org was co-founded by wealthy Hollywood star Matt Damon and the non-profit is helping to ensure clean water and proper sanitation is available throughout the globe for all people. Water.org works with "**microfinance** institutions" making **microloans**. Damon's co-founder, Gary White, says "traditional philanthropy was never going to be enough"[377] which is why Water.org is pushing the limits with pathbreaking, new ideas and alternative partnerships and approaches. They launched an affiliated non-profit to raise more money called WaterEquity. WaterEquity falls in the category of

---

[374] *The Good Society*, Galbraith. Pp 136
[375] *The Good Society*, Galbraith. Pp 136
[376] https://mobile-nytimes-com.cdn.ampproject.org/c/s/mobile.nytimes.com/2017/06/20/opinion/jeff-bezos-bill-gates-philanthropy.amp.html
[377] https://www.cnbc.com/amp/advertorial/2017/06/28/sustainable-investment-the-value-of-clean-water.html

"**catalytic philanthropy**" or "**impact investment**" where money is raised to solve specific problems.

Thus, philanthropy—as it is supposed to be—is pretty amazing.

55
ALTERNATIVE FUTURES
UTOPIA AND ANARCHY

Pathbreaking conversations for the financial system of the long-term future are likely to include 'extreme' concepts such as utopia and anarchy. These radical words are not necessarily the right ones to *implement*; however, suffice to say they are closer to conveying the *direction* we need to be *thinking* than many other concepts and ideas

Utopia because it sets the conversation toward the best possible end. Why wouldn't we want to create a perfect, flawless society?

Anarchy because it frames, and aims, the discussion around the most decentralized result possible.

Neither is probably achievable. And, in fact, a rationale case can be made that we *wouldn't even want* either of them. The point however is that we must aim big. We must push far beyond. We are locked around quaint, tight notions of what is possible. Anarchy and utopia take us outside the box.

The key question is: what do we really want? What is the bottom line goal? Is this not the most fundamental question of creating utopia? Building the system we truly want. All questions and ideas need to be on the table.[378]

UTOPIA

Is the goal utopia? What is utopia?

Thurow wrote that the modern conversation from the liberal perspective

---

[378] *All* questions and ideas. For example: what if the goal is not even to better oneself, or better society?

has "sold two visions of utopia- socialism and the social welfare state."[379] The ideals of utopia go far beyond such simplistic objectives.

Utopia essentially means a perfect society. Perfect.

Sir Thomas More wrote a book 500 years ago that basically entered the word into our lexicon.[380] More wrote of freedom from poverty and suffering. Five-hundred years later and we are still struggling with the same questions: how to end poverty? How to end suffering?

We all can quickly envision and imagine *our* own utopia.

Each of us would have unique versions of utopia, with the differences among us likely ranging to radically opposing ideas. Some might wish to smoke marijuana all day—work a little in the morning, surf in the afternoon. Others want to see peace and no more wars and no more Pentagon and no more military industrial complex. Some want the sanctity of human life protected including for the unborn. Our own most important values are each unique.

Regarding utopia, life doesn't work out perfectly so why would we expect society ever could? Our individual lives are unpredictable and society at large even more unpredictable. Storms, earthquakes, and on. There is so much unforeseen that is possible in society at large. Thus, utopia is, really, impossible.

Galbraith says there is a difference between "utopia and the achievable."[381] In other words, utopia simply may not be achievable (which is perhaps why the root of the word utopia, deriving from Greek, is "not" a "place").

What is realistic? What can we really achieve?

One thing is for sure is that just because a "perfect society" may be impossible does not at all mean we should not discuss trying to bring it about. Don't accept 'unachievability' as a reason to settle for what we have today.

How *could* we move *toward* utopia?

Fairhope was an attempt. Many other cities have been an attempt including Pleasant Hill, Nonesuch (Woodford County) and Bardstown (a monastery); all of these examples from Kentucky.[382]

Henry David Thoreau personalized the search for utopia on his retreat to the woods of Walden Pond.[383] Local, and small-scale experimentations, are indeed ways to achieve utopian ideals.

---

[379] *The Future of Capitalism*, Lester C. Thurow 1996 pp 256

[380] *Utopia*, by Thomas More was published in 1516 was a fictional account of a utopian society on an island.

[381] *The Good Society*, John Kenneth Galbraith, 1996

[382] *Utopia Drive: A Road Trip Through America's Most Radical Idea*, Erik Reece. 2016.

[383] *Walden*, Henry David Thoreau, 1845.

ANARCHY

Anarchy is as radical as utopia but in a completely opposite direction. To many the term can seem scary. Anarchy is easy to frame as being 'no rule of law' or 'complete lawlessness.' *That* is not the type of anarchy I would ever bring to the conversation. The point, to me, is rather to move toward 'no one being in charge.' That is a concept I see value in. That is the ultimate in decentralization—a basic premise of this book, that our financial system needs to be dramatically decentralized.

Can we have a society free of hierarchy?

Can we have a society where we don't have a "bipartisan commission" or all-powerful leader setting us on the course toward utopia but rather that utopia flourishes amid leadership-less freedom?

Some might call this chaos. It is a conversation that must be had. We need to understand anarchy.

What is anarchy? It is—perhaps not surprisingly—defined differently by different people. Pierre-Joseph Proudhon is now recognized as an originator of anarchist political philosophy. Proudhon based his anarchy around radical concepts of land and property. Publishing *What is Property?* in 1840, it is probably his views had an impact on the philosophy of Fairhope's _____ Henry George. Proudhon famously declared in his book that "property is theft." Or rather, Proudhon said "What is property?" and answered, "It is robbery!"[384]

Anarchy is anything from simply rejecting any hierarchy to, perhaps at the least leaderless hierarchy. In terms of government it could mean "no system" or without central rule; in which society is run via voluntary association and without traditional government or institutions; in effect, "stateless."[385] Self-government. Interestingly, from these basic ideas, anarchy can be supportive of total individualism of every person for themselves to "complete collectivism" in which everyone works together for mutual benefit but without leadership, a kibbutz.[386]

Anarchy helps as an anchor—in a similar manner as utopia—for the most insightful conversations. Whether it is global, national, state or local; politicians at any level can become too powerful.

Can we put the individual in charge? How can we maximize freedom?

Can we take leadership out of society and out of the economy?

Anarchy is often linked with chaos. And, delving the depths of anarchist thought can be intimidating. Even democracy is rejected by some anarchists, "even the most decentralized" democracy would still have rules. Anarchy is not rule "by the people."[387]

---

[384] https://en.wikipedia.org/wiki/Property_is_theft!
[385] https://en.wikipedia.org/wiki/Anarchy
[386] *The Kibbutz: A New Way of Life*, Dan Leon, 1969. Pp 33.

Where anarchy becomes quite relevant for conversations that shape the best future is in the concept of the "collective practice of freedom," "force-free society"[388] or a "self-managed society." These are ideas that can spur thought and conversation. And, from here, anarchy starts to become like utopia. Because it gets conceptual and hypothetical in ways that are hard for any of us to put a finger on. Isn't society without leaders and with complete individual freedom practically impossible?

In some cases, anarchy is as simple as filling in where the state is not getting the job done. For example, the Portland Anarchist Road Care organization was founded in 2017 to fix potholes faster than the city.[389]

Anarchists also view, for example, a worker's union such as the AFL-CIO as a "top-down" organization that, while pushing for a few more dollars and rights for workers, does not push far enough toward a better objective such as "worker control of society."[390]

The rub against anarchy is: how can you even have an organization if you are a true anarchist? And to some extent that debate is actually carried out within the range of anarchist thought. Some anarchists find it completely consistent to reject both capitalism *and* socialism. In other words, government ownership and control does not solve the problems of capitalism as a socialist would like to believe. Instead, the best of society would truly impower "the people," and workers as owners. And to realize this end of the people in control does rely on a form of organization, or "polity" that works to self-manage the interests the people.[391]

Suffice to say that a "purist" interpretation of anarchy is used as a means of discrediting the idea. In other words, we will limit our long-term potential if we reject anarchy on its surface without really delving into the philosophy embedded in the idea.

STRETCHING, AND DEEPENING, THE CONVERSATION

The reason anarchy and utopia are paired together in this book is that neither is probably achievable.

The value is that both anarchy and utopia challenge us.

We can deepen the conversation by stretching our imaginations and reaching for the best aspects of either or both anarchy and utopia.

Right, economic *outcomes* we could probably make fair but that is not likely to make us all equally happy and satisfied. And even if the economic

---

[387] https://theanarchistlibrary.org/library/wayne-price-are-anarchism-and-democracy-opposed

[388] http://www.anarchism.net/anarchism_structureofanarchistsociety.htm

[389] https://en.wikipedia.org/wiki/Portland_Anarchist_Road_Care

[390] https://workersolidarity.org/

[391] https://workersolidarity.org/

outcomes were made to be fair somehow, everything in life would *still* not be fair. We all experience life differently and life comes at us in dramatically different ways. Relatives pass away, accidents occur, natural disasters. More, we are sometimes in the right place at the right time and other times not. Life is not fair. It really never will, or can, be.

In America we have the preamble to the Constitution promising "life, liberty and the pursuit of happiness." Those are incredibly powerful, uplifting, positive words. Creating the spirit of America. It is that foresight that is indeed why over 200 years later the country is thriving as the best nation on the planet.

It is not "happiness," but "the pursuit of happiness."

Now it is time for equally radical concepts to carry humanity forward another 200-plus years. We cannot be stagnant.

Could we take "life, liberty and the pursuit of happiness" as an intrinsic aspect of our government, economic and societal fabric? And then set three more aspirational words on top of them to direct our future? Many among us are connecting the dots. Seemingly disparate dots. Free market anarchists, market socialists. That is the direction the future is heading. Bringing different folks together to the table for discussions that include seemingly radical concepts to enable bold action for a better future.

56
ALTERNATIVE FUTURES

SMALL-SCALE EXPERIMENTS

Every possible idea for the future does not need to win out over everything else. We do not have to debate it all and figure out a "comprehensive" solution that can pass Congress at 3am by a vote of 218 to 217.[392]

We often limit our debates over the economy to winner-take-all, red-or-white, 'battle royal' end games. Perhaps that is because of politics. If only our political side wins we could implement our own desires.

Rather, we should think small.

And, in small-scale thinking, all can win.

**In small-scale
thinking and implementation
all can win.**

We don't have to impose capitalism on everyone. We don't have to impose socialism on everyone. We don't need corporations ruling over everyone.

By allowing small-scale experimentation we can try just about any kind of idea; test it out. If it does well, expand it to more areas. If it doesn't work, cast

---

[392] The number of representatives in the U.S. House of Representatives is fixed, by law, at 435 (https://www.house.gov/the-house-explained) since the Apportionment Act of 1911, however subsequent apportionment acts have redefined the actual allocation of the 435 seats according to the states and population.

it away or tweak and improve it.

We need to unleash more experimentation in society.

In so doing, we can press the limits and give a lot more ideas a chance. We don't have to continually restrict ideas.

By trial of various proposals and concepts we can learn whether they can work; and we can start to understand ways in which they can be enhanced to work even better.

Fairhope itself was a small-scale test. And the general principle of a "single-tax" has worked. It is still in place. Fairhope is not an economy unto itself and so the single-tax is part of all the other taxes and complexities of the rest of the local, state and federal systems.

Fairhope has tried other innovations. Being on the far side of the bay from Mobile upon its founding, the only way to get to Fairhope back then was by a boat from Mobile across the bay. As such, a pier (which in Fairhope is often referred to as a "wharf") was needed for boarding and unloading from the boat—extending out past the shallow waters near the shore.

The founders of Fairhope didn't have the money to build the wharf. Where would they come up with the money? Their own governing documents prohibited issuing debt. They needed to get creative.

The solution? "Wharf certificates."[393] Everyone that contributed to the construction (whether it be with money, materials or labor) were provided a credit in the amount of $1.25 for every $1.00 invested. When the wharf opened, the investors would be able to exchange their certificates at face value for the transport of passengers and/or freight via the wharf.

Put some money down, up front; and once the wharf is open for use you can freely use it up to the amount you invested, plus the 25% investors cushion.

When you don't test a big idea you end up 'swinging for the fences' as they say in baseball. In other words, you either hit a home run or miss the ball and strike out badly. Bill Gates recently confided that rolling out "Common Core" nationally before trial-and-error on a smaller basis was a mistake.[394] We need to test things. And then, if they work, 'roll-them-up' to bigger usage.

Communes are almost little societies unto themselves and may have potential for experimentation.

Whether it be financial anarchy, a utopian village or a socialist economy, or founding a needed project—allowing experimentation will benefit all of us.

Will the government and Goldman Sachs banks allow small-scale experimentation?   Probably   not.

---

[393] *Fairhope, 1894-1954, The Story of a Single Tax Colony,* 1956, Paul E. and Blanche R. Alyea. Pp 74.

[394] http://thefederalist.com/2017/10/25/bill-gates-tacitly-admits-common-core-experiment-failure/

57
ALTERNATIVE FUTURES

EXTREME, RADICAL CAPITALISM AND "FREE ENTERPRISE"

Do we spend any time thinking about how to delve deeper into capitalism? More rugged, raw free markets? Seems when it comes to socialist ideas, there is much published and no shortage of media coverage.

Perhaps 'popular culture' is the glorification of raw capitalism. Rappers, musicians, sports stars, tech titans, stock market traders. And the signs of capitalist achievement—the nice homes, fancy restaurants, eye-catching cars. Maybe it is right to talk about ways to balance against the excesses of capitalism.

What if, however, we aren't going far enough?

What if our society could become even better if only we embraced *a lot more* capitalism? Wow. So counterintuitive!

Is it possible our best future is only if we become *more* capitalist?

The point we need to, at least, go there.

Milton Friedman says the "ordinary man" has experienced the most improvement under "freedom" and "free market economics". The "free enterprise system" and the "free market" have been the best economic model in history for eliminating poverty.[395]

MARCUS R. BOWMAN

There is nothing close to capitalism. Nothing can handle all the complexity of humanity and society as well as freedom, free markets, democracy. There is so much complexity to all of us individuals in society that there is almost no other way then freedom. So why are we afraid?

It is hard to believe we would be anywhere near the level of advancement under a socialist/worker dominated society. Consider for example the hardware of laptops and iPhones to the software running them to the apps and platforms such as Facebook and Google that have fostered continued innovation. There is steady advancement and innovation in the 'cutthroat economy.' Growth is largely idea driven. People at meetings talking about how to design and layout the store, the system, the new product or device.

The benefit of capitalism is that the freedom involved actually creates hard incentives toward efficiency as well as continual improvement. Businesses want to lower their costs to improve their profits.[396] They also want to make their products better so more people will want them. At the same time, individual employees work as best they can so that they might earn more money and/or to get a better job. The great characteristic of capitalism is that it spurs innovation through competition. Each of us, as individuals as well as through the many corporations/businesses, can compete and make any products people are likely to buy.

Innovation through competition
Hard work to earn more money or move up to a better job

Adam Smith put this a slightly different way by pointing out the individual **self-interest** that comes into play to make capitalism succeed: "It is not from the benevolence (kindness) of the butcher, the brewer, or the baker that we expect our dinner, but from their regard to their own interest." Self-interest does not mean selfish or greedy. It may include the selfish and the greedy; however, self-interest is merely seeking to reach goals. That could be happiness, more relaxation, money or a myriad of things. We are making decisions based on a general life direction we are aiming to achieve.

One essence of capitalism is the presumption that people want to better themselves. That is a key driving aspect of the success of capitalism. That people want to continually improve their situation is what makes the capitalist economic system thrive. People are able to keep most of the rewards of their hard work and innovative ideas. Essentially it is decentralized markets with free-floating prices that determine much of the supply of goods in capitalism. If a company believes people will buy a product they will produce it. And if too much of a product is produced then prices drop. There is motivation to

---

[395] https://www.goodreads.com/author/quotes/5001.Milton_Friedman
[396] https://www.thebalance.com/capitalism-characteristics-examples-pros-cons-3305588

make smart decisions. There is no dictate of what should be produced. It is the ambition, invention and imagination of individuals and companies that determine products and services.[397]

Many economists would definitively say that "extreme capitalism" is a bad thing.[398] Others contend it is the "diluting" of capitalism that creates problems. That so-called "hyphenated capitalism" or "hybrid capitalist" systems create inefficiencies.[399]

Going down a path of even more radical capitalism—in the aggregate—is probably not likely. However, the implementation of elements of more radical capitalist ideas would surely be beneficial. Jennifer Morone put a spin on "extreme capitalism" by outlining an economic system in which all of us, as an individual, could register as corporations. That would allow all individuals to protect their individual talent, knowledge and expertise they bring to any job.[400]

More important than any of how the future is defined (heck, capitalism could be left behind all together) is to delve into understanding the foundational aspects of what has made our economy thrive. What are those elements? We must not let them go.

THE RIGHT TERMINOLOGY

What is the right word? Is it "freedom," "free markets," "free enterprise"? What term correctly captures the very essence of what must be retained in how we currently live. "Capitalism"? Too controversial.

Would we have the iPhone today if not for our current economic and political framework?

"Free enterprise" is perhaps the best at capturing both the underlying principle of a free society as well as the organizing principle of "enterprise," that is also itself, free. People freely associate, and freely develop the world around them. That is the essence of what I believe needs to be unleashed. And whatever it is that you say you are not able to truly freely associate and freely develop, the screws likely should be taken off. In other words, if you feel you should be able to create your own organization that works in a new direction (be it 'corporate-like' with radically different goals: such as sustainability and no CEO, or a socialist-style sharing of profits), I believe that "free enterprise" would not limit that. Capitalist elements seem to

---

[397] *The Capitalist's Bible*, Gretchen Morgenson, 2009, Pp xvi-xvii (introduction written by Robert J. Samuelson
[398] *One Market Under God: Extreme Capitalism, Market Populism and the End of Economic Democracy*, 2000, Thomas Frank.
[399] https://www.wsj.com/articles/costs-and-benefits-of-hyphenated-capitalism-1511553625
[400] https://www.youtube.com/watch?v=b4tr4-J9cCg

demonstrate that they have, do and will limit competition and protect their own interests. However, if we embrace individual freedom and the freedom to organize under alternative means than I believe a radically better future can, and will, result.

Merriam-Webster dictionary defines "free enterprise:"

> *freedom of private business to organize and operate*
> *for profit in a competitive system without interference by government*
> *beyond regulation necessary to protect public interest and keep the national economy in*
> *balance.*[401]

Replace "business" with "organization" and add "or non-profit" after 'profit' and then I believe you have a workable definition of "free enterprise" that unleashes creativity. Remember the structure of our modern corporations has been around a long time. There are other ways of organizing together and a minimally-altered definition of "free enterprise" unleashes new entities. The principle of "free enterprise" could and should carry over in to politics. Just as economic establishment elements limit it us via archaic legislative codes to one kind of money (incentive structure) and a handful of limited organizing methods (such as corporations) so too does the political establishment limit competition. "Free enterprise" is needed on our ballots where other parties are allowed to compete against the entrenched Republicans and Democrats.

---

[401] https://www.merriam-webster.com/dictionary/free%20enterprise

58
ALTERNATIVE FUTURES
THE "GIG ECONOMY" AND SHARING

The internet, social media and other technology advances have enabled the growth of the so-called "Gig economy" in which people can become experts in an independent field of their choosing.

The difference is these workers don't "have a job" in the traditional way.

Workers can set their own schedule as they, basically, build a small business around themselves. The benefit is that it is enabling people to both a) bring in extra income and/or b) pay the bills in a purposeful way other than collecting unemployment.

Gig jobs do not tend to pay that well, although at times the pay can be extraordinary. For example, an Uber driver may on average barely make $9/hour, but then catch a long ride and make $60 in the next hour. For the meager pay that an Uber driver averages the sad reality in the gig economy is that it does not include the costs. Uber drivers use their own cars and buy their own gas. Bye-bye some of that pay. And Uber drivers have no benefits. The company does not provide vacation time or healthcare or any other such benefits. There are perks to being an Uber driver, including healthcare offers and discounts at oil change centers; however, these benefits are the equivalent of being a AAA member.

There are now numerous ways to make money, 'on the side' via the internet on so-called 'digital marketplaces:' Etsy, Airbnb, Uber/Lyft, Rover, FlexJobs, TaskRabbit, Behance, Upwork and Fiverr.

These websites take a percentage cut from the earnings. Usually, the website has little, or no, involvement in the actual task. They enable the pairing of the person placing the order with the person performing the work. Then, the work is done by the gig worker.

The gig workers complain about the lack of benefits and the low pay, though at the same time benefit from having basically no boss and no set schedule or commitment. A gig worker could walk away from the job anytime.

A wide range of serious policy issues are being raised with respect to these freelance workers, including minimum wage requirements, benefits and government entitlements; let alone the work conditions, and costs borne by the worker.[402]

The shift into the "gig economy," or freelance work, has become so pronounced that some estimates are that as many as 43% of American workers will be freelancers by 2020.[403] This makes the need for action in defining the terms of this new branch of labor all the more pressing.

Making it in the "Gig economy" runs deeper than these websites and apps that match a customer with a freelancer. Halsey made it big in the music industry starting only by posting videos on YouTube.[404] Successful bloggers, such as Glenn Reynolds,[405] could also be considered a part of the Gig Economy.

A lot of the "gig economy," however, seems to rely on having an asset. A home with space available for Airbnb. Your car to make money with Uber/Lyft. If you own those assets you can make extra income. Call it the "asset-based economy." You can only share and make money if you own assets.

The next stage of these types of innovations might be able to cut off the middleman. Make it a non-profit. For, say Uber/Lyft-type driving, all of the profit could go to the driver. Uber developed an app, but a non-profit could come up with an app. Another advantage of Uber is working out all the deals with municipalities to have legality for this new way of transportation. Overall though Uber just gets a cut from someone else working. Uber has nothing to do with the car, the costs of the car, the people in the car. And yet Uber takes a cut. Sitting in Silicon Valley, they get a cut of a driver using their own vehicle in cities far away. As Ann Pettifor writes, "the rentier class based in Silicon Valley... almost effortlessly extract rent from the worker and her asset."[406] That could be the next big change. Wall Street, banks and big money don't

---

[402] https://www.theguardian.com/business/2017/oct/17/sometimes-you-dont-feel-human-how-the-gig-economy-chews-up-and-spits-out-millennials

[403] https://www.forbes.com/sites/sleasca/2017/07/17/highest-paying-jobs-gig-economy-lyft-taskrabbit-airbnb/#2291005e7b64

[404] https://en.wikipedia.org/wiki/Halsey_(singer)

[405] https://pjmedia.com/instapundit/

[406] August 8, 2017 accessed 8/22/17 http://www.redpepper.org.uk/the-economic-crash-ten-years-on/

want *that much* freedom for people!

59
ALTERNATIVE FUTURES
NORDIC MODEL

The so-called "Nordic Model" for economic-political systems is romanticized as the path to lower inequality; as well as a happier population. Reality might be that we don't have a deep enough understanding of these economies to justify conclusions of either a) what it is that makes them successful or even b) whether they are indeed successful. In other words, some say it is more of a "Nordic Myth" than a model.[407]

First, what is Nordic? Five Nordic countries: Denmark (which includes Greenland and the Faroe Islands), Finland, Iceland, Norway and Sweden.

In attempting to turn what could be a myth into a measurable fact, the United Nations now tracks "happiness." Three of the Nordic countries ranked 1, 2 and 3 in the UN "World Happiness Report 2017:" Norway, Denmark and Iceland (Finland was 5th, Sweden tied for 9th).[408] Part of Norway's success (in the Happiness ranking) is attributed to rich reserves of oil and the finding that they manage their valuable oil resources effectively. The rankings score countries based on such concepts of "caring, freedom, generosity, honesty, health (life expectancy), income and good government" as well as "mutual trust (absence of corruption in business and government), shared purpose and having someone to count on in times of trouble."[409]

---

[407] http://www.nationalreview.com/article/438331/nordic-democratic-socialist-model-exposing-lefts-myth
[408] http://worldhappiness.report/wp-content/uploads/sites/2/2017/03/HR17-ESv2_updated.pdf

But happiness doesn't really capture what it is these Nordic countries are doing with their economy.

Proponents of the Nordic Model believe that recent years show that a far higher level of "government transfer" can occur in a society without impeding growth rates. That the Nordic countries economic growth has not been lower than that of the United States despite higher government benefits for all people.[410]

The Nordic Model basically includes socialist attributes such as comprehensive "universalist" welfare state and national collective bargaining; operating in combination with free market capitalism (such as private ownership, free trade and free markets). The Nordic Mode" also includes inclusion of "tripartite" corporatism, in which business, labor and government are to act as partners to create economic policy in a cooperative and compromising manner.[411]

An objective and balanced conclusion might be that the Nordic Model does not offer either capitalists or socialists a total win. Rather, the Nordic Model seems to blend the best of socialism and the best of capitalism, or as sociologist Lane Kenworthy said it is "social democracy" *within* the framework of capitalism.[412] The Nordic Model is not a replacement of capitalism. Others define the Nordic Model as "embracing globalization and sharing risks."[413]

The mystery of the Nordic Model and whether it is the key to our future success perhaps traces back to Sweden.

Sweden is not ever thought of as the mecca and origination of modern capitalism. And maybe that is because we are not really capitalist in the way we think we are. Whatever it is, a lot traces back to Sweden. Chapter 34 the modern commercial corporation dates back to Sweden. Chapter 11, the first modern central bank? Established in Sweden.

Nordic success? Nothing new?

Bitcoin? Probably will be adopted by Sweden first. Will Nordic ideas continue leading us into the future?

---

[409] http://worldhappiness.report/wp-content/uploads/sites/2/2017/03/HR17-ESv2_updated.pdf

[410] http://www.demos.org/blog/10/8/14/why-property-theft-and-why-it-matters

[411] http://encyclopedia.uia.org/en/problem/155119

[412] https://www.foreignaffairs.com/articles/united-states/2013-12-06/americas-social-democratic-future

[413] https://economics.mit.edu/files/5726

60
ALTERNATIVE FUTURES

THE SOCIALIST ALTERNATIVE
AND PROGRESSIVE MOMENTUM

Somedays you could wonder if we in the United States are more along the path of socialism than we would like to admit. How much longer before we all get our goods from one store? Wal-Mart.

Usually, the first thoughts that come to mind with the word socialism are the U.S.S.R., Cuba and other miserably failed states. Next might be the philosophy of Karl Marx, author of the 1948 Communist Manifesto and the 1867 socialist *Das Kapital*.

In America, a modern hero of socialist ideas is an elder statesman; the congressmember from Vermont. U.S. Senator Bernie Sanders calls himself "the longest serving independent in congressional history."[414] He tweeted on Black Friday, America's biggest retail shopping day of the year that "today and every day, our workers deserve $15 an hour, decent working conditions and the right to form a union."[415] In his college activism and politics in Vermont, Sanders was more proudly a socialist.[416] Today, he downplays that label; however, he is America's most-prominent politician and activist for socialist objectives.

---

[414] https://twitter.com/SenSanders

[415] https://twitter.com/SenSanders/status/934098051693760513

[416] https://www.washingtonpost.com/archive/politics/1990/11/11/for-vermonts-sanders-victory-followed-long-path/36a3036c-d738-4039-a728-891ae9aba9f5/?utm_term=.23c2a11a44e0

Despite continual attempts to pose socialism as a failed experiment of the past, it remains a continued theory of interest to both the future and here-and-now. Rebels of the past are romanticized, including Che Guevara, Fidel Castro, Leon Trotsky and Mao Zedong. Lesser-known is, say, Eugune Debs; lacking the cool, revolutionary status of those from faraway lands as all Debts did was run for U.S. President five times representing the Socialist Party of America around the turn of the 20th century.[417]

It is hard to capture all aspects of socialist thought just as it is difficult to try and trivialize the many nuances within capitalism. Here is a list of recent direction[418]:

- A minimum wage increase (such as to $15/hour), or "living wage"
- Protecting the environment, most notably a Green Party philosophy and/or "sustainability," including opposition to oil drilling
- The right to organize into unions and the expansion of workers' rights
- More government spending to solve social problems
- Opposition to tax cuts and opposition to less government spending (so-called 'anti-austerity')
- Expanded social programs, including welfare, unemployment insurance and such
- Higher taxes for corporations and high-income individuals
- Wealth redistribution and "social justice"
- Greater worker ownership of the instruments of production
- Wage equality (for example, women's pay)
- Student loan forgiveness
- Healthcare for all in society
- Tighter regulations of corporations, banks and markets

More radical elements exist within the green/eco movement, the newer Black Lives Matter (BLM) as well as the Occupy movement (formerly Occupy Wall Street). For example, rent control[419] and even nationalization of large corporations[420] are among the more radical proposals among socialists.

Prior to all the movements of today was the "Progressive Era," in the late 1800's and early 1900's, most notably led by President Theodore Roosevelt as a national, populist backlash to the monopoly power of the Gilded Age[421]

---

[417] https://www.biographyonline.net/people/famous/socialists.html

[418] Socialist viewpoints are defined here by their economic characteristics, as opposed to liberal moral positions which may be held by the same supporters. Not intended as an all-inclusive list but a best-attempt has been made to cover all important positions.

[419] https://en.wikipedia.org/wiki/Kshama_Sawant#Campaign_issues

[420] https://en.wikipedia.org/wiki/Kshama_Sawant#Economic_policies

mega-wealth and mega-corporations of the financial tycoons such as John D. Rockefeller and J.P. Morgan.

Perhaps ironically, socialist/populist ideals reached their height of political power before they really ever got going. And subsequently never have gotten going. Like the electric automobile, however, perhaps their time has finally come?

Certainly, there are numerous movements that have sprung up (aided by social media) in recent years, and all around the globe. The "Socialist Alternative" has attempted to consolidate all efforts as part of one movement. Grabbing global inspiration, the movement has found a foothold in local elections, such as Kshama Sawant. Ms. Sawant was elected to the Seattle City Council in 2013 and won re-election to a four-year term in 2015.

In London, Hilary Wainwright has quickly popularized a socialist ("green-left") publication, "Red Pepper," (green for the environment, red for socialism/communism) in parallel to the political rise of long-time British socialist Jeremy Corbyn.[422] Hilary Wainwright has been a revolutionary economic leader of late in forging ahead with radical ideas.[423]

The momentum in England was, in part, born out of the Greek economic crisis and the anti-austerity backlash. In Spain the 15-M Movement and Indignados Movement attracted masses of protestors to rally against high unemployment and welfare cuts.[424] A year prior to that were the strikes and demonstrations in Greece, including protests by "Direct Democracy Now!"[425]

Within the depths of any of these movements are truly innovative ideas that could make valuable contributions to our future. For example, consider the concept of "Freedom Under Planning," a 1945 book by Barbara Wootton.[426] Is such a counterintuitive process possible?

Socialism used to be as simple as more government spending or less government involvement in the economy. John Maynard Keynes, author of *The General Theory*, perhaps mainstreamed socialist ideas without receiving any credit. After all, the anti-austerity campaigns of radical activists are nearly anything more than a reflection of Keynesian economics; more government spending stimulates the economy.

Now the objectives for socialists are both so much more specific as well as

---

[421] https://hsp.org/education/unit-plans/the-progressive-era-and-economics

[422] https://www.bloomberg.com/news/articles/2017-09-27/corbyn-tells-may-to-step-aside-and-let-labour-govern-britain

[423] Arguments for a New Left: Answering the Free-Market Right, Hilary Wainwright, ISBN: 978-0-631-19191-9, 346 pages, January 1994, Wiley-Blackwell

[424] https://en.wikipedia.org/wiki/Anti-austerity_movement_in_Spain#/media/File:Puertadelsol2011.jpg

[425] https://en.wikipedia.org/wiki/Anti-austerity_movement_in_Greece

[426] Reviewed here https://www.jstor.org/stable/2144738?seq=1#page_scan_tab_contents and available online here https://archive.org/details/freedomunderplan00wootrich

so much more impactful.

In the green movement, environmentalists are increasingly stating that capitalism itself is the key problem that is obstructing any long-term ability to control and manage the problem of climate change. From Naomi Klein's 2014 book, *This Changes Everything: Capitalism vs. the Climate* to a 2016 *New York Times* op-ed "The Climate Crisis? It's Capitalism Stupid" the momentum is growing within the environmental movement to dump capitalism to save the planet.[427]

Recently, definitions of socialism have trended toward anarchy in the sense of moving definitively away from the state-controlled socialism that has been tried in the past. For example, the WSM (World Socialist Movement) defines socialism as "stateless" with a "post-monetary economy:" "a system of society based upon the common ownership and democratic control of the means and instruments for producing and distributing wealth by and in the interest of the community."[428]

Post-monetary economy. Stateless. Common ownership. Democratic control of the tools of production. Democratic control of distributing wealth. That's not the socialism of the U.S.S.R. That is, flushing it all through. That is vision.

---

[427] https://www.investors.com/politics/editorials/climate-change-crisis-capitalism/ and
https://www.nytimes.com/2017/11/20/opinion/climate-capitalism-crisis.html
[428] https://en.wikipedia.org/wiki/World_Socialist_Movement#Socialism

61

PARALLEL TRACKS

There is more than one way to skin a cat.[429]

We don't all have to be in the same economy. The Federal Reserve maintains a monopoly over our financial system. One way of doing business.

How about some other ways to make it in the world? Beyond traditional money. Outside the capitalism of loans, bonds, interest rates.

I call this "parallel tracks," in which other competing models are allowed to operate alongside the current economic system. People can participate in whichever system they would like, or both.

Like the Federal Reserve model? It has served us well. I think we are going on to better things. Are you happy and content within the existing Federal Reserve economic system? Stay in it.

However, that should not preclude other ways of operating. In other words, the Federal Reserve should not be able to maintain a monopoly over *all* economic activity. We should also allow the existence of other economic frameworks.

Parallel Economies

Parallel tracks would a) eliminate the Federal Reserve monopoly, while b) not eliminating the Federal Reserve and allowing those that wish to stay in that economy to do so, while c) enabling new ideas to flourish. The idea of "parallel tracks" offers the most freedom. It enables us to implement new,

---

[429] http://grammarist.com/phrase/more-than-one-way-to-skin-a-cat/

and potentially better financial systems without totally disrupting what we have.

Numerous economic systems could run simultaneously. Multiple universes of finance.

One kickoff to this new era could, for example, be as simple as a law permitting alternative currencies. This is a simplistic example of a parallel economy in which people could choose to be paid in Federal Reserve Notes (our dollar bills are "Federal Reserve Notes") or in another currency. My view is Bitcoin is part of the existing system and very tightly controlled by global, establishment interests (as explained primarily in Chapter 44).

"Alternative currencies" means completely different, competing currencies. Say, Texas with its own currency, or a rural town with its own money, or just someone operating out of their garage starting a new currency that people begin to trust and adopt.[430]

Beyond competing currencies, there are other ways that people could 'operate' (for lack of a better word) outside the existing Federal Reserve Note economy. Collecting 'points' (an idea described in Chapter 44) is another conceptual idea in which people could work and spend in an economic system outside the current way.

A "parallel track" is as simple as 1 new law to unleash competition to the Federal Reserve and the Federal Reserve Note. No longer would the Federal Reserve have a monopoly over everyone in the economy. Americans could establish alternatives and choose to work and live within another system. And the ultimate beauty of this solution is that it both a) enables radically different futures with b) the least disruption, as the existing Federal Reserve system continues to operate.

Parallel tracks. It doesn't have to all be the same.

---

[430] There are lots of cryptocurrencies that could be said to be started up by anyone in a garage, but they are all within the Bitcoin system, derivatives of bitcoin and not the totally different ways I am envisioning are possible.

62
ALTERNATIVE FUTURES

RADICAL ECONOMIC IMPROVEMENT

Change?

Or improve.

Jack Ma, founder of Alibaba, "many years ago I wanted to change the world, now I think if you want to change the world then change yourself. Change yourself is more important; and easier. Secondly, I want to improve the world."

Change yourself. Improve the world.[431]

That is a bit of the message in this book. It is perhaps too difficult to outright change the financial system. But we must improve it. And, in my opinion, radically so.

The internet, Netflix, Google, social media—all of this new technology has been revolutionary in breaking through to a new era.

However, what is coming on its heels, is likely far more radical. But it must be permitted. So far, we have forged new ground. Very little disruption to the status quo. Netflix eclipsing Blockbuster. Not that big a deal.

Coming breakthroughs have the potential to take us into a radically different future. Not just technology breakthroughs in the sense that we think of them. Learning breakthroughs. Breakthroughs developed *because* of various

---

431 Jack Ma at the World Economic Forum, June 25, 2016. https://youtu.be/6SuFGpYQt0E

technologies. Technologies *applied* to *real-world* applications.

Think: new ways of transportation and getting around. Super high-speed trains, self-driving cars.

New ways of living.

New ways of packages being delivered.

Amazon eclipsing retail outlets. Alibaba eclipsing Amazon.

The telecommunications industry, or cable industry—entire industries—eclipsed in short order.

Computing giants and others.

Banking revolutionized.

Democracy revolutionized.

There are some rather big changes that *could* happen. However, you can be sure that entire industries are not going to be eclipsed without a fight.

And this is the type of establishment collusion that is holding us back.

Many of the ideas are there already. However, freedom is being lost.

We need to make economic changes that unleash true freedom… for the benefit of a lot more people.

Radical simply means far-reaching, thorough and "affecting the fundamental nature of something."

A complete, exhaustive, sweeping, wide-reaching, profound overhaul.

Totally new people in charge. A totally new culture.

Brand new institutions or leadership that has an entirely different focus.

Nothing like the past.

Closing down the Federal Reserve; with the Fed closed: Who picks up the pieces? What happens without a Federal Reserve?

What happens without stock exchanges running the show from New York City? Crowdfunding, Kickstarter and similar innovations and new ways not yet even introduced can be used to raise capital and guide the economy to better and higher heights. Congress approved the "Jumpstart Our Business Startups" Act in the summer of 2012. However, the innovation in that bill does not go far enough and many of its provisions are not being fully implemented.

The private enterprise system works. Competition works. More banks. Totally different banks. The criticism is that totally new banks would be "wildcat banks." Like Ron Paul says we have "wildcat restaurants" and "wildcat shoe companies".[432] People go where they go. We have wildcat businesses all around town and throughout our counties and states. Let there be freedom.

Radical means short-term and long-term thinking. Some changes can be so bold as to believe they can't be implemented right away. And yet they can; and will. At the same time, it isn't over until it's over. One cool thing or a bunch

---

[432] *End the Fed*. Ron Paul. 2009. Pp 190.

of cool things does not mean radical overhaul. Complete overhaul will take time. This is going to be a long, ongoing process. Big, longer steps sometimes and inching along throughout.

Overnight Change

We are witnessing the results of new research and learning across so many parts of society. Revolutionary new technologies being developed.

Technology and new inventions are going to increasingly make whole industries obsolete overnight.

With Blockbuster it was kind of cool and just a tad bit sad. It was like, wow. I don't need to go to a Blockbuster store anymore to get movies? Woah. What is going to happen to all those Blockbusters?! But then you process that it is just a retail outlet and there are lots of retail stores and so most people will just go to work in a different retail store. And… Blockbuster isn't all that big right. And so, ok, bye bye Blockbuster. And the world keeps on rolling around.

Now what may come next is a bunch of similar type of innovations.

First, taking a whole business and turning it on its own head… overnight. Except this time a much bigger business.

Then, a whole industry is going to change.

And the disruption is going to be flipping enormous. It is quite possible to have tens of thousands of jobs simply unnecessary overnight. Or massive change from one way of doing things to another.

Consider UPS deliveries. Currently a host of drivers deliver packages the last mile to your door. Well, in the future, it is likely you will go pick your package up. Not necessarily at the main hub UPS facility that is across town, on the other side of the rail road tracks, in that one industrial district that no one ever otherwise ventures to. They will just have one big truck that will take packages to little neighborhood pickup hubs. It might be a deal with Wal-Mart or your near-by dollar store. Somewhere you pass by most days. Or somewhere you go once a week anyways, like a grocery store or maybe even a gas station.

Electricity: another industry where increasingly people can live outside the utility grid. Government doesn't like that. The electric utility doesn't like that. Currently, government and the utilities are winning the battle. They get laws and regulations passed that outlaw people from using their own electricity?

Government and Big Business
Holding Back Our Potential

It is the 21st century! Change may come to the global financial system whether we are ready or not. It is time to get out in front of financial revolutions that may come. It is time for an economy that works for more people. Life is too short to struggle year after year. Life is too short for a Federal Reserve that worries about ensuring the stock market goes up every single day after day after day the stock market is up. While incomes are stagnant year after year after year employees go to work for the same pay.

The world is changing so fast. So rapidly. And yet the government structure is stuck. We are not modernizing finance and government anywhere close to fast enough.

> **The world is changing so fast. So rapidly.**
> **And yet the government structure is stuck.**
> **We are not modernizing finance and government**
> **anywhere close to fast enough.**

In part this is because corporate involvement with government works counterproductively to perpetuate the status quo.

Existing industries do *not* want these changes that are coming. It could get worse before ultimately improving. They will outlaw and ban competition directly. At the same time, powerful banking interests may continue grabbing even more control then they already do. And it could be frustrating to watch as they are adept in dressing everything up so rosy, enough to make someone like me want to puke. However, I do believe a better result is inevitable and will come about one way or the other.

A lot of change is going to happen in the economy simply as a productive of innovation. Two types of innovation working together.

1. Innovative Thinking
2. Technology Innovation

New technologies enable the implementation of innovative thoughts.

The world *will* be drastically changing. If not the innovation/technology one-two punch it will be the will of the people. Or a combination of the two.

> **The forces of the people and new technology**
> **will—eventually—overwhelm any attempts**
> **to continue this status quo.**

Frustration is building in the minds of others. Most frequently seen by the activist demonstrations of the left. There are some that would like to see a near total breakdown of society. They are frustrated not only with the economy, but they link the economy to economic disparities affecting race and many other problems. We very well may see radical change come along in unpredictable ways in sporadic bursts spurred by revolutionary protest and centered from one location moving to another.

How? Who?

Who will bring all of this about? Our current big money congress members will clamor that they **need** to mold it and shape it. Wall Street will contend that it must be certain, highly educated economists, Harvard professors and MIT mathematics geniuses.

But, why can't it be you?

Do you know a lot about economics and finance?

As Milton Friedman famously quipped: you don't ask to get treated for cancer only by a doctor that has had cancer before.[433]

You don't ask to get treated for cancer only by a doctor that has had cancer before.

The financial system and economy of the future does not need to be developed and brought about by those in the thick of the system currently.

The only requirement is the interest in molding a solution. Whatever that solution might be.

Are you passionate about bringing about a new and better economy? Then you are qualified. You are indeed needed.

In fact, it will not come about without you.

Take the ideas in this book. Mold them. Talk and take action that helps brings about a radically new and better path for our collective future.

To solve poverty, you don't have to be poor yourself.

It might help. It might not. You probably want to immerse yourself deep amid poverty to build an experience that helps to bring about the best solution—either by learning and/or by taking action directly. But don't hold yourself—or others—back. Don't listen to naysayers. And don't like the current power brokers dampen your spirit.

I am convinced that the big names and big ideas of today are not where to look for how the future will be shaped. Goldman Sachs struck it big by getting into the IPO business back in the 1890's. What will the future of IPO's look like? Who will invent an IPO that is completely outside the Wall Street umbrella? Who will invent an IPO concept that is completely outside our

---

[433] https://youtu.be/Rls8H6MktrA?t=4m24s

existing financial system? No one will be talking about them when these truly innovative ideas pop up. They will be quietly breaking a path that will be the highway we all go down in the future?

63
ALTERNATIVE FUTURES
THE COLLECTIVE

Thomas Paine was a revolutionary at the founding of the United States. Considered a great political writer, we rarely see Thomas Paine mentioned as an economist.[434] Yet, here will be the second time Paine is referenced in this financial book.

Paine saw the earth as "common property" and that everyone born to the earth had a right to some stake in that "common property."[435]

Paine went on to outline how the value of land (the earth) that is captured by its existing owners could slowly over time be divided among the entire population, "rich or poor." "Successive generations" would be made to make payments to all. The basic premise behind all of this is that no person should be born on to this planet worse off.[436] The philosophy runs quite deep and it is clearly quite similar to the later economic expressions of Henry George and Pierre-Joseph Proudhon.

Paine expressed this perspective of "common property" with respect to land. So...

Could a group of Americans start

---

[434] In fact, as of November 25, 2017 the Wikipedia entry for Thomas Paine referred to him as a "political activist, philosopher, political theorist, and revolutionary" but makes no mention of him in economics. https://en.wikipedia.org/wiki/Thomas_Paine

[435] http://www.constitution.org/tp/agjustice.htm

[436] http://www.constitution.org/tp/agjustice.htm

to take *ownership* of this country?

The political process is one way to achieve big changes in society.

Another way is by acquiring land and assets.

Could a group of Americans pool money together and buy a park? Start their own nature preserve? Buy a rundown city building and fix it up?

Buy things. Like the Federal Reserve buys things.

And once owned. It is for keeps so to speak.

That is the rough sketch of an idea called "The Collective."

As we have uncovered regarding the Federal Reserve, they have a balance sheet that exists in outer space—beyond and outside our existing economy.

Anything that the Federal Reserve buys, they have no obligation to sell.

Any expansion of assets or liabilities of the Federal Reserve has no accountability to the markets. The Federal Reserve balance sheet is accountable to no one.

In a similar way, the future of our economy may develop completely outside our existing financial system.

Can assets that are part of our current economy be pulled outside of it?

One way to do that is to outright purchase land and/or certain assets.

Once owned, it is—more or less—yours.

So, for example, if environmentalists pulled money together and started buying land they would own that property. And as the owner of that property they could protect it. They could enhance it. They could, in effect, do what they wanted with that property. With free and clear ownership of that property, theoretically, they can hold that land outside of the existing financial system.

This is the concept behind what I am calling "The Collective."

The Collective (TC) is assets that are collectively owned by the group and members belonging to the collective. There could be just one collective, or many collectives—a decentralizing of ownership.

The idea is raising money among a group of people with shared values. And then taking the collected money and using it to make purchases that are in line with the values of those contributing the money.

Land could be purchased for a park in your town. Then the park could be managed and operated in a number of different ways. For example, the park could be a) open only for the use of TC members and their guests, or b) open to the public for free, or c) open to the public for a fee. Option (c) is interesting in that the revenue raised from the public could be used for a) ongoing operations and maintenance of the park or b) additional revenue for The Collective to expand by making more purchases of other properties.

A key notion behind The Collective is cooperation. Many of varied backgrounds have written of cooperation. Including Milton Friedman, an influential economist of the 20th Century, and one considered to be quite to the right of the political spectrum and as free market conservative as they come. "Our society is what we make it. (We can shape our institutions. Physical and human characteristics limit the alternatives to us. But none prevents us, if we will, from building) a society that preserves and expands human freedom, that keeps government in its place, keeping it our servant and not letting it become our master."[437]

An essential element of this book is aimed to provide pathbreaking solutions. New, radical ideas that stir minds and spur bold action. We are capable of a much better economy.

**The Collective is an idea in which
the system is changed through playing by the rules.
It rests on the concept of private property.
Property can be purchased and it
becomes part of The Collective.**

What could be part of TC?

A hotel. That any member of TC could stay at? Perhaps, TC members would each get 1 night per year to stay at the hotel. It could be a very nice property. Right in the middle of activity of a fun, large city. Or right on the beach; oceanfront!

Who works at the hotel? TC volunteers. To get more staff there can be benefits to being an employee or volunteer. Such as nights at the hotel.

Where TC can really become different is in how the property can be shared. So many people in the world never get to stay at the nice fancy hotel or stay oceanfront. And so, TC can make rooms available to a wide array of people. This is how TC can sit outside of the regular economy.

As more property is acquired you can see how it can become *The Collective*.

Any kinds of assets could be purchased.

The hotel could have a room that is full of musical instruments for anyone to use and practice. Another room could have art supplies. Another room could be a computer lab. Conference and meeting rooms to hold networking events and group meetups and discussions.

There are certain rules that could be established by the members of TC.

You put money into TC as if the money vanishes and no longer exists.

---

[437] *Free to Choose*. Milton and Rose Friedman. Pp 37.

The money is used to purchase assets that become part of The Collective.

As they become part of The Collective. They are taken out of the current economy. They become part of a non-money economy.

And "The Collective" would continue to grow and gain even more ability. TC can partner with cities to get other assets. People could donate assets into The Collective.

A core of common principles could arise toward how you must use items in The Collective. Perhaps there are no paper cups. People must reuse their own mugs and canteens. Perhaps there are no bags. People have their own bag they bring around to carry items they purchase, such as groceries.

The Collective then serves as a test run. An experiment. A totally different economy can arise—through real-life trial and error. The rules established by TC to use properties and assets can become the rules of a next generation economy. Do you need any money at TC hotel? No. That one property—and all the properties of TC—could be outside our current concept of economy. Whole new methods of arranging society could spring forth.

TC could have one approach in New Orleans, another in New York City and yet another in Seattle, Washington. What works? Share the best practices and best ideas and concepts that stick and catch on.

Another way to look at this or say it is "The Commons." In computing there is the concept of the "Creative Commons." And that in essence is the concept. Linux. Sharing. Building together. Volunteering to help TC.

COMMON, COOPERATIVE, PRIVATE-PUBLIC OWNERSHIP

In the traditional view of society privatization is bad and it is the opposite of the public good. TC is a form of privatization that is good for society and better for all the people.

Talk about a ton of contradictions!

Private ownership for the public good?

Public ownership facilitated by private action?

A version of TC is seen in cooperatives. One popular cooperative is in Berlin. Holzmarkt got off the ground in the last 5 years or so and has been a big success due to help from investors.[438]

The Collective (TC) could also be viewed as a private version of public ownership. So, instead of government/public ownership of land and items it can be owned 'collectively' by the people. An ironic mind twist. Hard to conceptualize based on typical, status quo mentality. We are basically taught to believe that the government owning something is good for the public. However, that has proven problematic in many areas and ways. Moreover, to expand the concept of public ownership it is a difficult notion for more and

---

[438] https://www.shareable.net/blog/berlins-holzmarkt-shows-the-incredible-potential-of-urban-villages

more of society to be rolled into government. However, if ownership is put into private cooperatives, then it may actually be a purer form of "public ownership."[439] Goal to serve the public interest.

There are many ways to achieve the outcomes. Sometimes the solution could be counterintuitive. And in this case the result is common property owned by individuals for the public good.

Another way to look at this is that it is not necessarily the end goal or the name of the approach that matters. It is in the means. And it is more importantly in the nature of the means. The operation of the means. Whether it is government ownership or private ownership, the important end goal is that it is for the public good. And to that end, it is a matter of ensuring the end is properly served all the way through. It could be called "control." Who 'controls' the process? And if the process is properly controlled by the public it should, in the end, and throughout, serve the public.

---

[439] https://www.tni.org/en/article/public-ownership-in-the-21st-century

64
TAKING ACTION

FRANK DIALOGUE

The best path forward for the best possible future is frank dialogue and the cross-blending of different perspectives.

A liberal idea and a conservative idea, hashed out, reworked.

Blended, if you will.

The key is frank dialogue. Simplistic notions have to be left behind. It is not enough to say capitalism or socialism is the problem. First off, two people could hardly agree on what capitalism or socialism means. They are abstract words and concepts.

Not as simple as only blaming the government.
Not as easy as blaming business and the rich 1%.

Too much government, or too much cronyism by the 1% *is* a problem. To some degree, both contribute to holding back our best possible future.

The point is where we go from here?

Improving dialogue among us involves listening to ideas that challenge our own ideas and viewpoints.

If you want others to listen to you,
do you also have the ability to listen to them?

Bridgewater Associates founder Ray Dalio calls this "Radical Truth and Radical Transparency." Dalio says "openly and thoughtfully disagreeing on important issues" can open conversations to lead to our best futures.[440]

Beyond legislative changes and structural changes to our financial system and economic reforms, is necessary improvements to our collective mindset and individual mentality.

How will we ever find common ground when we can hardly communicate? There is a near total breakdown of communication in society. So many of us believe we are so right. We are losing friendships and such. Former employees of Facebook, insiders from the early days are pointing out how Facebook is changing society for the worse. We have taken the shouting over each other of CNN political pundits and put it to a typing argument on an internet website with our own friends and family![441]

How can lead us by example?

Who can rise above and be able to tolerate others?

We need to let it go and chill.

Let people be different.

Let some other parts of the country do it a different way. The NCAA removing tournament games from North Carolina because of a law is intolerant. North Carolina can work out its own problems. Just like marijuana is legalized in Oregon, other states need to be free to make different decisions. And if it comes to splitting up the country or making a different financial system for some people then we need to let it go. The whole world does not need to be the same. We do not need a technical knockout of the other political perspective.

Likewise, some are noticing it is even hard to talk about controversial ideas with those you agree with. You could agree with someone 95%, but express one ounce of a different position and look out! We are losing our ability to talk to each other.[442]

Everything Needs to be on the Table

Any, and all, of us must be able to bring our ideas to the table.

That the Federal Reserve came into existence merely by a law passed by Congress should open any creative, aspirational mind reading this to the awesome potential that *any idea* can be moved through Congress. In just a year or two from now, it is possible for radical change to be implemented. Just one new law. Impossible is nothing.

Thus, anything truly can be on the table. Odds of what is possible don't

---

[440] https://www.ted.com/speakers/ray_dalio

[441] https://techcrunch.com/2017/12/12/facebook-bats-back-after-a-second-former-exec-accuses-it-of-negatively-impacting-society/

[442] http://blog.samaltman.com/e-pur-si-muove

matter. Anything is possible.

The proposals in this book, and the ideas that will be triggered from reading this book (or books like this) and the ideas for the future that will be independently spawned—they are all so revolutionary to how we currently run our economy and financial system that massive changes to our laws and government structures are likely to result and coincide with the path forward.

Still, all of us—and in my humble opinion—mostly liberals, need to let their guards down and open up.

No idea should simply be shut down. We have to listen. To it all.

Listen to the religious. Ironically, what a progressive socialist liberal might be hoping for may lie in the words of someone you might not expect. In other words, when a Christian is bringing the words of Jesus and the Bible to a discussion to helping us create the best economy and financial system for all of us in the future, it doesn't mean we are sanctifying that the economy *is* a Christian one. It is merely that all of us must be able to put everything on the table for discussion. And bring it from our hearts and minds. Bring it from the worlds we live in. If it is Bible verses that inspires someone's ideas for a different financial system, that is how that person arrives at their ideas. This is what is important to them. That may not be *all* of how they arrive at a decision. It is just *a part of it all.* Just as a socialist liberal is influenced by what they see, read, learn and experience.

So, can we listen to each other?

Christian ideas need to be on the table for discussion just like any other ideas. And then we mold it into the best possible future.

We can talk about it all. "Zero to 100" as I like to say.

As with all aspects of moving to a new, better future there is good and bad to examine in all of the past; as well as all our future solutions. The best future is possible by facing the complexities of our past: in handling dialogue that looks at all angles. Be open.

65
TAKING ACTION
DEFINING TERMS FOR CONVERSATION

The same word means different things to different people. Different emotions can be stirred up. This is especially the case in politics and economics.

Capitalism. Socialism. Republicans. Democrats.

We are now 'pre-wired,' to either like or dislike something based simply on its association with one of those words above.

It would be nice if terminology didn't matter. But it does. We don't even listen anymore, past a certain keyword.

But one word doesn't tell even a bit of the story.

It shouldn't matter what we call it.
The description, the definition,
the place of that 1 word in a larger story,
are more important.

Listen to the full description. That is at least one way to move us forward.

We cannot 'shut down' at the first word you don't agree with. This is not an argument over semantics.

We need to work toward action. So, let a conversation 'flush itself out.'

The right and left can be saying the same exact word and yet have completely different meanings and conceptions. Also, the use of one word by a liberal or conservative can stir up very counterproductive emotions in the other, without any intention. A liberal mentioning 'socialism' to a conservative. A conservative mentioning 'capitalism' to a liberal. Look out. But it doesn't have to be this way. It is only words. Can we talk?

Even within the left and the right there are differences. Many on the right are so anti-establishment that they cannot even agree among themselves. The right has developed such a distrust of the system that many of them kind of are unwilling to fully trust each other. For the left, this is not so much a problem. In fact, the opposite is more so the case. On the left, they are quick to agree and quick to rally behind an idea or concept. There is a unified front. The danger, or problem with this is that the left does not engage in healthy debate. They form kind of a groupthink in which the issue is quickly settled and anyone that doesn't fully agree doesn't believe in solving the problem.

Common definitions are a pre-requisite for moving forward. Conversing toward common understandings is also essential to develop solutions that can impact the broadest number of people.

For or Against Capitalism?

Is this book for or against capitalism? Probably both socialists and capitalists wonder at points in this book. Both throw the book up against the wall.

Really, it depends on how you define capitalism.

Moreover, it depends what you mean when you say it.

And, it depends what another person thinks when they hear the word.

You and I talking together might get on the same page. And then someone overhears us talking about capitalism. That person thinks they know what we are talking about. Based on their own definition and interpretation of the word.

**Capitalism is
a loaded term if ever there was one.
Hearing the word
capitalism can get people worked up.
For, or against.**

Capitalism was not even a term until 1850. A lot of capitalism rests on the principle of loans and credit.

Credit comes from Latin "credere" which means "to believe".

In other words, credit is not just money you actually possess but what others believe you will be able to pay back. One economist called credit "money of the mind." Credit multiplies the amount of money in circulation.

So many of these terms are 'loaded.' Different meanings are conjured up in each of us. They stir up emotions in others. Really strong emotions.

You can be talking in a similar vein; however, use of one of these words the wrong way and you could lose half an audience.

It is important both to the writer/speaker as well as the reader/listener to allow the ability to flush through a thought. Capitalism means different things to each of us. From: opportunity, free markets, the stock market and small business. To corporate power, collusion, corruption and widespread inequality.

Defining Capitalism and Socialism

Capitalism and socialism. The appeal of these economic philosophies, is as with nearly all philosophies: it is in their ideal. The ideal of the free market and capitalism. The ideal of socialism. However, each of us individually define these terms ourselves; differently. The ideals behind the definitions shape each of our understandings.

What do we have in America? Capitalism? Noam Chomsky calls it an "international plutonomy." For the most part, it is widely acknowledged and agreed that the United States is a capitalist economy.

What is not necessarily clear is: what exactly does that mean? Capitalism, as generally understood, is free markets with fluctuating prices; economic freedom for people to work where they would like; and to pursue the economic opportunities they would like.

Each of us has a slightly different take on that definition and explanation. Defining words is, itself, a large part of the problem toward finding a solution.

Defining terms could be one of the biggest roadblocks to a better future. We all need to leave behind a bit of our own 'definition baggage.'

Focusing on the <u>solutions, ideas and proposals</u>
for the future—
regardless of whether they sound
liberal or conservative, or socialist or capitalist—
that is the key.

Evaluating each idea outside of a context that does not mean the same thing to each of us.

If you introduce an idea to the public and you call it a 'capitalist approach' you lose a whole bunch of people just by the inclusion of that word. They will not even consider the idea itself. Same if an idea is said to be a 'new socialist approach.' There will be a lot of people that will shut down at the word 'socialist' and not consider the idea.

That doesn't mean either of those approaches are wrong or can't work but we need to be aware of our differences. Don't fight against people so much.

Seek to understand. Don't presume everyone is for or against you on the first take. Give it all a chance.

So, when you see socialism or capitalism in this book, for example, focus on the actual outcomes. The intention is a much better society. Likely, more than 90% of us (whether we are pro-capitalism or pro-socialism) are such because we believe it can make the world a better place. And for the parts that make any of us feel that way we just might be right. Something about that idealist socialist or passionate capitalist should make sense even to an opponent. Listen for it.

What is capitalism?

> Merriam-Webster defines "capitalism":
> *"An economic system characterized by private or corporate ownership of capital goods, by investments that are determined by private decision, and by prices, production, and the distribution of goods that are determined mainly by competition in a free market."*
>
> Their dictionary for "English learners":
> *"A way of organizing an economy so that the things that are used to make and transport products (such as land, oil, factories, ships, etc.) are owned by individual people and companies rather than by the government."*
>
> Their student dictionary:
> *"An economic system in which resources and means of production are privately owned and prices, production, and the distribution of goods are determined mainly by competition in a free market."*

That is—for all intents and purposes—the textbook definition of capitalism.

The definition of socialism? I would say it is evolving. The Merriam-Webster definition is easily eclipsed online by more succinct definitions by leaders and associations within the socialist movement.

Suffice to say, socialism is "collective or governmental ownership" of "the means of production" and "distribution of goods" and it may include "no private property."[443]

Critics define socialism and "democratic socialism" by what has occurred under prior attempts of socialism. For example, socialism "horrifies" Charlie Kirk. Socialism has failed everywhere it has been tried. "The poor will never get richer. You will all be equally poor." Socialism is "immoral, it is evil, it is impractical." Kirk says "100 million people died under democratic socialism." There is no moral justification for people dying under a form of government, or economic framework. So, the fact people have died under democratic

---

[443] https://www.merriam-webster.com/dictionary/socialism

socialism is horrifying. One person dying would be too many. Kirk's criticism also rightly points out that at the top, a "couple thousand people" (those running the government and their partners) "will be so magnificently rich."

However, Kirk's take down of socialism[444] offers little to a rational discussion *for the future*.

Like capitalism, socialism is a loaded term and a loaded subject. There are a couple significantly different ways to take socialism. The first, quickly, is the Marxist interpretation of which we are most conceptually familiar with. The second is a modern, fresh take that evokes the "social" of "social media" and Facebook. The concept of the "socialization of finance" uses "social" in the sense of social media as opposed to socialism.

What, really, does democracy in finance mean? Does democracy in finance mean socialization?

20th century economist F.A. Hayek defines socialism as 1) nationalization of the means of production and 2) central economic planning, including a) redistribution of incomes through taxation and b) welfare state. All with good intentions but leads to totalitarianism.

In the words of the Socialist Labor (political party) Platform in the 1890's "the true theory of politics is that the (machinery of) government must be owned and controlled by the whole people." Reasonable enough. And, by extension "the true theory of economics is that the machinery of production must likewise belong to the people in common." "Through the perversion of democracy (to the ends of plutocracy), labor is robbed of the wealth it alone produces."

"Our despotic system of economics is the direct opposite of our democratic system of politics" which "can plainly be traced the existence of a privileged class" and "the corruption of government by that class."[445] More things change the more they stay the same?

What we have today in finance and economics is the exact opposite of the democracy we have in politics and government.

Capitalism and socialism. It is not so much what they can be ideally. It isn't how they have failed. Rather, how can they be tweaked? Perfected? What parts can be utilized? What are the best pieces of either?

Communal, and community, are positive terms. Communism? Not so much. Communism has been deployed in the world with detrimental results. But are there aspects of communist theory that can be utilized in a positive way.

Test. Experiment. Try small. Experiments; "models of what the larger society might become."[446] What can fit into frameworks that can work for a

---

[444] https://www.facebook.com/prageru/videos/1364556833593029/

[445] Socialist Labor party platform from the 1890's, various sources including http://projects.vassar.edu/1896/slpplatform.html

modern world and for our best economic future.

Taking Politics out of the Conversation

Ground discussion outside of politics and government. This is not to say that they are not interrelated. They absolutely are. However, to have a discussion that gets to a solution, the words of economics need to be read for what they are (or can be) and not the emotions, politics and feelings we attach to them.

Discussing the economy does not have to be socialist or capitalist. We can discuss terms that may sound capitalist or socialist without linking the entire meaning. A socialist concept does not make the entire system socialist. A capitalist concept does not make the entire system capitalist.

Can each of us take a step way back? Way, way back to just have a reasonable conversation. And to make change.

We don't define words the same way. We don't hear the same thing. Or have similar understandings.

Moreover, none of us understand the problems properly. None of us know all the right solutions.

To move forward, we need to leave a lot behind.

We can't bring so many preconceived notions to the conversation.

We need to hope to learn; and yearn to understand.

We don't spend enough time on definitions.

If we just say "hey, this book is about capitalism," we are leaving everyone on different, or even wrong, pages.

And we don't spend enough time just listening.

**Instead of listening for the word you can
pick apart to win an argument...
listen for the one word or idea
you can find some agreement on.**

And go from there. Wow. That would be powerful!

---

[446] *Man and Mission*, Paul Gaston. 2012.

66

TAKING ACTION

HUMANITY AND THE FINANCIAL TERMINOLOGY OF THE FUTURE

"All you need is love."

"All you need is love." July 1967. The Beatles. Written largely by John Lennon.

Bono, of U2, 2017: "Love is bigger than anything in its way."[447]

When Jesus was asked "which is the greatest commandment?" Jesus replied, "Love the Lord your God," and "Love your neighbor as yourself."

The greatest minds… when digging deep to find one message to share.

Love.

Where does a concept and word like 'love' fit in our financial system and our economic framework?

That can change the whole conversation.

Can we get a roundtable discussion of the future financial system and begin with brainstorming ideas based on love?

What is love? Love is an emotion. Or a mental state.[448] Love is what you are attracted to. What you have a devotion to. Or a particular attachment, and

---

[447] http://www.allu2songslyrics.com/2017/09/love-is-bigger-than-anything-in-its-way.html
[448] https://en.wikipedia.org/wiki/Love

admiration. Love is even "unselfish" and "benevolent."[449]

If we wrap a conversation of our economic future around these defining words of love, what would result? What do we pull out that is relevant?

There are a lot of directions we can take this. We can examine the existing economy and financial system that we have and see what aspects of it do seem to reflect love. Then we can think more abstractly about how we can deeply incorporate love.

What are we 'devoted to' in our current economy?

Money.

Can we instead find a way to ensure we are devoted to the work right in front of us? Could we love what we work on and create? Could we have a purpose that is higher and more valuable than collecting a paycheck? We work to spend. We love to spend.

Some of 'do what we love' right? Many of us believe this. For example, a sports star surely does. A yoga instructor probably does. And on and on. It is a talking point in society to 'do what you love' so that you 'never have to work a day in your life.' In other words, if you enjoy your work and feel rewarded in your work it isn't really work.

So, how do we enable all of us to have that feeling? That we are devoted to the right thing.

Some of us may simply enjoy 'working hard.' Doesn't matter what. Just breaking a sweat (to borrow a lyric: "get my back into my living"). Working hard, that alone may be doing what you love. Digging a ditch. Building something.

So, while some people want to be the boss; other people want to just be told what to do. Some people have multiple passions. Others invest themselves in a singular pursuit.

This all starts to blend in to some of the valuable aspects of a **free society**. Not necessarily capitalist, per say. Perhaps. Perhaps, mostly. But, *definitely* **free**. The best, for all of us, is that we are free for our unique talents and skills to develop and shine through.

That is perhaps a digression because the point here is not to have any of the answers.

The conversation must change
A different conversation will yield a
better, improved world.

We can spur our minds to new thoughts, words and topics in order to change the direction of society. To help us toward better economic results.

I strongly believe it involves using a completely different vocabulary than

---

[449] https://www.merriam-webster.com/dictionary/love

we have become accustomed too.

Using a Completely Different Vocabulary

There are two key thoughts regarding vocabulary and definitions. The first, the subject of the preceding chapter.

1- Using common *definitions* (or at least some mutual understanding) so we can move dialogue forward
2- Using a completely different vocabulary than we have become accustomed to.

The second part is the focus here: we need to build a completely different vocabulary for discussing our economic future. And, the second part could, itself, be said to have two sub-categories.

First, we need "humanity" in our future financial system. We need to be thinking about the economy and financial system in completely different ways. Words that are not traditionally part of the financial system need to be a part of the discussion. So, for example, many words are 'over-played' such as: capital, interest rates, banks, etc. Those words can be replaced in the discussion with trying to integrate 'honesty,' 'authenticity,' 'love.' We need to solve problems of poverty.

Then, second within this point is that those who do want a completely different financial system and come to the table bringing these new ideas and 'outside-the-box' notions may need to 'brush up on' and learn to respect or accept that certain aspects of modern finance are indeed acceptable and/or beneficial to build on. Put another way, progress will only come by accepting that ideas you may not agree with may actually have value. A capitalist must come to respect some alternative perspectives. A radical socialist must similarly come to respect some aspects of our current financial system.

Lots of New Terminology:
Orienting Around New Questions

Have we the right level of humanity in our current financial system?
Are we "being humane?" Benevolent? Are we showing "brotherly love?" To whom? Why?
To those closest to us? Are we succeeding because of our own brilliance? And anyone around us that acknowledges our own brilliance?
Who among us is in it for their neighbor as much as themselves? Lach

Walesa called this "solidarity."

Can we live in a society that rewards helping everyone succeed?

Is that possible? How?

In these ways the conversation is not about what is this new economy called or what type of economy is it. Is the future populist? Capitalist? Socialist? Yes, probably each one… to some extent. However, such aiming misses the point. The point is what are we trying to achieve? What is the foundation? What are the core values?

Consider words like:

Love

Happiness

Honesty

Authenticity

Essence

Kindness. How can we get kindness into our world and our economy?

Mercy

Justice

Sacrifice

Serve

Redemption

Forgiveness

Hope, beauty, honor, striving, virtue.

Atonement

As referenced in the chapter on religion, in the bible there is a string of words we could consider: "love, joy, peace, forbearance, kindness, goodness, faithfulness, gentleness and self-control."[450]

How about we need to start being really nice to everyone else in the world because we might need them one day.

What are the words to orient building the right financial system of the future? "Finance" itself might not even be the right word. Probably it shouldn't be "financial" at all.

Can we have a feeling inside—in our soul—that our lives are moving on a daily basis for what is truly right. That we feel good about our daily contributions to society.

Is any of this really inside us?

These are deep questions. Are we meant to be all about kindness and love? Perhaps not entirely. It is likely a matter of balance and to what degree. One thing is crystal clear for me however. The needle needs to move in this direction. The conversation needs to be primarily wasted deep in the depths of these outside-the-box, alternative economic and financial terms.

---

[450] Galatians 5:22-23
https://www.biblegateway.com/passage/?search=Galatians+5&version=NIV

How are they economic and financial terms?!

One classic economic book that captured part of the essence to completely different concepts is called *Small is Beautiful*. Published in 1973, E.F. Schumacher's book included the sub-title "economics as if people mattered."[451]

What kind of financial system can incorporate sacrifice, kindness and forgiveness?

Focus on the End, and Find the Best Means

E.F. Schumacher draws the conversation to Buddhist economics in pointing out that the economic objectives of our society actually do not align with a proper understanding of the bottom-line, fundamentally valid objectives of individuals. We value consumption almost in and of itself. Consumption brings well-being. The means satisfies the end thus it must be the right means. And Schumacher points out that we cannot lose sight of the end. We need to keep the end goal in mind. And then find the best way to achieve the end.[452]

How can we maximize well-being?

Completely different principles need to be the center of our future financial system and economic way of life. Entirely alternative concepts.

Conversations involving totally different words.

Not a conversation to be 'won.' A conversation that must dig deep.

Focusing on different end objectives.

And, then, most importantly not just accepting the first means that achieves that end. Too often a means is heavily promoted, and it seems it can reach the end. That is not enough. We need conversations that penetrate to deeper levels.

For example, it is not the word "capitalism" to be defended at all costs.

It is the use of capitalism to achieve the right goals and objectives that is far more important.

In the words of Hernando de Soto, when capitalism "is a success story not only in the West but everywhere" that would be an achievement. Currently, the poor are left behind. Capitalism fails in that. De Soto says the more important ends are finding the right path that preserves "freedom," has "compassion for the poor, respect for the social contract, and equal opportunity."[453]

---

[451] *Small is Beautiful*. E.F. Schumacher. 1973.

[452] *Small is Beautiful*, E.F. Schumacher. 1973. Pp 61.

Beyond Traditional Philosophy: Questioning What We Do and Why

To put this whole issue of "terminology" another way, we study philosophy and have numerous philosophers. However, we don't really study morality. We study morality in our own religion. However, we do not connect morality or religion to society. That is the disconnect that must be unlocked and bridged. Sigmund Freud is perhaps an originator of breaking outside the traditional confines of abstract philosophy.[454] Freud's "psychoanalysis" (study of disorders and our subconscious mind) can be pragmatically applied to the real world. We need a lot more of moving beyond questions such as 'why do we exist.' The future must take us into the realm of studying morality. Studying not just why we exist but how we can exist better.

**Studying not just why we exist but
how we can exist better.**

We do this within an industry. Certainly, businesses and industries are constantly working to improve. How do we make a better medical treatment? A better diagnostic instrument in healthcare? A more efficient car or truck? And on and on. We do look to innovate and make the world better. All the time.

Not necessarily in the aggregate, however. We are not connecting the dots and pushing society to a better place. We are not solving problems within society as a whole.

There must be more discussion. The benefit of global organizations such as the United Nations is that they are, at least, a forum for exchange of information and ideas between different countries, societies and peoples. We need a lot more of that aspect. While making it more 'real,' at a common level.

And then looking at individual industries, there is not an outside observer questioning, are we doing the right things?

**Are we heading in the right direction?
Is the business or industry moving us—as a society—
in a better direction? Are we improving society?**

Perhaps the closest we have come to *any* study of this kind is the idea of

---

[453] *The Mystery of Capital*, Hernando de Soto, 2000. Pp 228

[454] *A Passion for Wisdom*. Robert C. Solomon and Kathleen M. Higgins. 1997. Pp 118.

"applied philosophy."[455] This is a very valuable direction. While it is so important to have research and study in the direction of Freud and scientific philosophers (theoretical physicists) such as Michio Kaku toward understanding and knowing the conscious and unconscious mind, it is fundamentally more important to practically study making the here and now better. Branching beyond Freud and Kaku into studying collective decision-making and the path society is on would be more relevant. Are we merely "getting better and better at playing the wrong game?"[456]

Consumption, Production and Public Goods

The process of "stuff" can be examined as a chain system: from extraction to production to distribution to consumption to disposal. Extraction is getting the materials to make the product.

This chain system that we are running is, essentially, a "linear system" on a "finite planet." That might be a kind description because within the "linear system" are "exponential" processes. Exponential processes conducted within a finite planet.[457] Even worse.

Thus, extraction is the most critical of the problems. Trees, metals, water, oil and on and on. All the materials needed for a world of 7 billion people. Seven billion consumers. Well, extraction is the most visible problems. However, production and distribution (and even consumption) require energy—more resources; and chemicals. And the final step, disposal. Well, it rapidly gets going into a whole new conversation.

One important aspect of branching off is the idea of "public goods." Fresh air can be considered a public good. In that we all have equal access to it. Whether rich or poor, whatever your nationality or race, when you step outside each of us, we breathe the same air. Basically. When you start thinking about the outliers to that statement is when it connects back to the problems of consumption (extraction, production and disposal). And this is where the conversation of the future can take off to a whole new level. The earth is finite. And thus, technically, should or could be considered a public good. Henry George focused on land taxation in large part for this very reason. Here come connections into revolutionizing how we think about our place in the

[455] http://www.appliedphil.org/view/about.html
[456] The *Story of Solutions* documentary, 2013 as watched via https://www.youtube.com/watch?v=9GorqroigqM
[457] The *Story of Stuff* documentary, 2007 as watched via https://www.youtube.com/watch?v=9GorqroigqM

world and how our financial system and economy could best operate.

Wanting the world to want to stop consumption is admirable. However, breaking the problem down into the sub-issues can help to actually make a difference in improving how our economy can operate in the future.

We are outsourcing problems.

Trees that we cannot see
are cut down for
the paper we print and read on.

67
TAKING ACTION

TAKING RESPONSIBILITY; ACTING RESPONSIBLY

Responsibility. From the successful among us to the struggling.

We all need to act with more responsibility.

If you make money, it is not all about you, yourself and your amazing effort. Be responsible for your position in society. Whether you want to call it helping another brother out, or "pay it forward," the point is there is no higher moral ground in saying 'how hard you work.' A lot of people work hard.

And for those that just want to blame the system and screw the rich people who just seem to catch all the breaks, take some personal responsibility.

To me, there is a lot of grey in the world. Can we be more balanced? More balanced about our own success. More balanced about our own failure. Positive we can make a difference. All of us. Whether rich or poor, make a difference. Give back. All of us can give back to others. If you are making it in the world, who can you help? If you feel you aren't making it, still, how can you help?

When it comes to some of the changes mentioned in this book… it's easy to support proposals that you believe will help you. And, it's easy to oppose proposals that you believe will hurt you.

What if we can… do the right thing?

Mike Huckabee says he doesn't look at things as whether they help the left or right, but rather on a vertical scale.[458] Will it make us worse, or better, off?

Detachment of Hard Work from Reward

Success comes to some people because they work harder than others. In the literal sense, that is—and should—be true. If you work hard you will be successful. As a basic tenant of what capitalism *should be* that is true and *should* be true.

The harder you work the more you will be rewarded.

I totally agree with that; for numerous reasons.

However, the capitalist mindset and the American psyche of today presents kind of an inverse of this principle, that if you are successful it is due to your hard work. You earned it. You deserve it. If you have money it is because you must have worked hard.

Hard work is an important value of a successful society.

We will go nowhere without hard work.

However, we don't reward hard work as much as we think we do.

Work and effort are detaching from the amount of money and reward that is received. On both ends of the stick.

The very rich and the very poor
Make most of their money without labor.
And too much 'work' in our existing society
Is not really 'doing' anything.

The connection between success and hard work is not necessarily there anymore in our current economy and society. At the bottom, if you can't make it, you are just given money. You don't have to work, and you get money. Sends the wrong message and it rubs people that *are* working the wrong way.

At the top, simply knowing the right people—and using connections, influence and power gains advantages that are not earned from work. In politics, is the biggest problem. Politicians in there to help the friends that pay for their campaign. Personally, I don't have that in me. I view politics and government as trying to make a positive difference for society and the area and people you represent. That doesn't win elections. The well-funded campaigns are politicians that are in it for themselves. Local, State, Federal. For too many politicians, it is all only about them. And we suffer with narrow growth oriented around the few people they aim to help. Locally, it will be construction firms. Nationally, it is the corporations and big banks.

---

[458] https://www.youtube.com/watch?v=YaAqnrpev44

MARCUS R. BOWMAN

68
TAKING ACTION

NOT GOING TO BE EASY

One thing is certain: rest assured there is one segment of society working hard to build the economy of the future. The current establishment.

First, they will work to delay any changes. And they will work to make any changes they don't like virtually impossible to implement (think, trying to get a third party on a political ballot anywhere).

Second, they will have their own way forward. It will receive lots of glamorous media coverage. It will be innovative. It will be cool. And it will lead right back to the same people in charge. Just moving the cheese around.

Third, any good ideas that do start to make traction the establishment will co-op. They will either get their people moved into the idea. Or they will acquire the competition.

All of this will work against any possibility of a new path.

Finally, there need to be people smart enough with the alternative ideas as well as those with the work ethic to implement new ways. And they will need to stick to their own path.

Those building a new way will need to keep up the efforts in the face of insurmountable odds. And persist amid rules meant to exclude them and to make their efforts twice as hard. They won't receive much media attention.

The tide of public opinion is likely to be strong as anyone tries to wade into the water with a new idea. Finding a new financial system or new way of structuring our economy will be a difficult road versus entrenched interests. The banks will not allow change; might even outlaw or ban some alternatives.

How do I suspect real positive change will come about?

1. Expect crying. If establishment bankers, corporate titans and Washington DC aren't screaming mad and literally throwing a temper tantrum then it is not change.
2. Expect threats. If it is truly different we will hear how terrible the outcome will be if we dare to try another way.[459]

It will take a concerted effort. The current system is not only way out in front by virtue of money, power, control of existing institutions, etc. They are also thinking 3, 4, 5 steps ahead.

It is like chess. Or billiards. A good pool (billiards) player is thinking 2 or 3 shots ahead. They will be aiming to make 1 shot while thinking of where they will be leaving the cue ball for the next shot. And then they will play this out as far as their brain can handle it. How many shots in advance do they believe they can have reasonable control over where the cue ball will be ending up. So, a really good pool player may quickly size up a table and know the next 4 or 5 shots they are planning to take. And make. Same in chess. The best chess players are not just making 1 move. They are making 1 move with a series of subsequent moves planned. Chess is even more difficult to plan ahead—because of alternating turns. The chess player needs to make a move based on the anticipation of what move their opponent will make after their own move. *And*, try to think ahead and play out those scenarios. Exponentially more possibilities because your opponent may make any number of different moves and you yourself will be adjusting your planned moves based on their move.

Control of government (elections), financial markets, the economy and even more importantly and specifically control of the banks, money printing and financial system are the same way. Those in power are working to maintain that control. And they are thinking ahead.

They work to stay one or more steps ahead of everyone. The Federal Reserve is ahead 15 points in the fourth quarter. They are so far entrenched there is hardly any opposition. We can't imagine how it could be possible to have any other way for our financial system. Time for a comeback.[460]

---

[459] Think TARP bailout and how it had to be passed or else dire consequences.
[460] http://www.nba.com/bulls/news/bullsclassics_smith_111206.html

324

69
TAKING ACTION

TAKING ACTION,
BE OPEN!

Be not afraid.

The U.S. did not have a Federal Reserve up until 1913. Even the Dow Jones Industrial Average only goes back a little further to 1896.

Microsoft was formed in 1975. Amazon was founded in 1994. Google was started in 1998. Mark Zuckerberg started with Facemash in 2003. Nike shoes 1964. A lot of what we can't imagine ever being different is pretty fresh.

The world we know today could be so much different 20 years from now. And, we should expect it to be.

Be open to new and different.

Enable someone. Enable something. Unleash some freedom.

Be open to radical changes in how our economy works.

Innovation is what is needed in America. Openness to new ideas and different people. We are stagnating by thinking the current borders, businesses and politicians are how it always must be. And we are bogging down. Becoming too politically correct on one hand and also letting the establishment businesses and politicians regulate away all competition. From ballot access to mega-mergers we are losing our ability to innovate.

America has led the world for a long time. And to continue leading we need to innovate. And we cannot afford to stifle discussion and different viewpoints. From ultra-conservative, far-right Christians to BLM, just let people be people. Free people to pursue some new ideas and do things differently.

There is entirely too much regulation. Federal, State and local. Want to start a business? So many fees and certifications. We need to let people be free to start and run a business without so much red tape. "Cut it, cut it, cut it, cut it."[461]

"Freedom!"[462] or was it "Freeeeedommmmmm"[463] – Mel Gibson,
last words of the character William Wallace in the movie Braveheart

I wrote this book believing we are on the cusp of leaping into a new financial system that is so much better, and for so many more people. A financial system that makes society better. And makes our lives have more meaning and purpose.

So many good, decent, honest-working people. Everyone deserves better. So many lost and left behind in America. So many more around the world not yet, or ever, lifted up.

It is time for a big leap. Quantum-like changes are coming. If you feel it, believe it. Work toward it starting from this moment.

"Without action, the best intentions in the world
are nothing more than that: intentions."
-- Jordan Belfort, Wolf of Wall Street[464]

I am optimistic we will get to that better future.

Your initiative and work, or even a simple, short message might be a game changer. You might instill the bug in someone else that spurs *them* to action.

In practice I have learned in markets and life (my own experience and seeing that of others) that things often get even worse before they get better. I don't want that to be a discouragement. Let's say we already hit the low and it is all up-and-away to a better world from here. The point is, what if it's not. I want to prepare innovators to persevere.

And to think differently.

LaVar Ball[465], Colin Kaepernick.[466] Roy Moore? Do we have any room for

---

[461] https://youtu.be/qMwcslY1GYE?t=33s

[462] https://www.youtube.com/watch?v=oU5wYEAVmZU

[463] https://youtu.be/y-y5fpZR8ek?t=1m19s

[464] https://cdn4.geckoandfly.com/wp-content/uploads/2014/08/jordan-belfort-quotes-wolf-wall-street10-830x467.jpg#.WibmQloELvs.link

[465] Took me a minute to warm up to LaVar. I thought he was way too bombastic. Now, I see him as kind of a business rebel. He has tapped into something. He is passionate about it. And he seems anti-establishment. Probably really going to shake things up and/or inspire a lot of other people to dream big and accomplish big. Now I am a big fan of LaVar.

[466] I think sitting during the National Anthem was ridiculous and wrong. I think the NFL condoning the behavior in the face of customer (fan) disapproval was an unbelievably

different? Some progressives and liberals plus the establishment media ridicule every person that dares to have Christian values.[467]

The future isn't going to be what you think it is going to be.

Some of the best things are likely to be hard to embrace.

I imagine that consumerism, markets, capitalism and the pursuit of money is going to become even more popular.

Going to have to endure and persevere to get to a better way. If you live in the 'hood don't be surprised when some old lady living in the country with Christian values has an idea that puts something together in your life. And vice versa! Be open. Could come in ways you wouldn't expect from people you wouldn't expect. Be true and right. Humble.

When the people realize they are ultimately in control it could be quite revolutionary. And when the establishment grasps that they are actually losing their control it will hit them hard. *Their* reactions (that of the establishment) are likely to be violent. When we have the U.S. Senate floor filled with a guy that was a truck driver, an inner-city rapper and a waitress… that will be the day. Not the fake pictures (Scott Brown in a pick-up truck[468]… please) and stories of the media. When the establishment and media are freaking out that someone made it to the Senate and doesn't fit the mold.

Institutionally, the advantage is enormous. Media influence. Global organizations. Academic, government bureaucracy, corporate, big banks. The advantage is staggering.

There is no reason why in the 21st century there should be so much concentration of power. It won't get any better by those in power suddenly wanting to share their own power and positions. And they don't see any problem. Hard to think anything can be improved when you are chaufered to the airport for your first-class flight to a five-star resort in Davos, Switzerland to eat caviar for lunch, fine wine after dinner and meet among your corporate, multi-millionaire peers. 'Hey, did you the unemployment rate went down 0.1%.'

Decentralize.

Democratize.

New distribution.

Different outcomes.

---

terrible decision, business and morally. Nevertheless, Colin marches to his own drum. He is passionate about some policy issues. Let Colin be Colin. I don't think the NFL 'blackballed' him as much as Kaepernick was increasingly taking his head too much outside football. Kaepernick seems to be more interested in politics than playing football. And maybe he could do well and make an even bigger impact outside football. Probably some of his most radical policy ideas should be talked out.

[467] http://religion.blogs.cnn.com/2013/05/05/when-christians-become-a-hated-minority/

[468] https://blogs.wsj.com/washwire/2010/01/19/pickup-truck-politics-in-massachusetts-senate-race/

70
TAKING ACTION
PULLING IT ALL TOGETHER

Who will win the future?

All of us should win.

Look in the other direction. The narrow gate. Little ideas can overrun entire industries overnight. It will be fought. Establishment interests are not going to let go easily.

This is America and we need to do better.

Our economy must get better. *Way better.*

Not at growing GDP. Not at creating jobs.

Growing a GDP that matters. Creating good jobs with purpose. The distribution of power down to the people.

Building with real purpose.

Do we have purpose? Denzel Washington, "You can run in place all the time and never get anywhere."[469]

What are we creating? And what are we leaving behind?

What is the vision? What are the ideas?

Is this the best economy and country ever? Ok, how do we take it into the stratosphere of awesome?

Are we enabling enough innovation?

Is the "mushy middle" of centrist compromising actually snuffing out a lot of America's potential? Political correctness of a corporate-banker centrism is not giving results to enough people.

Sometimes the extreme free market proposal is probably our best choice.

---

[469] https://youtu.be/BxY_eJLBflk?t=4m39s

Other times… a radical, socialist proposal might could benefit us the most. How about try something different?

We need to accept a little bit from both extremes to make progress. Our best economy and most optimum financial system is likely neither totally socialist nor totally capitalist.

Capital is old. Bonds, interest rates, stocks, GDP. 1600's old. The arch of history is freedom. Free markets are to capitalism as democracy was to Kings. However, neither our economy or our political system has been truly unleashed to freedom. Both need to leap ahead to the next level of our capability.

Decentralize.

Democracy.

Distribution.

Different outcomes.

As simple as changing 1 law. Just 10 years from now could be as different as social media and smart phones have flipped the internet over.

Unleash free markets. Crony capitalism is not free markets. Even capitalism does not mean free markets. Freedom is essential, and we are losing dynamism with its erosion.

We can close the New York Stock Exchange (and/or regulate it for the casino that it is; and/or provide some real, fresh competition). We can End the Fed. America was awesome before the stock market. And America was super innovative before the Federal Reserve. Someday there will be different ways of doing the economy and we will be fine. My contention is actually that we need to speed up the change so that we can truly stay out in front in innovation. Moreover, the Federal Reserve is not constitutional; and neither is bitcoin for that matter.

Bitcoin is not different. Bitcoin? Blockchain? Blockchain is different. I am convinced Bitcoin is a Goldman Sachs creation for a global currency that will ultimately be government-regulated and controlled by a world central bank. Blockchain, however, is a technology that can be utilized a lot of different ways.

Break up the monopoly over our financial system.

Change the structure of corporations.

Start small. Fix locally. Think the traditions of small towns like Fairhope. Think like the founders of Fairhope. Think about Pritchard.

Give things a chance. Everybody does not need to follow one way. Why does every business and job have to be layered in regulation?

Christians and conservatives. I believe they are increasingly being written out of politics and the economy. Liberal areas of the country have the money and the legal organization.

Let people be free. It must be ok to be different. It is ok to hold traditional values and positions. Not everyone can change and not everyone needs to change. Who cares?

Let people have a different perspective.

Democracy. Democratization of Finance. Get more people involved in decision-making of our financial system and economy.

Distribution. Get more money into the rest of the population.

Maybe the fact that the Federal Reserve theoretically can buy anything is a great thing. Let's put that idea to work? Take it over and start spending. On the rest of us; not the bankers in New York. Takeover the Fed and just redirect money to everywhere else. To pockets it hasn't been going. Truck drivers. Waitresses. The rest of the people! Or better yet, just close the Federal Reserve.

Radical changes are ok.

Close the U.S. stock market. Or allow some unregulated competition against it. Allow some competition to the Federal Reserve. See if they can compete if they don't monopolize control over the entire economy.

We are the greatest country on earth. Surely our self-proclaimed smartest bankers ought to be able to manage a lot more than 2 economic targets. The world record for juggling is 10 balls at once. How about a baby step from two? The Federal Reserve governors can manage the economy to 5 economic indicators.

Is this like frogs in a pot? The establishment consolidating global power day-by-day. No one can put a finger on it without sounding like a conspiracy nut. It is "large changes in small, scarcely noticeable increments."[470] Likewise going in another direction. It doesn't have to all happen at once. And it surely won't. And all of it isn't going to be *your* cup of tea. But if you can let the people across town sip their coffee then they let you have your tea.

Kshama Sawant on her position with the Seattle City Council and increasing the minimum wage, "we took it up not because we believe that fifteen dollars an hour will cure all ills, but because that's a demand that a mass number of workers are willing to come together, get organized, and fight for."[471] In other words, sometimes you have to fight for what you can win. You have to try to move the needle a little in your direction. You can't always win your ideal situation. Perhaps Mick Jagger and Keith Richards said it best with the Rolling Stones, "you can't always get what you want. But if you try sometimes, you get what you need."[472] A different approach to our economy is not a fringe movement or a radical movement, or even a left or right one. This is a broad, mainstream movement recognized by leading economic observers such as James Grant as well as the curiosity of authors such as

---

[470] From *The Death of Money*, James Rickards, 2014 pp 292
[471] https://jacobinmag.com/2017/08/kshama-sawant-interview-seattle-city-council
[472] https://en.wikipedia.org/wiki/You_Can%27t_Always_Get_What_You_Want and https://www.youtube.com/watch?v=7S94ohyErSw

James Rickards writing *The Death of Money*, and U.S. Representatives such as Ron Paul and former insiders like David Stockman.

If we focus on different outcomes we will get better results.

The economy is not working for enough people. The focus is on economic targets that don't mean anything. The stock market should not drive the economy; it must be the other way around

Pull more people in to a better life. Our country is capable of so much better. Discuss new ideas. Intellectually. Fundamentally. For more opportunity. Muhammad Yunus, a pioneer in the industry of "micro finance," or super small loans to the poor in third world countries calls his ideas for the future financial system, "social business."[473] His ideas are out there innovative.

Beyond what the goal is, the question ultimately becomes: What is possible? What are the means? How can we achieve that end? Or, how can we come close to achieving the end? What tract do we start down?

The ultimate goal is new and better jobs. New and better infrastructure. Higher incomes across the board for the population. A structure of economy that has a lot less control by a few. A lot less ability for insider manipulation. A lot less ability—or no ability—to rig systems.

The goal is not fairness. The goal is to unleash the freedom of entrepreneurs. Artists. Alternative talents.

Life, liberty and the pursuit of happiness.

The *pursuit* of happiness. Not just a happiness delivery system.

And take it up a notch. Life, liberty and the pursuit of happiness is so 1770's. Add to it. Delve into it.

The goal is not *your* happiness. And it is not your style of happiness. The goal is not the happiness of your people, or your side, or your world view. It is the collective happiness of all via individually.

> **"Our happiness cannot come from its solitary pursuit,**
> **but from the liberty of living together**
> **and engaging in the democratic politics**
> **that will help us value our common future."**

That is the last sentence of Raj Patel's book, *The Value of Nothing*. It is a deep comment. Political, and philosophical.

Patel's points seem to be merely, first, 'don't try so hard.' It is not so much for you to solve how everybody must live and believe. Second, the overriding point "happiness cannot come from its solitary pursuit." The goal is not pursuing happiness anyways. Happiness is not the goal. Happiness is the result of effective coexistence.

Can we let go? Can we let other people succeed? Can we let other people

---

473 http://www.muhammadyunus.org/index.php/social-business/social-business

be themselves? Can we live free? Sacrifice some of our own 'A' to find a solution that mixes in a little 'Z.'

And that is the essential element of the free market approach and democracy. We must always have the freedom that allows people to create new. A better democracy. A better free economy.

A higher purpose. More than simply growing GDP. More than stock prices. More than just a job. Less to control. Humility. Let's take it up a notch!

The counterfeiting of the Federal Reserve system is a totally unfair advantage to corporations and big banks. Doesn't mean the people themselves are bad. Doesn't mean their actions in that system are necessarily bad.

Decentralization and democratization of the distribution of money is the path of the future.

How about this though as a question for Wall Street. What are they afraid of? So smart? So much initiative? Can you put that to work in someone else's system?

APPENDIX:
SELECTED SOURCES

Influential books. Here is a list of books that impacted me in writing.

1. *The Creature from Jekyll Island: A Second Look at the Federal Reserve*, G. Edward Griffin, 1994
2. *What Has Government Done to Our Money?*, Murray N. Rothbard, 1963 (note many of Rothbard's books are available free, online via The Mises Institute).
3. *Small is Beautiful*, E.F. Schumacher, 1973.
4. *The Road to Serfdom*, F.A. Hayek, 1944.
5. *Free to Choose*, Milton Friedman, 1980
6. *Progress and Poverty*, Henry George, 1880
7. *Social Problems*, Henry George, 1883
8. *The Heretic's Guide to Global Finance*, Brett Scott, 2013.
9. *Building Social Business*, Muhammad Yunus, 2010
10. *Compassionate Capitalism*, Rich DeVos, 1993
11. *Economics in One Lesson*, Henry Hazlitt, 1946
12. *The Work of Nations*, Robert B. Reich, 1991
13. *Democratic Promise*, Lawrence Goodwyn, 1976
14. *The Future of Capitalism*, Lester C. Thurow, 1996
15. *The Zero-Sum Society*, Lester C. Thurow, 1980
16. *Capitalism, Socialism and Democracy*, Joseph A. Schumpeter, 1942
17. *For the New Intellectual*, Ayn Rand, 1961
18. *Post-Capitalist Society*, Peter F. Drucker, 1993
19. *The Mystery of Capital*, Hernando de Soto, 2000
20. *The Bully Pulpit*, Doris Kearns Goodwin, 2013

21. *Capital in the Twenty-First Century*, Thomas Piketty, 2014
22. *The Innovators*, Walter Isaacson, 2014
23. *The Commanding Heights*, Daniel Yergin and Joseph Stanislaw, 1998
24. *The Alchemists*, Neil Irwin, 2013
25. *Titan*, Ron Chernow, 1998
26. *Market Wizards*, Jack D. Schwager, 1989
27. *The Secrets of the Federal Reserve*, Eustace Clarence Mullins, 1952
28. *The Wealth of Nations*, Adam Smith, 1776
29. *The Great Index Mania*, Jeffrey B. Little, 1997
30. *Reminiscences of a Stock Operator*, Edwin Lefevre, 1993
31. *Money: Whence It Came, Where It Went*, John Kenneth Galbraith. 1975
32. *Web of Debt: The Shocking Truth about Our Money System and How We Can Break Free*, Ellen Hodgson Brown, 2012
33. *Man, Economy, and State with Power and Market*, Murray N. Rothbard, 2009
34. *Anatomy of the State*, Murray N. Rothbard, 1974
35. *The Mystery of Banking*, Murray N. Rothbard, 1983
36. *For a New Liberty: The Libertarian Manifesto*, Murray N. Rothbard, 1973
37. *A History of Money and Banking in the United States: The Colonial Era to World War II*, Murray N. Rothbard, 2002

ABOUT THE AUTHOR

Marcus Bowman moved to Fairhope, Alabama in 2012 following 12 years in Washington, DC where he earned a Masters of Public Policy (MPP). In the nation's capital Marcus worked for a Japanese owned company researching transportation and energy policy and legislation for several years. Marcus earned a B.S. in Finance with a minor in Economics from Iowa State University after growing up in the suburbs of Chicago, Illinois. In 2016, Marcus was blessed with his first and only child.

www.ingramcontent.com/pod-product-compliance
Lightning Source LLC
Chambersburg PA
CBHW071249220526
45468CB00001B/54

* 9 7 8 1 9 8 1 7 9 1 1 6 3 *